Preliminary Edition Notice

You have been selected to receive a copy of this book in the form of a preliminary edition. A preliminary edition is used in a classroom setting to test the overall value of a book's content and its effectiveness in a practical course prior to its formal publication on the national market.

As you use this text in your course, please share any and all feedback regarding the volume with your professor. Your comments on this text will allow the author to further develop the content of the book, so we can ensure it will be a useful and informative classroom tool for students in universities across the nation and around the globe. If you find the material is challenging to understand, or could be expanded to improve the usefulness of the text, it is important for us to know. If you have any suggestions for improving the material contained in the book or the way it is presented, we encourage you to share your thoughts.

Please note, preliminary editions are similar to review copies, which publishers distribute to select readers prior to publication in order to test a book's audience and elicit early feedback; therefore, you may find inconsistencies in formatting or design, or small textual errors within this volume. Design elements and the written text will likely undergo changes before this book goes to print and is distributed on the national market.

This text is not available in wide release on the market, as it is actively being prepared for formal publication. Accordingly, the book is offered to you at a discounted price to reflect its preliminary status.

If you would like to provide notes directly to the publisher, you may contact us by e-mailing studentreviews@cognella.com. Please include the book's title, author, and 7-digit SKU reference number (found below the barcode on the back cover of the book) in the body of your message.

Crime Victimization
Patterns, Impact, and System Response

Preliminary Edition

Karol Lucken

University of Central Florida

Bassim Hamadeh, CEO and Publisher
Natalie Piccotti, Director of Marketing
Kassie Graves, Vice President of Editorial
Jamie Giganti, Director of Academic Publishing
Jennifer McCarthy, Acquisitions Editor
Amy Smith, Project Editor
Casey Hands, Associate Production Editor
Jackie Bignotti, Senior Graphic Designer
Sara Schennum, Licensing Associate

Cover image Copyright © 2012 Depositphotos/Nejron.

Printed in the United States of America.

ISBN: 978-1-5165-4664-0 (pbk) / 978-1-5165-4665-7 (br)

Contents

SECTION I

Definitional and Historical Issues on Crime Victimization

The Rediscovery of Crime Victims

by Andrew Karmen

THE DISCOVERY OF CRIME VICTIMS

Each law that prohibits a certain act as being harmful defines the wrongdoer as a criminal subject to punishment, and at the same time specifies that the injured party is a victim deserving some sort of redress. The laws forbidding what are now called **street crimes**—murder, rape, robbery, assault, burglary, and theft—can be traced back several thousand years. When the 13 American colonies were settled by immigrants from Great Britain, the earliest penal codes were based on religious values as well as **English common law**. Hence, victims of interpersonal violence and theft were "discovered" ages ago, in the sense that they were formally identified and officially recognized.

THE DECLINE OF CRIME VICTIMS

Scholars of the history of the legal system report that in past centuries, victims played a leading role in the resolution of criminal matters. To discourage retaliation by victims and their families—acts that could lead to endless feuding if offenders and their kin counterattacked—societies in simpler times established direct repayment schemes. Legal codes around the world enabled injured parties to receive money or valuables from wrongdoers to compensate for the pain, suffering, and losses they endured.

This process of victim-oriented justice prevailed mostly in small villages engaged in farming, where social relations were based on personal obligations, clear-cut family ties, strong religious beliefs, and sacred traditions. But the injured party's role diminished as industrialization and urbanization brought about business relations that were voluntary, secular, impersonal, rationalized, and contractual. Over the centuries, victims lost control over the process of determining the fate of the offenders who harmed them. Instead, the local governmental structure dominated judicial proceedings and extracted fines from convicts, physically punished them, or even executed them. The seriousness of the wounds and losses inflicted upon victims were of importance only for determining the charges and penalties wrongdoers faced upon conviction. Restoring injured parties to the condition they were in before the crimes occurred was no longer the main concern. In fact, the recovery of damages became a separate matter that was handled in another arena (**civil court**) according to a different set of rules (**tort law**) after criminal proceedings were concluded (Schafer, 1968).

Historically, in the United States and in other parts of the world, the situations of victims followed the same evolutionary path from being at the center of the legal process to being relegated to the sidelines. During the colonial era, police forces and public prosecutors had not yet been established. Victims were the key decision makers within the rudimentary criminal justice system and were its direct beneficiaries. They conducted their own investigations, paid for warrants to have sheriffs make arrests, and hired private attorneys to indict and prosecute their alleged attackers. Convicts were forced to repay those they harmed up to three times the value of the goods they had damaged or stolen (Schafer, 1968).

But after the American Revolution and the adoption of the Constitution and the Bill of Rights, crimes were reconceptualized as hostile acts directed against the authority of the government, which was defined as the representative of the people. Addressing the suffering imposed upon individuals was deemed to be less important than dealing with the symbolic threat to the social order posed by lawbreakers. **Public prosecutors**, acting on behalf of the state and in the name of the entire society, took over the powers and responsibilities formerly exercised by victims. Federal, state, and county (district) attorneys were granted the discretion to decide whether to press charges against defendants and what sanctions to ask judges to impose upon convicts.

The goals of deterring crime through punishment, protecting society by incapacitating dangerous people in prisons or through executions, and rehabilitating transgressors through treatment came to overshadow victims' demands to be restored to financial, emotional, and physical health.

Over the last two centuries, the government increasingly has assumed the obligation of providing jail detainees and prison inmates with food, clothing, housing, supervision, medical care, recreational opportunities, schooling, job training, psychological counseling, and legal representation—while leaving victims to fend for themselves. As they lost control over "their" cases, their role dwindled to just two contributions: filing a complaint with the police that initiated an investigation and, if necessary, testifying for the prosecution as another piece of evidence in the state's presentation of damning facts against the accused.

When **plea negotiation** (a settlement worked out by the prosecutor and the defense attorney) replaced a trial as the most common means of resolving criminal cases, victims lost their last opportunity to actively participate in the process by presenting their firsthand experiences on the witness stand to a jury. Victims rarely were included and consulted when the police and prosecution team decided upon their strategies and goals. To add insult to injury, often they were not even informed of the outcomes of "their" cases. Thoroughly marginalized, victims frequently sensed that they had been taken advantage of twice: first by the offender and then by a system that ostensibly was set up to help them but in reality seemed more intent on satisfying the needs of its core agencies and key officials (see Schafer, 1968; McDonald, 1977; and Davis, Kunreuther, and Connick, 1984).

THE REDISCOVERY OF CRIME VICTIMS

After centuries of neglect, those on the receiving end of violence and theft were given renewed attention and, in effect, were rediscovered during the late 1950s and early 1960s. A small number of self-help advocates, social scientists, crusading journalists, enlightened criminal justice officials, and responsive lawmakers helped direct public concern to a serious problem: the total disregard of the needs and wants of victims. Through publications, meetings, rallies, and petition drives, these activists promoted their message: that victims were forgotten figures in the criminal justice process whose best interests had been systematically overlooked but

merited attention. Discussion and debate emerged during the late 1960s and has intensified throughout the following decades over why this injustice existed, and what could be done about it. Various groups with their own distinct agendas formed coalitions and mobilized to campaign for reforms. As a result, new laws favorable to victims are being passed and criminal justice policies are being overhauled.

Social Movements: Taking Up the Victims' Cause

Aside from suffering harm at the hands of criminals, victims as a group may have very little else in common. They differ in terms of age, sex, race/ethnicity, religion, social class, political orientation, and many other important characteristics. Therefore, it has been difficult to organize them into self-help groups and to harness their energies into a political force for change. Despite these obstacles, a crime victims' movement emerged during the 1970s. It has developed into a broad alliance of activists, support groups, and advocacy organizations that lobbies for increased rights and expanded services, demonstrates at trials, maintains a variety of websites, educates the public, trains criminal justice professionals and caregivers, sets up research institutes and information clearinghouses, designs and evaluates experimental policies, and holds conferences to share experiences and develop innovative programs.

The guiding principle holding this diverse coalition together is the belief that victims who otherwise would feel powerless and enraged can attain a sense of empowerment and regain control over their lives through practical assistance, mutual support, and involvement in the criminal justice process (see Friedman, 1985; Smith, 1985; Smith, Sloan, and Ward, 1990; and Weed, 1995).

The victims' movement has greatly benefited from the work of advocates, who, by definition, speak in behalf of someone else, especially in legal matters. Originally, advocates were referred to as "ombudsmen." Rape crisis centers and shelters for battered women were the first to empower their clients in the early 1970s by furnishing them with the services of dedicated and knowledgeable consultants who understood how the criminal justice process worked and how to make the system more responsive to their clients' needs. These pioneers in advocacy usually were former victims who knew firsthand what the injured parties were going through. A Florida police department and a Chicago legal services organization were the first components of the justice system to routinely provide advocates in the mid-1970s. Shortly afterward, prosecutors' victim–witness assistance programs (VWAPs) and family courts (responsible for assigning *guardians ad litem* to represent the best interests of abused children) followed suit. In addition to survivors and volunteers, professionals in the helping fields (such as social workers, nurses, psychologists, psychiatrists, counselors, and lawyers) began to offer their specialized skills. Agencies provided short-term training in crisis intervention techniques and practical assistance with financial claims, court proceedings, and referrals to medical, mental health, and legal services. Courses and career preparation became available on college campuses. Two forms of advocacy developed: Case advocacy involves a one-on-one relationship with a client who needs specific assistance and focused guidance for a short period of time. System advocacy involves representing an entire group as part of an organized lobbying campaign to bring about procedural reforms that will ease their plight (Dussich, 2009a).

Major Sources of Inspiration, Guidance, and Support Several older and broader social movements have greatly influenced the growth and orientation of the victims' movement. The most important contributions have been made by the **law-and-order movement**, the **women's movement**, and the **civil rights movement**.

The law-and-order movement of the 1960s raised concerns about the plight of victims of street crimes of violence and theft. Alarmed by surging crime rates, conservatives adopted the "crime control" perspective and campaigned for a hard-line, get-tough policies. They insisted that the criminal justice system was society's first line of defense against internal enemies who threatened chaos and destruction. The "thin blue line" of law enforcement needed to be strengthened. A willingness to tolerate too much misbehavior

was viewed as the problem and a crackdown on social and political deviants who disobeyed society's rules and disrupted the lives of conventional people was offered as the solution. To win over people who might have been reluctant to grant more power to government agencies—police, prosecutors, and prison authorities—they argued that the average American should be more worried about becoming a victim than about being falsely accused, mistakenly convicted, and unjustly punished (Hook, 1972). Conservative crime control advocates pictured the scales of justice as being unfairly tilted in favor of the "bad guys" at the expense of the "good guys"—the innocent, law-abiding citizens and their allies on the police force and in the prosecutor's office. In a smooth-running justice system that they envisioned, punishment would be swift and sure. Attorneys for defendants would no longer be able to take advantage of practices that were dismissed as "loopholes" and "technicalities" that undermined the government's efforts to arrest, detain, convict, imprison, deter, incapacitate, and impose retribution on wrongdoers.

"Permissiveness" (unwarranted leniency) and any "coddling of criminals" would end: more offenders would be locked up for longer periods of time, and fewer would be granted bail, probation, or parole. Liberals and civil libertarians who opposed these policies as being too repressive and overly punitive were branded as "pro-criminal" and "anti-victim" (see Miller, 1973; and Carrington, 1975).

In contrast, liberal activists in the women's movement have focused their energies since the late 1960s on aiding one group of victims in particular: females who were harmed by males and then failed to receive the support they deserved from the male-dominated criminal justice system. Feminists launched both an antirape and an antibattering movement. The antirape movement set up the first rape crisis centers in Berkeley, California, and Washington, D.C., in 1972. These centers were not just places of aid and comfort in a time of pain and confusion. They also were rallying sites for outreach efforts to those who were suffering in isolation, meeting places for consciousness-raising groups exploring the patriarchal cultural traditions that encouraged males to subjugate females, and hubs for political organizing to change laws and policies (see Rose, 1977; Largen, 1981; and Schechter, 1982). Some antirape activists went on to protest the widespread problem of sexual harassment on the street, uniting behind the slogan "Take back the night" (see Lederer, 1980).

Other feminists helped organize battered women's shelters. They established the first "safe house" in St. Paul, Minnesota, in 1974. Campaigns to end battering paralleled activities to combat rape in a number of ways. Both projects were initiated for the most part by former victims who viewed their plight as an outgrowth of larger societal problems and institutional arrangements, rather than as personal troubles stemming from their own individual shortcomings. Both sought to empower women by confronting established male authority, challenging existing procedures, providing peer support and advocacy, and devising alternative places to seek help in a time of need. The overall analysis that originally guided these pro-victim efforts was that male versus female offenses (such as rape, wife beating, sexual harassment in the streets and at work, and incest at home) pose a threat to all women; and that this kind of illegal sexual oppression slows progress toward equality between the sexes. The gravest dangers are faced by women who are socially disadvantaged because of racial discrimination and economic insecurity. According to this philosophy, girls and women victimized by boys and men cannot count on the privileged males at the helm of criminal justice agencies to lead the struggle to effectively protect or assist them—instead, women must empower each other (see Brownmiller, 1975).

Similarly, liberal activists in the civil rights movement focused their energies on opposing entrenched racist beliefs and discriminatory practices that encouraged members of the white majority to intimidate, harass, and attack people of color. Over the decades since the 1950s, this movement has brought together organizations representing the interests of a wide range of minority groups, in order to direct attention to the special threats posed by racist violence, from lynch mobs to Ku Klux Klan terrorism in the form of bombings and assassinations.

In recent years, one of the movement's major concerns has been convincing the government to provide enhanced protection to individuals who are the targets of **bias crimes**, which are motivated by the perpetrators' hatred of the "kind of person" the victim represents. Bias crimes can range from harassment and vandalism to arson, beatings, and slayings. Civil rights groups have been instrumental in lobbying state legislatures to impose stiffer penalties on attackers whose behavior is fueled by bigotry and in establishing specialized police squads to more effectively deter or solve these inflammatory violations of the law. Otherwise, these divisive crimes could polarize communities along racial and ethnic lines and thereby undermine the ongoing American experiment of fostering multicultural tolerance and the celebration of diversity (see Levin and McDevitt, 2003).

Civil rights organizations also try to mobilize public support to demand evenhandedness in the administration of justice. A double standard, although more subtle today than in the past, may still infect the operations of the criminal justice system. Crimes by black perpetrators against white victims always have been taken very seriously—thoroughly investigated, quickly solved, vigorously prosecuted, and severely punished. However, crimes by white offenders against black victims, as well as by blacks against other blacks (see Ebony, 1979) have rarely evoked the same governmental response and public outrage. The more frequent imposition of the death penalty on murderers who kill whites, especially blacks who slay whites, is the clearest example of a discriminatory double standard (see Baldus, 2003). Civil rights activists also point out that members of minority groups continue to face graver risks of becoming victims of official misconduct in the form of police brutality—or even worse, the unjustified use of deadly force—as well as false accusations, frameups, wrongful convictions, and other miscarriages of justice.

Additional Contributions by Other Social Movements Social movements that champion the causes of civil liberties, children's rights, senior citizens' rights, homosexual rights, and self-help also have made significant contributions to bettering the situation of victims.

The **civil liberties movement**'s primary focus is to preserve constitutional safeguards and due-process guarantees that protect suspects, defendants, and prisoners from abuses of governmental power by overzealous criminal justice officials. However, civil liberties organizations have won court victories that have benefited victims of street crime in two ways: by furthering police professionalism and by extending the doctrine of "equal protection under the law."

In professionalized police departments, officers must meet higher educational and training requirements and must abide by more demanding standards. As a result, victims are more likely to receive prompt responses, effective service, and sensitive treatment. If they don't, channels exist through which they can redress their grievances. Guarantees of equal protection enable minority communities to gain access to the police and prosecutorial assistance to which they are entitled and to insist upon their right to improved, more professional law enforcement in contrast to the underpolicing they endured until recently. This improves the prospects for sensitive and responsive handling for complainants whose calls for help were given short shrift in the past when officials discriminated against them due to their race, ethnicity, sex, age, social class, disability, or some other disadvantage (Walker, 1982; and Stark and Goldstein, 1985).

Children's rights groups campaign against sexual abuse, physical abuse, severe corporal punishment, gross neglect, and other forms of maltreatment of youngsters. Their successes include stricter reporting requirements of cases of suspected abuse; improved procedures for arrest, prosecution, and conviction of offenders; greater sensitivity to the needs of victimized children as complaining witnesses; enhanced protection and prevention services; and more effective parenting instruction programs. Activists in senior citizens' groups have pressured some police departments to establish special squads to protect older people from younger robbers and swindlers and have brought about greater awareness of the problem of **elder abuse**—financial, emotional, and physical mistreatment by family members or caretakers (see Smith and Freinkel, 1988).

The **gay rights movement** originally called attention to the vulnerability of male homosexuals and lesbians to blackmail, exploitation by organized crime syndicates that ran bars and clubs, and police harassment of those who deserved protection (see Maghan and Sagarin, 1983). The movement now focuses on preventing street assaults ("gay-bashing") against suspected homosexuals and lesbians—hate crimes that are motivated by the offenders' disdain for the victims' presumed sexual orientation.

Groups that are part of the **self-help movement** have set up dependable support systems for injured parties by combining the participatory spirit of the grassroots protest movements of the 1960s with the self-improvement ideals of the human potential movement of the 1970s. The ideology of self-help is based upon a fundamental organizing principle: that people who have directly experienced the pain and suffering of being harmed and are still struggling to overcome these hardships themselves can foster a sense of solidarity and mutual support that is more comforting and effective than the services offered by impersonal bureaucracies and emotionally detached professional caregivers (Gartner and Riessman, 1980).

Even the prisoners' rights movement of the late 1960s and early 1970s may have inspired victim activism. Inmates rebelled at a number of correctional institutions, often in vicious and counterproductive ways. They protested overcrowded conditions; demanded decent living standards; insisted on greater ways of communicating with the outside world (via uncensored mail, access to the mass media, more family visits and meetings with lawyers); asked for freedom of religion; called for more opportunities for rehabilitation, education, and job training; and complained about mistreatment and brutality by guards (see ACLU, 2008). Many people harmed by these incarcerated offenders surely asked, if convicts deserve better treatment from the authorities, don't we, too?

The task for victimologists is to assess the impact these other social movements have had on shaping the course of the victims' movement over the decades, as well as on alleviating the suffering of persons harmed by criminals these days. How

7

effective and influential have the victories of these campaigns really been?

Elected Officials: Enacting Laws Named after Victims

Legislators engaged in the political process of enacting new laws have helped rediscover and publicize the plight of victims. Starting in the 1980s, federal, state, and local representatives realized that if they proposed a new law and named it after someone who had suffered terribly in a highly publicized crime, their campaign would gain a great deal of favorable media coverage that would help build support for the law's passage and for their own reelection. All suggestions for revisions and additions to the existing body of laws can be controversial and might provoke opposition, but officeholders who dare to argue against proposed legislation that enshrines the name of an innocent person harmed by a vicious predator run the risk of being branded "antivictim."

Probably the best-known example of a law bearing the name of a crime victim is this *"Brady Bill," Handgun Violence Prevention Act*. The title honors James Brady, President Reagan's press secretary, who was shot in the head in 1981 by an assassin trying to kill the president (the gunfire killed two persons guarding the president). This *"Brady Bill,"* which Congress passed in 1993, imposed a computer-based FBI criminal background check on anyone who seeks to buy a firearm from a federally licensed dealer, in a stepped-up attempt to prevent arms purchases by individuals deemed to be dangerous (which had been forbidden by law since 1968, as a reaction to the assassination of President Kennedy in 1963).

The *Jeanne Clery Disclosure of Campus Security Policy and Campus Crime Statistics Act* (originally referred to as the Crime Awareness and Campus Security Act) was signed into law in 1990. Named to memorialize a 19-year-old freshman who was raped and murdered in her dorm by another student, the law requires all colleges that receive federal aid to maintain and disclose annual reports about a long list of crimes that take place on or near their campuses.

The *Emmett Till Unsolved Civil Rights Crime Act* went into effect in 2008. It set up a cold case unit within the Department of Justice to reinvestigate bias-motivated murders committed before 1970 that had violated a person's civil rights. Emmett Till, a 14-year-old black teenager, was kidnapped, tortured, shot, and dumped into a river in 1955 by two white racists for flirting with the wife of one of the two men at a grocery store in rural Mississippi (see Anderson, 2011).

The *Matthew Shepard and James Byrd Jr. Hate Crimes Prevention Act* was passed by Congress in 2009. Named to commemorate a gay college student who was beaten to death by bigots, and an African-American man who was dragged to his death behind a pickup truck by white supremacists, the legislation expanded the coverage of the federal government's hate-crime law, which was originally passed in 1969.

The *Adam Walsh Child Protection and Safety Act*, also known as the Sex Offender Registration and Notification Act (SORNA) was enacted by Congress in 2006. Named in the memory of a six-year-old who was abducted from a department store and then viciously murdered, the act strengthened sex offender registration requirements, stiffened the penalties of existing laws forbidding sexually abusing and exploiting children, and extended federal authority over kidnappings.

Over the decades, many state legislatures have passed statutes named after victims, such as New Jersey's *Megan's Law*. Commemorating a seven-year-old girl slain in 1994 by her next door neighbor, a habitual child molester, each state's version of *Megan's Law* mandates that convicted sex offenders register with their local police department, and that community residents be notified of their whereabouts, so that parents—in theory, at least—can take steps to better shield their children from these potentially dangerous strangers.

Since the 1980s, state and county legislatures nationwide have enacted thousands of new laws named after victims (see Lovett, 2006; and Editors, *New York Post*, 2006). The rediscovery of the victim's plight by lawmakers can evoke two very different responses. The first is to view certain highly publicized tragedies as a "final straw" that focused much-needed attention on a festering problem, mobilized public opinion, and triggered long overdue legislative action by well-meaning elected officials. The other response is to suspect that vote-seeking politicians are exploiting the media attention surrounding highly emotional but very complicated situations for their own personal advantage (to advance their careers). They grab headlines by proposing a change in the existing body of law that will allegedly prevent such an incident from happening again. The strong feelings evoked by a recent tragedy make it difficult for opponents to question the wisdom of implementing the reforms proposed in the name of the victim.

The task for victimologists is to start out as impartial observers and to gather data to see whether the legislation bearing the name of a victim actually offers any tangible assistance to ease the plight of individuals harmed in this particular manner. Also, are these measures really effective in preventing innocent people from being hurt by these kinds of offenses in the future, or do they just punish offenders more severely in behalf of those they already injured? Some of these recent legal reforms enacted to ostensibly reduce the occurrence of a certain kind of victimization might turn out to be ill-conceived, seriously flawed, ineffective, or even counterproductive (for example, see Cooper, 2005).

The News Media: Portraying the Victims' Plight

The news media deserve a great deal of credit for rediscovering victims. In the past, offenders received the lion's share of coverage in newspapers, magazines, and on radio and television stations. Stories delved into their backgrounds, their motives, and what should be done with them—usually how severely they should be punished. Scant attention was paid to the flesh-and-blood individuals who suffered because of the offender's illegal activities.

But now those who are on the receiving end of criminal behavior are no longer invisible or forgotten people. Details about the injured parties are routinely included to inject some human interest into crime stories. Balanced accounts can vividly describe the victims' plight: how they were harmed, what losses they incurred, what intense emotions

distressed them, what helped or even hindered their recovery, how they were treated by caregivers, and how their cases were handled by the legal system. By remaining faithful to the facts, journalists can enable their audiences to transcend their own limited experiences with lawbreakers and to see emergencies, tragedies, and triumphs through the eyes of the injured parties. Skillful reporting and insightful observations allow the public to better understand and empathize with the actions and reactions of those who suffered harm.

In highly publicized cases, interviews by journalists have given victims a voice in how their cases are resolved in court, and even how the problem (such as kidnappings, easy access to firearms, or collisions caused by drunk drivers) should be handled by the criminal justice system. Media coverage has given these individuals with firsthand experiences a public platform to campaign for wider societal reforms (Dignan, 2005).

However, victims—and if they perish violently, their next of kin—often complain about **sensationalism**, a kind of coverage that has been branded as "scandal-mongering," "pandering," "yellow journalism," and "tabloidism." Newspapers, magazines, radio stations, and television networks are prone to engage in sensationalism because they are profit-oriented businesses. Shocking stories attract readers, listeners, and viewers. Blaring headlines, gripping accounts, colorful phrases, memorable quotes, and other forms of media "hype" build the huge audiences that enable media enterprises to charge advertisers high rates. Producers, editors, and reporters who seek to play up the human-interest angle may exploit the plight of persons who have suffered devastating wounds and losses, having found that crime stories attract a lot more notice if they are spiced up with a heavy dose of sex, gore, and raw emotions. In the quest for higher ratings, coverage can sink to an "If it bleeds, it leads" orientation that infects commercially driven "infotainment." If reporters turn a personal tragedy into a media circus and a public spectacle, their intrusive behavior might be considered an invasion of privacy. Overzealous journalists frequently are criticized for showing corpses lying in a pool of blood, maintaining vigils outside a grieving family's home, or shoving microphones into the faces of bereaved, dazed, or hysterical relatives at funerals. The injured party receives unwanted publicity and experiences a loss of control as others comment upon, draw lessons from, and impose judgments on what he or she allegedly did, or did not do, or should have done. It appears that incidents receive intensive and sustained coverage only when some aspect of the victim–offender relationship stands out as an attention-grabber: The act, the perpetrator, or the target must be unusual, unexpected, strange, or perverse. Causing harm in ways that is typical, commonplace, or predictable is just not newsworthy. Editors and journalists sift through an overwhelming number of real-life tragedies that come to their attention (largely through contacts within the local police department) and select the cases that are most likely to seize center stage, shock people out of their complacency, or arouse the public's social conscience.

The stories that are featured strike a responsive chord in audiences because the incidents symbolize some significant theme—for example, that anyone can be chosen at random, simply for being at the wrong place at the wrong time; that complete strangers cannot be trusted; and that bystanders might not come to a person's aid, especially in anonymous, big-city settings (Roberts, 1989). Historically, heinous crimes that have received the most press attention have had one or more of these elements in common: Either the injured party or the defendant is a child, woman, or a prominent or wealthy person; intimations of "promiscuous" behavior by the victim or defendant help explain the event; and some doubts linger about the guilt of the convict; and the circumstances surrounding the slaying seemed unusual (Stephens, 1988; and Buckler and Travis, 2005). For example, it is predictable that the unsolved Christmas Eve murder of a six-year-old beauty contest winner in her own upscale home, with her parents and brother upstairs, would be the subject of incessant tabloid sensationalism (Johnson, 2008). Similarly, the disappearance of a 24-year-old intern after jogging in a park set off an avalanche of lurid speculation when it was revealed that she was having an affair with a married

Congressman (the case was solved years later when her killer turned out to be a complete stranger who had attacked other women in that same park at about the same time) (Tavernise, 2011). Furthermore, media coverage may reflect the unconscious biases of talk show hosts, correspondents, and editors who work in the newsroom. For example, members of minority communities have charged that national news outlets, especially those on cable TV, focus relentless attention on the disappearance of attractive white people, particularly young women and children, but overlook equally compelling cases involving individuals who do not share these characteristics (see Lyman, 2005; Memmott, 2005; and Gardiner, 2008).

If these charges are true, the problem may go deeper and may reflect the shortcomings of market-driven journalism. The gatekeepers, under organizational pressures to sell their product, sift through a huge pool of items and select stories they perceive will resonate with the general public, at the expense of presenting an accurate sampling of the full range of tragedies taking place locally, nationally, and around the world (see Buckler and Travis, 2005).

And yet, it can be argued that media coverage of crime stories is an absolute necessity in an open society. Reporters and news editors have a constitutional right, derived from the First Amendment's guarantee of a free press, to present information about lawbreaking to the public without interference from the government. Illegal activities not only harm particular individuals but also pose a threat to those who may be next. People have a right as well as a need to know about the emergence of dangerous conditions and ominous developments, and the media has an obligation to communicate this information accurately.

The problem is that the public's right to know about crime and the media's right to report these incidents clash with the victim's right to privacy. Journalists, editors, and victims' advocates are addressing questions of fairness and ethics in a wide variety of forums, ranging from blogs and posted comments on the Web and letters to the editor in newspapers, to professional conferences and lawsuits in civil court.

Several remedies have been proposed to curb abusive coverage of a victim's plight. One approach would be to enact new laws to shield those who suffer from needless public exposure, such as unnecessary disclosure of names and addresses in news coverage or on websites. An alternative approach would be to rely on the self-restraint of reporters and their editors. The fact that most news accounts of sexual molestations of children and of rapes no longer reveal the names of those who were harmed is an example of this self-policing approach in action. A third remedy would be for the media to adopt a code of professional ethics. Journalists who abide by the code would "read victims their rights" at the outset of interviews, just as police officers read suspects their Miranda rights when taking them into custody (see Thomason and Babbilli, 1987; and Karmen, 1989).

Victimologists could play an important role in monitoring progress by studying how frequently and how seriously news reporters insult and defame the subjects of their stories and how successfully the different reform strategies prevent this kind of exploitation, or at least minimize abusive invasions of privacy.

Then there is the question of accuracy in media imagery. For example, the most publicized stories about mass killings center on a lone gunman who randomly shoots complete strangers in a public setting. However, a careful analysis of multiple homicides reveals that the most frequent category of mass killings is the head of a household slaying all the members of his family, so the widely disseminated image misidentifies the greatest source of danger (Duwe, 2000). Journalists often put forward intriguing possibilities without sufficient documentation in their coverage of victims' issues. A story in the news might hypothesize that there are a great many battered women living in insular, devoutly religious communities who are extremely reluctant to turn to outside authorities for help. It is up to victimologists to treat these plausible assertions as research hypotheses to be tested, to see if the available data support or undermine these impressions circulating in the media.

Commercial Interests: Selling Security Products and Services to Victims

Just as the rediscovery of victims by elected officials and the news media has benefits as well as drawbacks, so too does the new attention paid to injured parties by businesses. The development of this new market of people seeking out protective services and antitheft devices simultaneously raises the possibility of commercial exploitation. Profiteers can engage in fear mongering and false advertising in order to cash in on the legitimate concerns and desires of customers who feel particularly vulnerable and even panicky. In situations where entrepreneurs issue bold claims about their products' effectiveness, objectivity takes the form of scientific skepticism. Victimologists must represent the public interest and demand, "Prove those assertions! Where is the evidence?"

Consider the question of whether expensive automobile security systems actually work as well as their manufacturers' advertisements say they do. For instance, do car alarms really provide the layer of protection against break-ins that their purchasers want and that sales pitches claim? In New York, the City Council passed regulations restricting the installation of new car alarms because the devices were deemed to be largely ineffective as well as a serious source of noise pollution. Rather than agreeing with frustrated motorists that the wailing sirens do no good, or trying to defend the alarm industry's reputation and profits, nonpartisan victimologists can independently evaluate the effectiveness of these antitheft devices. Are car alarms really useful in deterring break-ins; in minimizing losses of accessories such as car stereos, navigation systems, or air bags; in preventing vehicles from being driven away; and in aiding the police to catch thieves red-handed?

VICTIMOLOGY CONTRIBUTES TO THE REDISCOVERY PROCESS

The emergence and acceptance of victimology has furthered the rediscovery of new groups of victims. This process—in which people whose plight was recognized long ago, neglected for many years, and now again gains the attention it deserves—goes on and on with no end in sight. Such rediscovered groups include battered women; females who have suffered date rapes; kidnapped children; people targeted by bigots; drivers attacked by enraged fellow motorists; pedestrians, passengers, and drivers killed in collisions caused by drunkards; prisoners sexually assaulted by fellow inmates; and detainees killed while in government custody.

The rediscovery process is more than just a well-intentioned humanitarian undertaking, media campaign, or example of special pleading. It has far-reaching consequences for everyday life, and the stakes are high. Injured people who gain legitimacy as innocent victims and win public backing are in a position to make compelling claims on government resources (asking for compensation payments to cover the expenses they incurred from their physical wounds, for example). People who know from first-hand experience about the suffering caused by illegal acts also can advance persuasive arguments about reforming criminal justice policies concerning arrest, prosecution, trial procedures, appropriate sentences, and custodial control over prisoners. Finally, rediscovered victims can assert that preventing others from suffering the same fate requires a change in prevailing cultural values about tolerating social conditions that generate criminal behavior. Victims even can make recommendations that are taken seriously about the ways people should and should not behave (for instance, how husbands should treat their wives, and how closely parents should supervise their children) and even the proper role of government (such as how readily the state should intervene in "private" matters such as violence between intimates).

The process of rediscovery usually unfolds through a series of steps and stages. The sequential model that is proposed below incorporates observations drawn from several sources. The notion of developmental stages arises from the **self-definition of the victimization process** (Viano, 1989). The natural history, career, or life-cycle perspective comes from examining models of ongoing social problems (see Fuller and Myers, 1941; Ross and Staines, 1972; and Spector and Kitsuse, 1987). The focus on how concerns about being harmed are first raised, framed, and then publicized arises from the **constructionist approach** (see Best, 1989b). The idea of inevitable clashes of opposing interest groups battling over governmental resources and influence over legislation comes from sociology's **conflict approach**. The realization that there is an ongoing struggle by victimized groups for respect and support

in the court of public opinion is an application of the concept of **stigma contests** (Schur, 1984).

Stage 1: Calling Attention to an Overlooked Problem

The rediscovery process is set in motion whenever activists begin to raise the public's consciousness about some type of illegal situation that "everybody knows" happens but few have cared enough to investigate or try to correct. These **moral entrepreneurs**, who lead campaigns to change laws and win people over to their point of view, usually have firsthand experience with a specific problem as well as direct, personal knowledge of the pain and suffering that accompany it. Particularly effective self-help and advocacy groups have been set up by mothers whose children were killed in collisions caused by drunk drivers, survivors of officers slain in the line of duty, and parents who endured the agony of searching for their missing children, among others. Additional individuals who deserve credit for arousing an indifferent public include the targets of hate-driven bias crimes, adults haunted by the way they were molested when they were young, women brutally raped by acquaintances they trusted, and wives viciously beaten by their husbands. These victims called attention to a state of affairs that people took for granted as harmful but shrugged off with a "What can anyone do about it?" attitude.

These activists responded, "Things don't have to be this way!" Exploitative and hurtful relationships don't have to be tolerated—they can be prevented, avoided, and outlawed; governmental policies can be altered; and the criminal justice system can be made more accountable and responsive to its "clients." As Stage 1 moves along, activists function as the inspiration and nucleus for the formation of self-help groups that provide mutual aid and solace and also undertake campaigns for reform. Members of support networks believe that only people who have suffered through the same ordeal can really understand and appreciate what others just like them are going through (a basic tenet borrowed from therapeutic communities that assist substance abusers to recover from drug addiction).

Activists also state that victims' troubles stem from larger social problems that are beyond any individual's ability to control; consequently, those who suffer should not be blamed for causing their own misfortunes. Finally, activists argue that recovery requires empowerment within the criminal justice process so that victims can pursue what they define as their own best interests, whether to see to it that the offender receives the maximum punishment permitted by law, is compelled to undergo treatment, and/or is ordered to pay their bills for crime-related expenses.

To build wider support for their causes, moral entrepreneurs and self-help groups organize themselves into loosely structured coalitions such as the antirape and antibattering movements. Usually, one or two well-publicized cases are pointed to as symbolic of the problem. Soon many other victims come forward to tell about similar personal experiences. Then experts such as social workers, detectives, and lawyers testify about the suffering that these kinds of victims routinely endure and plead that legal remedies are urgently needed. Extensive media coverage is a prerequisite for success. The group's plight becomes known because of investigative reports on television, talk radio discussions, magazine cover stories, newspaper editorials, and the circulation of these accounts on blogs. Meanwhile, press conferences, demonstrations, marches, candlelight vigils, petition drives, ballot initiatives, lawsuits, and lobbying campaigns keep the pressure on and the issue alive.

Sociologically, what happens during the first stage can be termed the **social construction** of a social problem, along with **claims-making** and **typification** (see Spector and Kitsuse, 1987; and Best, 1989b), when a consensus about a pattern of behavior that is harmful and should be subjected to criminal penalties is constructed. This crystallization of public opinion is a product of the activities of moral entrepreneurs, support groups, and their allies. Spokespersons engage in a claims-making process to air grievances, estimate how many people are hurt in this manner, suggest appropriate remedies to facilitate recovery, and recommend measures that could prevent this kind of physical, emotional, and financial suffering from burdening others. Through the process of typification, advocates point out classic cases and textbook examples that illustrate the menace to society against which they are campaigning.

Stage 2: Winning Victories, Implementing Reforms

The rediscovery process enters its second stage whenever activists and advocacy groups begin to make headway toward their goals.

At first, it might be necessary to set up independent demonstration projects or pilot programs to prove the need for special services. Then government grants can be secured, or federal, state, and local agencies can copy successful models or take over some responsibility for providing information, assistance, and protection. For instance, the battered women's movement set up shelters, and the antirape movement established crisis centers. Eventually local governments funded safe houses where women and their young children could seek refuge, and hospitals (and even some universities) organized their own 24-hour rape hotlines and crisis-intervention services.

Individuals subjected to bias crimes were rediscovered during the 1990s. During the 1980s, only private organizations monitored incidents of hate-motivated violence and vandalism directed against racial and religious minorities, as well as homosexuals. But in 1990, the government got involved when Congress passed the Hate Crime Statistics Act, which authorized the FBI to undertake the task of collecting reports about bias crimes from local police departments. Achievements that mark this second stage in the rediscovery process include the imposition of harsher penalties and the establishment of specially trained law enforcement units in many jurisdictions to more effectively recognize, investigate, solve, and prosecute bias crimes. Self-help groups offer injured parties tangible forms of support.

The best example of a rediscovery campaign that has raised consciousness, won victories, and secured reforms is the struggle waged since the early 1980s by Mothers Against Drunk Driving (MADD). It is an organization of parents, mostly mothers, whose sons or daughters were injured or killed by drunk drivers. These anguished survivors argued that for too long the "killer drunk" was able to get away with a socially

13

acceptable and judicially excusable form of homicide because more people identified with the intoxicated driver than with the innocent person who died from injuries sustained in the collision.

Viewing themselves as the relatives of bona fide crime victims, not merely accident victims, these crusaders were able to move the issue from the obituary page to the front page by using a wide range of tactics to mobilize public support, including candlelight vigils, pledges of responsible behavior by children and family cooperation by their parents, and demonstrations outside courthouses. Local chapters of their national self-help organizations offered concrete services: pamphlets were distributed through hospital emergency rooms and funeral parlors, bereavement support groups assisted grieving relatives, and volunteers accompanied victims and their families to police stations, prosecutors' offices, trials, and sentencing hearings.

Buoyed by very favorable media coverage, their lobbying campaigns brought about a crackdown on DUI (driving under the influence) and DWI (driving while intoxicated) offenders. Enforcement measures include roadblocks, license suspensions and revocations, more severe criminal charges, and on-the-spot confiscations of vehicles. Their efforts also led to reforms of drinking laws, such as raising the legal drinking age to 21 and lowering the blood-alcohol concentration levels that officially define impairment and intoxication (Thompson, 1984). Along with the 55-mph speed limit, mandatory seat belt laws, improved vehicle safety engineering, better roads, and breakthroughs in emergency medical services, the achievements of MADD and its allies have saved countless lives (Ayres, 1994).

Stage 3: Emergence of an Opposition and Development of Resistance to Further Changes

The third stage in the rediscovery process is marked by the emergence of groups that oppose the goals sought by victims of rediscovered crimes. The victims had to overcome public apathy during Stage 1 and bureaucratic inertia during Stage 2, and they encounter resistance from other quarters during Stage 3. A backlash arises against perceived excesses in their demands. The general argument of opponents is that the pendulum is swinging too far in the other direction, that people are uncritically embracing a point of view that is too extreme, unbalanced, and one-sided, and that special interests are trying to advance an agenda that does not really benefit the law-abiding majority.

Spokespersons for a group of recently rediscovered victims might come under fire for a number of reasons. They might be criticized for overestimating the number of people harmed when the actual threat to the public, according to the opposition, is much smaller. Advocates might be condemned for portraying those who were harmed as totally innocent of blame—and therefore deserving of unqualified support—when in reality some are partly at fault and shouldn't get all the assistance that they demand. Activists might be castigated for making unreasonable demands that will cost the government (and taxpayers) too much money. They also might be denounced for insisting upon new policies that would undermine cherished constitutional rights, such as the presumption of innocence of persons accused of breaking the law (for example, allegations about child abuse or elder abuse can lead to investigations that permanently stigmatize the alleged wrongdoers even if the charges later turn out to be unfounded) (see Crystal, 1988).

When the antirape movement claimed to have discovered an outbreak of date rapes against college students, skeptics asked why federally mandated statistics about incidents reported to campus security forces showed no such upsurge. They contended that hard-to-classify liaisons were being redefined as full-fledged sexual assaults, thereby maligning some admittedly sexually aggressive and exploitative college men as hard-core criminals (see Gilbert, 1991; Hellman, 1993; and MacDonald, 2008a). When the battered women's movement organized a clemency drive to free certain imprisoned wives who had slain their abusive husband (in self-defense, they contended, but prosecutors and jurors disagreed), critics charged that these women would be getting away with revenge killings. When incest survivors insisted that new memory retrieval techniques had helped them recall repressed recollections of sexual molestations by parents, stepparents, and other guardians, some accused family members banded together and insisted they were being unfairly slandered because of a therapist-induced

false memory syndrome (see Chapters 8, 9, and 10 for an in-depth analysis of these three controversies).

Even the many accomplishments of the entire victims' movement can be questioned (see Weed, 1995). Under the banner of advancing victims' rights, pressure groups might advocate policies that undermine whatever progress has been made toward securing humane treatment for offenders and ex-prisoners and inadvertently "widen the net" of formal social control exercised by the police and prosecutors over deviants and rebels. Victim activism can unnecessarily heighten fear and anxiety levels about the dangers of violence and theft and divert funds away from social programs designed to tackle the root causes of street crime.

Groups that focus their energies on the plight of individuals harmed by street crimes also can distract attention from other socially harmful activities such as polluting the environment or marketing unsafe products, and their reforms can raise expectations about full recovery that just cannot be reasonably met (Fattah, 1986). It is even possible that what was formerly a grassroots movement run by volunteers who solicited donations has metamorphosed into a virtual "victim industry." It engages in a type of mass production, churning out newly identified groups of victims by dwelling on kinds of suffering that can arise from noncriminal sources such as bullying, emotional abuse, sexual harassment, sexual addiction, eating disorders, and credit card dependency (Best, 1997).

Stage 4: Research and Temporary Resolution of Disputes

It is during the fourth and last stage of the rediscovery process that victimologists can make their most valuable contributions. By getting to the bottom of unsolved mysteries and by intervening in bitter conflicts, victimologists can become a source of accurate assessments, helping evaluate competing claims about whether the problem has or has not been brought under control, and whether treatment and prevention measures are genuinely effective. By maintaining objectivity, victimologists can serve as arbiters in these heated disputes.

For instance, ever since the early 1980s, parents have been petrified about the specter of kidnappers

spiriting off their children. Highly publicized cases of vicious pedophiles abducting, molesting, and then slaying youngsters periodically rekindle this smoldering panic. Claims by some child-search organizations that each year tens of thousands of children were being kidnapped by complete strangers created near hysteria among parents until some journalists challenged their estimates as gross exaggerations. A blue-ribbon panel of experts convened by the U.S. Department of Justice in the 1980s and again in the late 1990s sought to make sense out of competing claims about just how often such unnerving and infuriating tragedies take place each year. The researchers concluded that killings and long-term abductions by complete strangers were, thankfully, very rare and did not pose a dire threat to the well-being of the next generation.

During the 1980s, a series of shocking shootings by disgruntled gun-toting employees led to the rediscovery of victims of "workplace violence." In the aftermath of these slaughters, worried workers insisted that employers call in occupational safety specialists to devise protection and prevention programs. Anxious managers usually acceded, fearing expensive lawsuits and lowered morale and productivity. But researchers have determined that these highly publicized multiple murders accounted for just a tiny fraction of a multi-faceted but far less newsworthy set of dangers. Most of the cases of workplace violence across the country involve robberies, unarmed assaults, and complaints about stalkers acting in a menacing way. Many incidents that disrupt the smooth functioning of factories and offices are not even criminal matters, such as instances of verbal abuse, bullying, and sexual harassment (Rugala, 2004).

During Stage 4, a standoff, deadlock, or truce might develop between victims' advocates who want more changes, and their opponents who resist any further reforms. But the fourth phase is not necessarily the final phase. The findings and policy recommendations of neutral parties such as victimologists and criminologists do not settle questions once and for all. Concerns about some type of victimization can recede from public consciousness for years, only to reappear when social conditions are ripe for a new four stage cycle of rediscovery of 1) claims making; 2) reform; 3) opposition; and 4) temporary resolution.

studies based on surveys completed by municipal and county police departments have concluded that most of these law enforcement agencies lacked sufficient policies and adequate training to accurately identify trafficking victims and successfully investigate their cases (Wilson, Walsh, and Kleuber, 2006; and Farrell, McDevitt, and Fahey, 2010).

The FBI and the U.S. Department of Homeland Security have compiled lists of behaviors and situations to help law enforcement personnel spot potential victims of human trafficking. Officers and others should be on the lookout for the potential signs of being trafficked for the purpose of exploitation in the sex trade or for debt peonage that appear in Table 2.1.

Clearly, the true level of seriousness of the problem and the effectiveness of government relief and rescue efforts remain subjects of controversy that require additional research. This is why the plight of trafficking victims within the United States can be considered to be currently at Stage 4 of the rediscovery process.

T A B L E 2.1   Possible Indicators That a Person Is a Trafficking Victim

Does the individual ...?

- Live on or near the work premises
- Live in a sparse place with many other occupants
- Lack personal space and possessions
- Frequently move from one work site to another
- Appear unfamiliar with how to get around the neighborhood
- Appear unable to travel around freely
- Admit that he/she cannot socialize with outsiders and attend religious services
- Disclose that he/she was recruited for one line of work but then was compelled to perform other tasks
- Disclose that earnings are garnished and held by someone else
- Indicate that identification and travel documents are held by someone else
- Appear to have been coached about what to say to immigration and police officers
- Appear unable to talk openly and to communicate freely with family and friends
- Look injured from beatings or show signs of malnourishment or lack of medical treatment
- Defer to someone else who insists on speaking or interpreting for him/her
- Claim to be represented by the same attorney that handles the cases of many other undocumented workers (illegal aliens)

SOURCES: Blue Campaign, 2010; Walker-Rodriguez and Hill, 2011.

A number of types of formerly overlooked victims have reached Stage 4 in the rediscovery process. Recently collected data can be analyzed to try to put the public's fears into perspective, to attempt to resolve ongoing controversies, and to assess the impact of countermeasures designed to assist those who are suffering and to prevent others from sharing their same fate (An example appears in Box 2.1).

REDISCOVERING ADDITIONAL GROUPS OF VICTIMS

Academics, practitioners, social movements, elected officials, the news media, and commercial interests continue to drive the process of rediscovery forward. A steady stream of fresh revelations serves as a reminder that neglected groups still are "out there" and that they have compelling stories to tell, unmet needs, and legitimate demands for assistance and support. Usually, they continue to escape public notice until some highly unusual or horrific incident reveals how they are being harmed and attracts the interest of the news media and criminal justice agencies. The types of victims whose plight is now being rediscovered—but who require much more scrutiny and analysis, and creative remedies—are listed in Box 2.2.

B O X 2.2 The Process of Rediscovery Goes On and On

These recently recognized groups of victims face special problems that require imaginative solutions. They eventually will receive the assistance and support they need as the rediscovery process continues to focus attention and resources on their plight:

- Disabled individuals (deaf, blind, mentally retarded, mentally ill, or afflicted in other ways) who were assaulted or molested (Office for Victims of Crime, 2003; and Barrow, 2008)

- People whose attackers cannot be arrested and prosecuted because they are members of foreign delegations granted "diplomatic immunity" and are able to escape justice by returning home (Ashman and Trescott, 1987; Sieh, 1990; Lynch, 2003; and Grow, 2011)

- Immigrants who feel they cannot come forward and ask the police for help without revealing that they are "illegal aliens" who lack the proper documents and are subject to deportation (Davis and Murray, 1995; Davis, Erez, and Avitabile, 2001; Chan, 2007; and Hoffmaster et al., 2010)

- Homeless adults robbed, assaulted, and murdered on the streets and in shelters (Fitzpatrick, LaGory, and Ritchey, 1993; and Green, 2008)

- Homeless runaway teens who are vulnerable to sexual exploitation and rape (Tyler et al., 2005)

- Hotel guests who suffer thefts and assaults because of lax security measures (Prestia, 1993; Owsley, 2005; and Ho et al., 2009)

- Tourists who blunder into dangerous situations avoided by streetwise locals and are easy prey because they let their guard down (Rohter, 1993; Glensor and Peak, 2004; Lee, 2005; and Murphy, 2006)

- Delivery truck drivers who are preyed upon by robbers, hijackers, and highway snipers (Sexton, 1994; and Duret and Patrick, 2004)

- Motorists and pedestrians slammed into during high speed chases by fugitives seeking to avoid arrest or by squad cars in hot pursuit (Gray, 1993; Crew, Fridell, and Pursell, 1995; and Schultz et al., 2010)

- Unrelated individuals, whose lives are snuffed out by vicious and demented serial killers (Holmes and DeBurger, 1988; Hickey, 1991; Egger and Egger, 2002; Pakhomou, 2004; Flegenheimer and Rosenberg, 2011; and AP, 2011); and especially prostitutes, hitchhikers, and stranded motorists, whose bodies are dumped near highways by violence-prone long-haul truckers (Glover, 2009; and Dalesio, 2011)

- Prostitutes soliciting customers on the streets or over the internet who face risks of being beaten, raped, and murdered that are many times higher than for other women in their age bracket (Boyer and James, 1983; and Salfati, James, and Ferguson, 2008)

- Newborns abandoned or killed by their distraught mothers (Yardley, 1999; and Buckley, 2007)

- Frantic relatives of "missing persons" who have vanished and are presumed dead but, since they were adults with the right to privacy, cannot be the objects of intense police manhunts unless there is evidence of foul play (McPhee, 1999; Gardiner, 2008; and NCMA, 2008)

- Suspects brutally beaten by police officers (Amnesty International USA, 1999; and Davey and Einhorn, 2007)

- Teachers attacked, injured, and even killed by their students (Fine, 2001)

- Youngsters sexually molested or physically abused through prohibited forms of corporal punishment by parents and teachers (Goodnough, 2003; and Larzelere and Baumrind, 2010)

- High school and college students subjected to abusive hazing and bullying by older students that results in injury or death (Salmivalli and Nieminen, 2002; and Montague et al., 2008)

- Students assaulted, robbed, even fatally shot by fellow students or by intruders in school buildings and schoolyards (Bastian and Taylor, 1991; Toby, 1983; NCES, 1998; DeGette, Jenson, and Colomy, 2000; and Booth, Van Hasselt, and Vecchi, 2011)

(Continued)

- Terrified residents whose homes were invaded by armed robbers (Copeland and Martin, 2006; and Thompson, 2011)
- "Mail-order brides," lured to the United States by unregulated international matchmaking services on the Internet, who fear deportation if they complain to the authorities about their husbands' violence (Briscoe, 2005; Morash, 2007; and Greenwood, 2009)
- Teenage girls and young women kidnapped and held captive as "sex slaves" by vicious rapists (Hoffman, 2003; and Jacobs, 2003)
- Unsuspecting people, usually women, who feel symbolically raped after being secretly videotaped during private moments by voyeurs using hidden spy cameras (Lovett, 2003; and Williams, 2005)
- Youngsters physically and sexually abused by child care workers and babysitters (Finkelhor and Ormrod, 2001)
- Female inmates sexually abused by corrections officers (Struckman-Johnson and Struckman-Johnson, 2002)
- Female motorists sexually abused by highway patrol officers (Tyre, 2001)
- People deceived by robbers and rapists impersonating uniformed officers as well as plainclothes detectives (Van Netta, 2011)
- Good Samaritans who try to break up crimes in progress and rescue the intended victims but wind up injured or killed themselves (Mawby, 1985; and Time et al., 2010)
- Innocent bystanders wounded or killed by bullets intended for others, often when caught in crossfire between rival street gangs or drug dealers fighting over turf (Sherman, Steele, Laufersweiler, Hoffer, and Julian, 1989; and Williams, 2009)
- People being blackmailed who are reluctant to turn to the authorities for help because that would lead to exposure of their embarrassing secrets (see Katz et al., 1993; and Robinson et al., 2010)
- Recipients, some of them children, of crank phone calls laced with threats or obscenities, made by individuals who range from "heavy breathers" and bored teenagers to dangerous assailants (Savitz, 1986; Warner, 1988; Leander et al., 2005; and Renshaw, 2008)
- Residents injured by fires or burned out of their homes, unaware that they were harmed by acts of arson until fire marshals determine that the suspicious blazes were intentionally set (Sclafani, 2005)
- Consumers who lose money in Internet cyber-swindles and "dotcons," such as online pyramid investment (Ponzi) schemes, bogus auctions, fake escrow accounts, and other computer-based frauds (Lee, 2003b; and Stajano and Wilson, 2011)
- Homeowners who become victims of mortgage fraud and foreclosure-rescue fraud and are evicted because they are swindled (FBI, 2008)

SUMMARY

Victimologists are social scientists who strive for objectivity when studying the characteristics of victims, the suffering they endure, their reactions to their plight, their interactions with offenders, and the way others (such as journalists, elected officials, and people allied with social movements and commercial interests) respond to them. Victimology's findings contribute to an ongoing rediscovery process, which constantly brings the plight of additional overlooked groups to the public's attention. The rediscovery process goes through several stages. After a group's plight becomes known and reforms are implemented, an opposition frequently arises that resists further changes that might be to the group's advantage. Victimologists can help resolve disputes by studying how newly rediscovered groups suffer and whether efforts to assist them are really working as intended.

SECTION II

Data Sources and Patterns of Crime Victimization

MEASURING CRIMINAL VICTIMIZATION
by William G. Doerner and Steven P. Lab

INTRODUCTION

Measuring the extent of criminal victimization has long been a goal of the criminal justice system and those who study crime. Researchers and policy-makers typically rely on three major data sources for measuring the level of crime (O'Brien, 1985). The first source, official records of police departments, is the traditional depository for crime information. However, dissatisfaction with police records prompted researchers to look elsewhere. Surveys that ask people about offenses they have committed became a popular alternative. Unfortunately, these surveys are not conducted on an annual or national basis, and they reveal very little about the victims of crime. A third tactic is to question individuals about instances in which they were victimized. As we shall see in this chapter, this is perhaps the most cited data source today. Despite the common goal of measuring crime, none of these strategies alone yields a definitive answer to the question of how much victimization occurs in society. Each scheme provides a slightly different angle from which to view the crime problem. Each one of these methods has its own distinct advantages and inherent flaws.

This chapter examines some issues involved in measuring victimization, paying particular attention to the development and use of victimization surveys. We will also examine the level of crime and victimization presented by official police reports of crime and the *National Crime Victimization Survey*. As you will see, victim surveys provide a wealth of data that is quite useful for studying victims and related issues.

OFFICIAL POLICE REPORTS

The most widely cited measure of crime is the *Uniform Crime Reports* (UCR), produced by the Federal Bureau of Investigation (FBI). The UCR was initially developed by the International Association of Chiefs of Police before being taken over by the FBI in 1931 (Chilton, 2010). The UCR was envisioned as a mechanism by which police departments in different jurisdictions could exchange relevant information about crime. Police administrators around the country were very supportive of this effort. They felt that such knowledge could help identify the magnitude of the crime problem, map changes over time, and guide actions to combat the criminal element. This reporting system was meant to be a tool for the law enforcement community throughout the U.S.A.

The UCR is characterized by a number of interesting and advantageous features. First, crime data are compiled annually from jurisdictions throughout the country. Such consistency and broad geographical coverage allows crime comparisons from year to year and from place to place. The fact that the UCR has been in operation since 1931 means that it is one of the longest-running systematic data collection efforts in the social sciences.

Second, the UCR has been influential in providing standardized crime definitions. Common definitions make it possible to draw comparisons across different times and jurisdictions. To achieve this goal, the FBI introduced what it calls the *Index*, or *Part I*, Offenses. The FBI divides these serious crimes into two groups. *Personal offenses* include murder, forcible rape, robbery, and aggravated assault. *Property offenses* consist of burglary, larceny-theft, motor vehicle theft, and arson. While state statutes and local codes are not bound to these definitions, the UCR does introduce a common metric among the 50 states.

WEB ACTIVITY

You can read a great deal about the UCR and the data that are available on the FBI website at **https://ucr.fbi.gov/ucr-publications.**

Third, the UCR gathers a large amount of information and details about the *Index* crimes. These data are especially useful when attempting to identify patterns and trends about crime and criminals. In addition, the UCR collects data on reported crimes and arrests for an additional 21 categories of offenses, known as the *Part II* Offenses. Included in this category are sex offenses (besides rape), offenses against the family, and vandalism. The same level of detail as found in the *Part I* Offenses, however, is not collected for these crimes.

The UCR is not immune from problems or disadvantages. Perhaps the greatest concern is that the UCR overlooks the *dark figure of crime*. In other words, these tabulations reflect only offenses that are known to the police. Any incidents in which victims or witnesses opt not to call the police are excluded from UCR figures. This drawback prompts critics to argue that the UCR grossly under-reports the true level of crime in society. The UCR reflects police—and not necessarily criminal—activity.

A second limitation with the UCR is its reliance on the "hierarchy rule." The *hierarchy rule* dictates that only one offense (typically the most serious offense) is recorded when multiple offenses occur at the same time (Chilton, 2010). For example, when an offender robs a bank with a weapon and simultaneously detains customers and takes their wallets, he or she is committing multiple robberies, theft, assault, and kidnapping—but only a single count of robbery is recorded. Under this rule, the number of crimes recorded falls short of the actual number of offenses.

Another major concern, particularly for our discussion, is the fact that the UCR offers little information on victims and offenders. The UCR gathers detailed data primarily on the more serious personal offenses (murder, forcible rape, robbery, and aggravated assault). Even then, most of the data deal only with persons who are arrested. There is very little information about the victim, the victim's circumstances, the context of the offense, and other potentially valuable information. This fact should not be surprising because law enforcement is oriented more toward dealing with offenders than with crime victims.

Interest in victims and the need to know more about individual criminal events has led to changes in the UCR system over the years. The *Supplementary Homicide Reports* (SHR) was initiated in 1976 and provides data on victim characteristics, location, offender characteristics, relationship between the victim and offender, the use of weapons, and the circumstances surrounding the homicide event. As such, the SHR offers information about the homicide victim and victimization not typically found in the balance of the UCR data. Data from the SHR are incorporated into the *Crime in the United States* reports produced each year by the FBI. Based on the SHR, we know that homicides rarely occur in commercial settings, occur more often on weekends, involve acquaintances or intimates, and typically occur with little planning (Schwartz & Gertseva, 2010). Despite the value of the SHR, problems with missing data and a lack of knowledge about the offender place limitations on its use (Schwartz & Gertseva, 2010).

The most recent set of changes in the UCR has been the introduction of the *National Incident-Based Reporting System* (NIBRS). The NIBRS grew out of a report completed in the mid-1980s that examined the changing needs for data collection and analysis that could assist law enforcement in combating crime. The NIBRS data have several major advantages over the traditional UCR data. First, the NIBRS collects detailed information on 23 categories with 49 total offenses (see Box 2.1) rather than just the eight Index Offenses. Second, rather than abiding by the hierarchy rule and counting only the most serious Index Offenses, the NIBRS reports on all of the offenses that occur during a criminal incident. Third, the NIBRS collects over 50 data elements, most of which are not found in the traditional UCR data, for each crime incident. Among the information included in this expanded data collection process is detailed

BOX 2.1 NIBRS OFFENSE CATEGORIES

Arson	Kidnapping/Abduction
Assault Offenses	Larceny/Theft Offenses
Bribery	Motor Vehicle Theft
Burglary/Breaking and Entering	Pornography/Obscene Material
Counterfeiting/Forgery	Prostitution Offenses
Destruction/Damage/Vandalism	Robbery
Drug/Narcotic Offenses	Sex Offenses, Forcible
Embezzlement	Sex Offenses, Non-Forcible
Extortion/Blackmail	Stolen Property Offenses
Fraud Offenses	Weapon Law Violations
Gambling Offenses	
Homicide Offenses	Source: Compiled from Federal Bureau of Investigation
Human Trafficking Offenses	(2015a).

BOX 2.2 INFORMATION COLLECTED BY NIBRS

Offense Information

- Bias motivation
- Location type
- Number of premises entered
- Method of entry
- Type of criminal activity/Gang information
- Type of weapon/Force involved

Property Segment

- Type of property loss/etc.
- Property description
- Value of property
- Date recovered
- Number of stolen motor vehicles
- Number of recovered motor vehicles
- Suspected drug type
- Estimated drug quantity
- Type of drug measurement

Offender Segment

- Age, sex, race, ethnicity

Arrestee Segment

- Arrest date
- Type of arrest
- Multiple arrestee segments indicator
- Arrestee was armed
- Age, sex, race, ethnicity
- Resident status
- Disposition of arrestee under age 18

Victim Segment

- Type of victim
- Age, sex, race, ethnicity
- Resident status
- Aggravated assault/Homicide circumstances
- Additional justifiable homicide circumstances
- Type of injury
- Relationship of victim to offender

Source: Federal Bureau of Investigation (2015a).

information on the victim, the victim–offender relationship, injuries, and property loss (see Box 2.2). Other information collected includes the location of the offenses, the presence of weapons, property lost, number of victims and offenders, and arrestee information.

The great advantage of the NIBRS data is the ability of law enforcement and researchers to gain a more in-depth picture of the crime problem and to use that information to decide on appropriate courses of action. Unfortunately, participation in the NIBRS involves increased data entry requirements and data-processing abilities on the part of local law enforcement. The agencies must also meet stringent guidelines for participation. Because of these requirements, in 2014, roughly one-third of the agencies who participate annually in the UCR submitted data through the NIBRS process (Federal Bureau of Investigation, 2015a). Consequently, NIBRS data are not nationally representative. The number of agencies participating in the NIBRS is increasing every year. Local agencies using the NIBRS, however, are able to undertake more sophisticated analyses of their crime problems.

Despite the problems with the UCR, the data have a long history and are helpful in answering a variety of questions. Increased involvement in the NIBRS system will enhance the value of official police crime data. Indeed, NIBRS data have been used to examine childhood victimization, intimate partner violence, and hate crimes (Addington, 2010).

 WEB ACTIVITY

The NIBRS system offers a great deal toward understanding crime. A large amount of information about the NIBRS may be found at **https://ucr.fbi.gov/nibrs/2014.**

VICTIMIZATION SURVEYS

While the UCR has a long history, victimization surveys are only about 50 years old. Victim surveys got their start with the work of the President's Commission in the mid-1960s. The Commission came about because of problems with increasing crime and civil unrest during that era. From its inception, the President's Commission (1967) recognized that an accurate description of the crime problem was lacking. As a result, it authorized a number of independent projects to gather information about crime victims.

From that modest starting point, victimization surveys have grown into an invaluable data source. A *victimization survey*, instead of relying on police reports or other official information, entails contacting people and asking them if they have been crime victims. In looking at the development of victimization surveys, one can divide them into various stages, or "generations" (Hindelang, 1976). Each successive generation is marked by the way it grappled with several methodological problems raised in earlier phases. Box 2.3 summarizes the four generations of victimization surveys since their inception in the mid-1960s.

First-Generation Victim Surveys

The initial victim surveys, undertaken at the behest of the President's Commission (1967), represented little more than a set of extensive feasibility studies.

BOX 2.3 THE DEVELOPMENT OF VICTIMIZATION SURVEYS

First-Generation Surveys

- Mid-1960s
- Carried out for the 1967 President's Commission
- Pilot studies of the feasibility of victimization surveys
- Showed much greater victimization than police data

Second-Generation Surveys

- Late 1960s and early 1970s
- Probed methods to address problems found in first-generation surveys
- City-specific surveys

Third-Generation Surveys

- Early 1970s to late 1980s
- *National Crime Survey* (NCS) initiated in 1972
- Business victimization surveys—1972 to 1977
- City surveys—26 cities from 1972 to 1975

Fourth-Generation Surveys

- 1988 to present
- NCS renamed the *National Crime Victimization Survey*—initiated in 1992

These efforts tested whether such an approach could elicit sensitive information from the public. The researchers also wanted to determine how the criminal justice system could use these victim-based findings.

Perhaps the best known of all the initial pilot studies was the poll sponsored by the National Opinion Research Center (NORC) and reported by Ennis (1967). This effort was the first national victim survey and targeted 10,000 households throughout the U.S.A. Interviewers initially asked participants to report on incidents that happened to them during the preceding 12-month period. Next, the interviewer sought more detailed information on the two most recent and most serious offenses.

What made this survey so well known was the subsequent claim that the UCR underreported by approximately 50 percent the crime rate indicated by the *NORC Survey*. Table 2.1 contains a comparison of crime rates based on the NORC data and the UCR figures. The *NORC Survey* uncovered almost four times as many rapes and more than three times as many burglaries as did the UCR. The lone exception to reporting discrepancies was motor vehicle theft, for which the data sources produced comparable rates. This similarity was probably due to the fact that most auto insurance companies will not issue a reimbursement check unless the victim files a police report. Combining the offenses into broader categories gave a much clearer picture. The *NORC Survey* unearthed 1.9 times as many violent episodes and 2.2 times more property offenses than official crime statistics had logged. Critics quickly pointed to the NORC findings as definitive proof that official crime records were inaccurate and unreliable because they neglected the "dark figure of crime" (Biderman & Reiss, 1967).

TABLE 2.1 Comparison of NORC Victimization Rates with UCR Rates

Crime Category	NORC	UCR	Ratio of NORC to UCR
Homicide	3.0	5.1	0.6
Rape	42.5	11.6	3.7
Robbery	94.0	61.4	1.5
Aggravated Assault	218.3	106.6	2.0
Burglary	949.1	299.6	3.2
Larceny $50+	606.5	267.4	2.3
Auto Theft	206.2	226.0	0.9
Violent Crimes	357.8	184.7	1.9
Property Crimes	1761.8	793.0	2.2

Source: President's Commission on Law Enforcement and Administration of Justice (1967).

Some Methodological Considerations

While the NORC results were dramatic, there were enough problems to compromise their usefulness. First, the claim that there was twice as much crime than what the police acknowledged was based on a very small number of victim accounts. Under normal conditions, someone conducting a victim survey might anticipate uncovering only a handful of rape and robbery incidents. Deriving estimates from a few observations can yield some questionable figures.

Second, the crime instances that victims reported were submitted to a panel of experts to assess whether these events were really crimes. Ultimately, the panel excluded more than one-third of the victim reports. An example of misclassification would be a person who returns home, finds all the furniture gone, and exclaims, "Help—I've been robbed!" The real crime here is a burglary, not a robbery. Employing a panel to check victim reports may help validate the results and impart a greater sense of confidence, but it also alerts us to the fact that the survey design included some major flaws in terms of question wording.

A third set of problems dealt with subject recall. Some participants experienced difficulties with telescoping. *Telescoping* takes place when respondents mistakenly bring criminal events that occurred outside the time frame into the survey period. For example, suppose that you are taking part in a victimization survey. The interviewer asks whether you had a car stolen during the past 12 months. In actuality, your automobile was taken 14 months ago. However, because you cannot remember exactly when the incident took place, you advise the interviewer that you were the victim of such a crime.

A related hindrance is faulty memory. *Memory decay* is evidenced when respondents were victimized during the survey time frame but forgot the event and did not provide the correct answer to the question. Researchers also found that respondent fatigue could influence the results. For example, the level of crime reporting decreased as the length of the survey increased. Because of these considerations, victimization estimates derived from these efforts contained an unknown margin of error. Unless telescoping and memory decay "exactly offset one another, the survey estimate of the amount of crime that occurred is inaccurate" (Schneider et al., 1978: 18–19).

Another major concern emerged from the selection of respondents. The study did not randomly select respondents from households, and individuals under the age of 18 were excluded unless they were married. In addition, all household offenses were counted as crimes against the head of the household. Each of these facts could add more bias to the results.

Besides the preceding concerns, a host of other imperfections contaminated the findings. There were definitional problems in the survey questions, an inability to locate where the crime actually took place, a problem in having a count of victims rather than offenses, and other nagging obstacles that plagued first-generation efforts. Despite these weaknesses, an important contribution had emerged. Criminologists and victimologists learned that the public were willing to answer questions about their victimization experiences. These early pilot studies clearly established the need for more refined victimization surveys and the avenues they should travel.

Second-Generation Victim Surveys

Preparations for the second generation of victim surveys began with several exploratory projects conducted during 1970 and 1971. These preliminary studies investigated a variety of methods for addressing the problems noted earlier with the first-generation surveys. Once these concerns received treatment, then it would be time to move on to running the surveys themselves.

Recall Problems

To test the accuracy of respondent recall, researchers in two different locations (Washington, DC and Baltimore) conducted their own record checks. Their strategy was to compare information derived from police records with victimization survey data. Two types of record checks were involved: reverse record checks and forward record checks.

A *reverse record check* starts by locating crime victim names in police files. The next step is to contact these people and administer a victim survey to them. Therefore, survey responses are checked against the police records to assess the degree to which a respondent confirms offense characteristics that appear in the official files.

The reverse record check comparisons revealed that memory decay grew more problematic as the time period increased. The most accurate recall usually occurred within three months of the incident. After that point, victims became more forgetful about the incident and its details. The results also showed that recall was better for some offenses than for others and that there was a noticeable degree of telescoping. In other words, victims erroneously moved up events that occurred outside the time frame and placed them inside the targeted interval. In addition, the wording of some questions and their order of presentation also affected the responses (Hindelang, 1976: 46–53).

Schneider and her associates (1978) approached the very same issues with the exact opposite methodology. They opted to conduct a *forward record check*. After asking respondents in a victim survey whether they had contacted the police about the incident, the researchers combed police records for a written case report. Police reports could not be found for about one-third of the victims who said they had filed such a report. When case records were located, police reports and victim accounts showed a great deal of similarity. However, there was evidence that telescoping could produce some major distortions unless specific steps were taken to counteract this tendency.

Despite the gains that these record check studies provided, there was still a need for caution. Skogan (1981: 13–14) warned of three assumptions imbedded within this strategy. First, there is an assumption that police incident records are the appropriate benchmark against which to assess victim accounts. Just because an officer responds to a call does not mean that an official report will be filed by the officer. Second, record check studies can deal only with situations that have come to the attention of the record-keeper. Third, crime victims are a very mobile group whose frequent address changes make recontact difficult. Checking reports at a later time, therefore, becomes problematic.

The problem of telescoping received further consideration in a panel study of households undertaken by the Bureau of the Census in 1971. A *panel design* surveys the same group of households or respondents at regular intervals over a period of time. The repeated interviews or surveys allow for *bounding*. In other words, the first survey serves as the calendar reference point for the second, the second for the third, and so on. The earlier interview gives the respondent a solid referent for separating one time period from the next. It also permits the researcher to check on whether the same victimization instance is reported in more than one time period. This provision can eliminate any obvious repetition in the events that victims report. This panel study found more accurate recall and less telescoping in a six-month time frame than over a 12-month format (Hindelang, 1976).

Respondent Concerns

Incorporating recommendations from earlier exploratory pretests, surveys in San Jose, CA, and Dayton, OH, sought to compare information gathered from self-respondents with household respondents. A *self-respondent* is a person who reports victimization incidents for him- or herself. On the other hand, a *household respondent* relays information about crimes committed against all members of his or her household. The San Jose and Dayton surveys revealed that self-respondents reported more personal crimes and experienced fewer recall problems than did household respondents (Hindelang, 1976: 57–68).

In addition to interviewing victims from the general population, surveys of businesses and commercial establishments were also being developed at this time. Problems with such issues as telescoping, memory decay, question wording, and bounding also existed in these evaluations. Sometimes, particular problems loomed even larger. For example, most reports of a business burglary or robbery would come from an employee who knew about the incident first-hand. Quite often, subsequent efforts to recontact the original informant were hampered by personnel turnover. The contact person, as well as anyone familiar with the episode, was sometimes no longer an employee of the business at the time of the second interview. Thus, the quality of record checks suffered from a lack of continuity among respondents.

The second-generation surveys were useful in identifying several factors that were incorporated into later survey instruments. First, it was found that more specific questions elicited more accurate information and better recall than did very general questions about prior victimization. Second, shorter recall periods (six months or less) significantly limited the problems of telescoping and memory decay. Third, bounding the time period by some concrete event (such as the last interview in a panel design) helped limit the problem of telescoping. Fourth, interviewing individuals themselves about their victimization experiences was preferable to asking a proxy (a household respondent) about the experiences of others. Finally, through careful wording of questions, it was possible to approximate UCR offense definitions in order to enable comparisons across the two data sources.

Third-Generation Victim Surveys

The third generation witnessed an ambitious schedule of activity. The federal government launched a national victimization survey, a survey of commercial businesses, and a special victimization survey in 26 American cities. The following subsections outline each of these endeavors.

The National Crime Survey

The National Crime Survey (NCS) was launched in 1972 with a probability sample of 72,000 households set up in a panel format. The plan was to interview each member of these households. This strategy would produce a study group of approximately 100,000 people after eliminating problems such as refusals to cooperate and incorrect addresses.

Workers contacted each household every six months over a three-year period for a total of seven interviews during this time. To avoid replacing the entire sample at the end of three years, the NCS staggered the beginning and ending points for each wave. Every six months, one-sixth of the households departed the study group and their replacements underwent the initial interview. Approximately 12,000 households were interviewed each month, making the survey process a year-round endeavor.

The NCS incorporated many features uncovered in the earlier exploratory studies. The panel design, for example, established a six-month bounding period for the study. The first interview was not used to estimate crime rates. Instead, it became the starting point or boundary. To guard against telescoping and memory decay, each subsequent interview was checked against previous reports.

One burden that confronted the NCS was the *mover-stayer problem*. Sampling of respondents was built on the residence, not the individual. If the original survey participants vacated the premises and somebody else moved in, the new tenants automatically joined the sample for the balance of the study period. Responses from the new residents were used even though bounding was not possible. The NCS made no effort to track the original respondents. Instead, it was assumed that the impact of relocation upon victimization estimates and the comparability of stable versus changed residences were minimal.

Unlike earlier generations, interviewers talked to each household member rather than to just a single household representative. Exceptions to this rule occurred when the contact person was a child, when the parent objected to an interview with a minor, or when repeated attempts to contact an individual family member proved futile. In these cases, one person acted as proxy for the entire household.

While the preceding is true regarding individual victimizations, crimes against the household were solicited from only one household representative. This procedure aimed to reduce interviewing time and to eliminate the overlap from talking to more than one person about the same things. Unfortunately, the selected household respondent may not always be aware of all crimes against the household or may not know all the details needed for accurate reporting.

The Business Victimization Survey

Along with the national survey, the NCS also launched a commercial victimization survey. This undertaking gathered information from businesses to assess their level of risk. The commercial survey, though, was discontinued in 1977 for two primary reasons. First, the sample of 15,000 businesses was too small to project reliable estimates. Second, the costs of the survey were not commensurate with the potential payoff.

City Surveys

Twenty-six large cities were selected for special surveys of both residents and businesses. A total of 12,000 households and 2,000 businesses were targeted for interviews in each city. While the single-city findings were interesting, there was a great deal of overlap with the national survey. The costs associated with these multiple projects were astronomical. Eventually, the city surveys were discontinued in 1975 after only three years of operation.

⬥ Fourth-Generation Victim Surveys

Today, we are in the fourth generation of victimization surveys. To emphasize this transition, the format and title of the national victim surveys have changed. The name is now the *National Crime Victimization Survey* (NCVS).

The redesign efforts began in 1979, partly as a response to issues raised in a National Academy of Sciences report (Penick & Owens, 1976). As before, a number of exploratory analyses were undertaken to test potential adjustments. Some of these considerations covered such items as improving accuracy of responses, identifying information by subgroups, adding new questions to tap different dimensions of crime and victim responses, and making the data more useful for researchers (Skogan, 1990; Whitaker, 1989).

Concern over recall accuracy returns to issues of question wording, bounding, memory decay, and telescoping. There was some worry that the *screen questions*—those inquiries that probe possible victimization experiences—could be misleading and in need of revision (Dodge, 1985). Redesign analysts suggested that improved screen questions could result in increased reports of crime by prodding the memory of respondents and providing clearer definitions of criminal victimization. To show how the NCVS does this, Box 2.4 displays current screen questions used in both the individual and household surveys. Each respondent is asked the questions in Box 2.4 as a means of probing victimization experiences in the past six months. These responses are then used as the basis for in-depth questions about the specific victimization occurrences.

To assess the impact of changes in screen questions, half of the interviews in 1992 were conducted using the old questions, while half of the subjects were asked the new questions. A comparison of the two formats showed that the revamped queries produced 44 percent more personal victimization reports and 49 percent more property incidents (Kindermann et al., 1997). As expected, reports for robbery, personal theft, and motor vehicle theft did not show substantial gains. However, rapes jumped by 157 percent, assaults rose 57 percent, burglaries increased by 20 percent, and theft moved upward by 27 percent. Inspection of the data led the analysts to believe that the new instrument made inroads into gray-area events. A *gray-area event* pertains to a victimization that does not conform to the usual common stereotype. For example, episodes involving non-strangers as the aggressors showed marked increases with the new questions. It would appear, then, that the revisions worked as intended.

A shorter reference period was also examined as a means to improve recall. This option, however, was rejected. The increased costs were simply too prohibitive.

The problem of bounding came up in reference to the mover-stayer issue. If you recall, newly relocated respondents at a household marked for inclusion in the NCVS provided unbounded information during their initial interview. One solution called for basing the sample on respondents, as opposed to household address. However, such a move would require interviewers to follow sample members to their new residences for subsequent questioning. This option was not feasible because it increased survey costs substantially.

36a. I'm going to read some examples that will give you an idea of the kinds of crimes this study covers. As I go through them, tell me if any of these happened to you in the last six months; that is since_____. 20__

Was something belonging to YOU stolen, such as:

a) Things that you carry, like luggage, a wallet, purse, briefcase, book—

b) Clothing, jewelry, or cell phone—

c) Bicycle or sports equipment—

d) Things in your home, like a TV, stereo, or tools—

e) Things outside your home, like a garden hose or lawn furniture—

f) Things belonging to children in the household—

g) Things from a vehicle, like a package, groceries, camera, or CD—*or*

h) Did anyone ATTEMPT to steal anything belonging to you?

Did any incidents of this type happen to you?

36b. How many times?

37a. (Other than any incidents already mentioned,) has anyone:

a) Broken in or ATTEMPTED to break into your home by forcing a door or window, pushing past someone, jimmying a lock, cutting a screen, or entering through an open door or window—

b) Has anyone illegally gotten in or tried to get into a garage, shed, or storage room—*or*

c) Illegally gotten in or tried to get into a hotel or motel room or vacation home where you were staying?

Did any incidents of this type happen to you?

37b. How many times?

40a. (Other than any incidents already mentioned,) since_____, 20__, were you attacked or threatened, *or* did you have something stolen from you:

a) At home, including the porch or yard—

b) At or near a friend's, relative's, or neighbor's home—

c) At work or school—

d) In places such as a storage shed or laundry room, a shopping mall, restaurant, bank, or airport—

e) While riding in any vehicle—

f) On the street or in a parking lot—

g) At such places as a party, theater, gym, picnic area, bowling lanes, or while fishing or hunting—*or*

h) Did anyone ATTEMPT to attack or ATTEMPT to steal anything belonging to you from any of these places?

Did any incidents of this type happen to you?

40b. How many times?

Note: *For each of these questions the respondent is asked to "Briefly describe incident(s)."*

Source: Compiled by the authors, from Bureau of Justice Statistics (2008).

Another exasperating problem has been the inability to examine subgroups within the survey data. Because of legal restrictions protecting respondent identities, it is difficult to analyze victimization data in anything but the national aggregate. The redesign efforts have demonstrated that it is possible to produce limited information based on cities or states without violating subject confidentiality. Such an ability allows for more direct and meaningful comparisons with the UCR and other data sources.

A major goal of the redesign was to enhance the analytical worth of the survey. Despite the wealth of information contained in the NCVS, many researchers would like to capture data on other related topics. The redesign team considered the feasibility of adding special supplements that would supply data on selected topics. A variety of supplements have been conducted over the life of the NCVS, particularly since the redesign was fully implemented in 1993 (see Box 2.5). These supplements have examined respondent perceptions of offense severity, school crime, workplace violence, and identity theft, among other topics.

Another suggestion in the redesign was to conduct longitudinal analyses. To date, victimization studies have been restricted to cross-sectional approaches. It has not been possible to match a person's file with responses from an earlier interview. The redesign team strongly recommended that procedures for more longitudinal analyses be adopted.

The redesign also suggested the move to *computer-assisted telephone interviews* (CATI). This technique uses a computer to prompt the interviewer with the proper questions. It automatically skips questions whenever appropriate. Computerization should also eliminate miscoded data by accepting only legitimate responses during the interview.

The NCVS began carrying out the redesigned survey in 1988 and had the full survey overhauled and in place by the end of 1992. The current survey targets approximately 160,000 respondents in some 90,000 households nationally (Bureau of Justice Statistics [BJS], 2016a). Typically, more than 90 percent of the households and individuals respond to the survey requests, and the size of the sample results in little sampling error (Rennison, 2010). The NCVS is currently undergoing redesign and testing to improve its efficiency and reliability

BOX 2.5 NCVS SUPPLEMENTS

National Survey of Crime Severity (1977)	*Workplace Risk Supplement (2004)*
• Asked respondents to rank severity of different offenses	• Assessed workplace violence and prevention efforts
Victim Risk Supplement (1984)	*Special Victimization Study (2006)*
• Assessed perceptions of safety and crime prevention behavior	• Focused on stalking
School Crime Supplement (1989, 1995, 1999, and biannually thereafter)	*Identity Theft Survey (2008, 2012, 2014)*
• Asked respondents aged 12 to 18 about school safety and security	• Assessed the extent and characteristics of identity theft
Public–Police Contact Survey (1996 and every three years thereafter)	Source: Compiled by the authors, from Rand (2010) and from http://www.bjs.gov/index.cfm?ty= dcdetail&iid=245.
• Examined police use of force	

(BJS, 2016c). Included is assessing the ability to incorporate more crime types. Victimization surveys have become a valuable tool within a very short time, both in the U.S.A. and other countries. [...]

COMPARING THE NCVS AND THE UCR

Recent years have witnessed a growing reliance on victimization survey data for assessing the crime problem. Perhaps the greatest reason for this change is the realization that the UCR suffers from systematic limitations. For some time now, criminologists have recognized that official reports underestimate how much crime there really is. Even the primitive early victim surveys uncovered much more crime than the UCR did. In addition, victim surveys capture data on the victim and the circumstances surrounding the criminal event. As a result, victimization surveys have earned an important niche in the measurement of crime.

According to the NCVS (Truman & Langton, 2015), almost 21 million crimes were committed in 2014. In comparison, the UCR tabulated fewer than half as many Index Offenses in 2014 (Bureau of Justice Statistics, 2016a). Even when one takes definitional differences into account, the gap between these two data sources is quite large. Clearly, victims reveal to interviewers incidents that have not come to the attention of the police. Table 2.2 shows that for most offenses, respondents report approximately half or less than half of their victimizations to the police. Aggravated assault (58.4%), robbery (60.9%), and motor vehicle theft (83.3%) are those offenses most often reported to the police. Cases of theft (29%) are the least reported offenses. Figure 2.1 graphically compares crime rates derived from both the UCR and NCVS for 2014. In virtually every category in which even rough comparisons can be made, the NCVS reveals significantly higher offense levels, with the largest differences appearing in burglary and theft.

Victimization surveys also provide additional information not addressed by the UCR. For example, males are more likely to be violent crime victims than females, blacks have higher robbery and aggravated assault rates than whites, never-married individuals are more likely to be victimized, and persons with lower incomes have a higher risk of becoming crime victims in every category than people who are wealthier.

TABLE 2.2 Percent of Victimizations Reported to the Police, NCVS, 2014	
Offense	% Reported
Violent Crime	46.0
Rape/sexual assault	33.6
Robbery	60.9
Aggravated assault	58.4
Simple assault	40.0
Property Crime	37.0
Burglary	60.0
Motor vehicle theft	83.3
Theft	29.0

Source: Compiled by the authors, from Truman & Langton (2015).

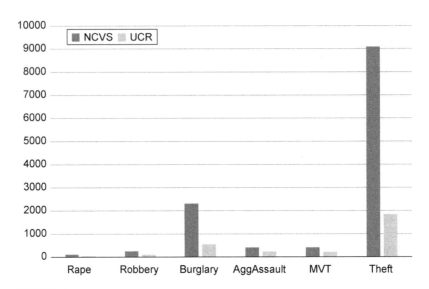

FIGURE 2.1
Comparison of 2014 UCR and NCVS Crime Rates

Source: Constructed by the authors, from Federal Bureau of Investigation (2015b); Truman & Langton (2015).

TABLE 2.3 Victim–Offender Relationships, NCVS, 2014

Relationship	Violent Victimization (%)	Rape/Sex Assault (%)	Robbery (%)	Aggravated Assault (%)	Simple Assault (%)
Intimates	11.8	24.7	10.7	11.4	11.1
Other Relatives	8.9	1.0	6.8	7.9	10.3
Well-Known/Casual Acquaintance	31.9	44.5	29.3	22.7	34.3
Stranger	40.4	24.3	47.2	50.2	37.5
Do not know relationship	4.2	3.1	4.3	6.2	3.6

Source: Bureau of Justice Statistics (2016c).

Victimization data also provide a great deal of information about victim–offender relationships (see Table 2.3). This information, however, is primarily for crimes in which the victim and offender have personal contact. In 2014, 11.8 percent of all violent victimizations were committed by intimates and another 8.9 percent by other relatives. Strangers were involved in a high of 50 percent of all aggravated assaults, followed by 47 percent of robbery victimizations. Strangers also committed 38 percent of all simple assaults, and a low of 24 percent of all sexual offenses (Bureau of Justice Statistics, 2016a). Acquaintances, either casual or well known, make up 32 percent of the offenders in all violent victimizations.

FEAR OF CRIME

Surveys of the public can provide insight into other issues related to crime and victimization. One of the most notable of these issues is fear of crime. Victimization surveys depict the objective odds of becoming a crime victim. They also present evidence of the subjective or perceived risk of becoming a crime victim. The fear of crime presents a view of criminal victimization that, although not necessarily real, leads to changes in personal activity and anxiety.

What exactly is fear? Despite the growth of interest in "fear of crime," there remains a lack of consensus on exactly what the term means. Perhaps the most recognized work on this issue is that of Kenneth Ferraro. Ferraro (1995: 8) defines *fear* as:

> [A]n emotional response of dread or anxiety to crime or symbols that a person associates with crime. This definition of fear implies that some recognition of potential danger, what we may call perceived risk, is necessary to evoke fear.

While this definition requires an emotional response, fear may manifest itself in various ways depending on the person involved and the basis for his or her anxiety. Some individuals fear walking on the streets in their neighborhood while others fear physical attack within their own homes. As a result, there may be a shift in physical functioning, such as high blood pressure and rapid heartbeat. Alternatively, the individual may similarly alter his or her attitudes about walking alone in certain places or avoiding various activities. To a great extent, the source of the fear for the individual will determine the response to the fear. Regardless of the source of this fear, it is real for the individual.

In an attempt to show the differences between various fear measures, Ferraro and LaGrange (1988) provide a classification scheme that considers the perceptions of the respondent being tapped and the degree to which the method addresses the individual or others. This classification taps *judgments* of risk— how safe the respondent or others are; *values*—how concerned the person is about crime or victimization; and *emotions*—how much the individual is afraid or worried about becoming a victim. Personal fear of crime measures would ask respondents directly about how afraid they are of being the victim of specific crimes, often without reference to any specific place or time. These types of questions directly tap the "emotions of dread or anxiety" of the individual.

Interestingly, while discussions of "fear of crime" are common, many researchers utilize measures that reflect risk or assessments of crime levels, rather than the emotional response of the individual (Ferraro, 1995). This diversity is seen in many of the common and large-scale surveys. Box 2.6 presents a sample of "fear" questions used in past surveys and research. Note that the questions vary from asking about perceptions on changes in crime (Gallup Poll), to feeling

BOX 2.6 COMMON "FEAR" QUESTIONS

National Crime Victimization Survey:

How safe do you feel or would you feel being out alone in your neighborhood at night?

General Social Survey:

Is there any area right around here—that is, within a mile—where you would be afraid to walk alone at night?

Taking a Bite Out of Crime Campaign Evaluation:

How likely do you think it is that your home will be broken into or burglarized during the next year?

Is having your home burglarized or broken into something that you worry about?

National Opinion Survey on Criminal Justice:

Do you worry very frequently, somewhat frequently, seldom, or never about:

- Yourself or someone in your family getting sexually assaulted?
- Being attacked while driving your car?
- Getting mugged?
- Getting beaten up, knifed, or shot?
- Getting murdered?
- Your home being burglarized while someone is at home?
- Your home being burglarized while no one is at home?

Gallup Poll:

- Is there more crime in your area than there was a year ago, or less?
- Is there more crime in the U.S.A. than there was a year ago, or less?
- Overall, how would you describe the problem of crime in the U.S.A.—is it extremely serious, very serious, moderately serious, not too serious, or not serious at all?

Fear of Crime in America Survey:

Rate your fear of: (1= not afraid at all; 10 = very afraid)

- being approached on the street by a beggar or panhandler.
- being raped or sexually assaulted.
- being murdered.
- being attacked by someone with a weapon.
- having your car stolen.
- having your property damaged by vandals.

Source: Compiled by the authors.

safe outside at night with no mention of crime (NCVS), to rating fear of specific criminal actions (Fear of Crime in America Survey). These differing measures all tap some aspect of the fear definition presented earlier.

Trying to delineate the actual level of fear is like trying to hit a moving target. No two studies provide the same results. This may be due largely to the use of varying measures of fear. Despite this fact, it is possible to offer some insight and "ballpark" figures for fear.

Many researchers report that 40 to 50 percent of the population express a fear of crime (Hindelang, 1975; Maguire and Pastore, 1995; Skogan and Maxfield, 1981; Toseland, 1982). In 2014, 37 percent of respondents to the Gallup Poll reported that there are areas near their home where they would be afraid to walk alone at night (Dugan, 2014). Questions asking about perceived changes in crime in the U.S.A. or a respondent's area often result in greater fear levels. Figure 2.2 tracks a series of annual Gallup polls spanning the 2000 to 2015 period. Respondents were asked two similar questions regarding their perceptions of crime. The first question read, "Is there more crime in the U.S. than there was a year ago, or less?" The wording of the second query was, "Is there

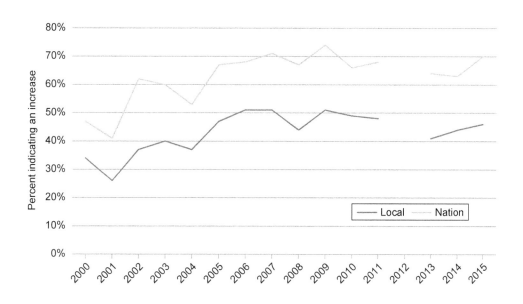

FIGURE 2.2
Percent Respondents Indicating Crime Has Increased by Year

Source: Compiled by the authors, from Gallup (2016).

more crime in your area than there was a year ago, or less?" The graph in Figure 2.2 shows that 47 percent of the respondents in 2000 thought the level of crime in this country had increased compared with the previous year. By 2015, that proportion had risen to 70 percent. The impression was that local crime also showed a similar upward climb. In 2000, 34 percent of the participants indicated that crime in their area had increased compared with the previous year. By 2015, 46 percent of the people in the survey said that local crime was on the rise.

The Gallup survey also asks Americans whether they worry about a variety of possible victimization episodes. As Figure 2.3 shows, approximately 70 percent of respondents are apprehensive about identity theft. Four out of ten are concerned about their car being stolen or broken into, and one-third worry about their child being harmed at school. Fewer than 30 percent are concerned about their homes being burglarized or getting mugged. Fewer than 20 percent are concerned about being sexually assaulted, murdered, attacked while driving, or being assaulted by a co-worker.

Interestingly, the level of fear (one's subjective odds) consistently outdistances both official and victimization measures of actual crime (one's objective odds). For example, Skogan and Maxfield (1981) illustrate the lack of a connection between crime and fear by showing that, in terms of robbery, approximately 48 percent of the non-victims report feeling somewhat or very unsafe, while

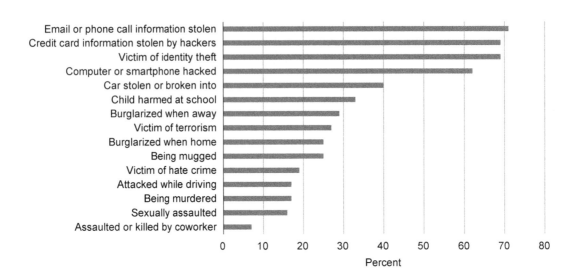

FIGURE 2.3
Respondents Reporting Concern about Types of Victimization, 2015

Source: Compiled by the authors, from Gallup (2016).

54 percent of the victims report the same fear. The expectation was that victims should express significantly more fear than non-victims. Similarly, both official and victimization measures show that less than 10 percent of the population is victimized, despite 40 percent or more fearing it.

The level of fear is also not consistent across all demographic groups in the population. It is principally an urban problem and affects the elderly and women to a greater extent than other groups. More than 60 percent of those persons living in urban areas express fear of crime. Conversely, only 30 percent of rural residents voice the same fears. A wide range of studies reveal that the elderly and women are the most fearful groups in society (Bennett and Flavin, 1994; Ferraro, 1995; Hindelang et al., 1978; McGarrell et al., 1997; Perkins and Taylor, 1996; Skogan and Maxfield, 1981; Will and McGrath, 1995). This persists despite the fact that the elderly and women are the least victimized groups. Some researchers argue that these fear results are an artifact of how fear is measured and that the young are actually the most fearful (Chiricos et al., 1997; Ferraro, 1995; Lumb et al., 1993).

Fear also varies along other demographic lines. Numerous studies report that fearful people tend to be black (Chiricos et al., 1997; Lab, 1990; Smith and Lab, 1991; Skogan and Maxfield, 1981), lower socioeconomic status (Bennett and Flavin, 1994; Greenberg et al., 1985; Riger et al., 1978; Will and McGrath, 1995), and live in large communities (Kennedy and Silverman, 1985; Liska et al., 1982;

Will and McGrath, 1995). Other studies, however, note the lack of a relationship or a reverse relationship between some of these demographic factors and fear (Gomme, 1988; Kennedy and Silverman, 1985; Lab, 1990; Smith and Lab, 1991; Ortega and Myles, 1987).

Two basic questions arise from an inspection of past research on fear of crime. First, how do you justify the levels of fear in light of the actual levels and chances of victimization? Second, why do different studies find divergent sets of characteristics among fearful individuals? There is no clear answer to these questions. Instead, there may be many contributing factors.

One possible explanation for inordinate levels of fear centers on victim vulnerability and the potential harm one encounters when victimized. Victimization has a greater impact upon some individuals than upon others. *Vulnerability* refers to the ease of being victimized and the impact the crime has upon the victim. The assumption is that people who would suffer the greatest pain or loss from a victimization episode will be the most fearful. The elderly, for example, live largely on fixed incomes, and any loss due to theft, property damage, or medical expenses cannot always be accommodated within their budgets. A minor dollar loss can translate into a major hardship. Similarly, physical injuries to elderly victims can result in lengthy, painful recuperation beyond that needed by younger individuals. The elderly and females also have a great physical disadvantage when faced with young male offenders, who hold an edge in strength and physical prowess. The perceived potential for physical harm is greatly enhanced when the victim and offender represent opposite positions in physical and social power. McCoy et al. (1996) and Smith and Torstensson (1997) find that perceived vulnerability is a strong predictor of fear among women and the elderly.

Vulnerability also appears in the form of social isolation (Akers et al., 1987; Bursik and Grasmick, 1993; Kennedy and Silverman, 1985; Riger et al., 1978). Many individuals, especially the elderly, live alone and have few family members or close friends living nearby. These individuals may feel they have no one to call on for assistance in the aftermath of a crime. They are socially isolated from networks that promote support.

The perceived risk of being victimized also contributes to fear. Many risk factors mirror vulnerability dimensions. Included here are an individual's economic resources, where the person lives, and if the individual lives alone. A person's economic status may dictate that he or she live in older, deteriorating neighborhoods; in areas that are more racially and ethnically diverse; and in neighborhoods with more transient populations. These types of neighborhoods are often very crime-prone. They frequently attract deviants as residents and draw in outsiders who commit crime. The prevalence of crime in these areas exacerbates feelings of fear.

Living alone also increases risk by making individuals more suitable crime targets. Dealing with a single individual lessens both resistance and chances of identification of offenders. There appears to be a relationship between living alone and victimization. The 2014 NCVS shows that people who have never married, or are divorced or separated have much higher violent victimization rates than people who are married or widowed (Truman & Langton, 2015).

A third possible explanation for the divergent finding in fear and victimization involves the idea of vicarious victimization. *Vicarious victimization* refers to knowing someone or hearing about others who have been the victim of a crime. This information may elicit a sympathetic reaction and empathetic fear of crime. Grohe and associates (2012), using a phone survey of residents in one southeastern U.S. city, report that fear of burglary is significantly related to actual burglary in the city. Analyzing fear among Houston residents, Zhao et al. (2015) note that local crime is related to fear of violent, property, and disorder offenses independent of actual victimization. Vicarious fear can also come from real or dramatic depictions of crime in the media, particularly television. Both fictional police dramas and the reporting of crime and violence in the news inundate the populace with a view that crime is a constant threat to every individual. It is also noteworthy that most depictions are not of everyday "street crimes." Instead, they focus on more heinous and frightening offenses such as murder, rape, and home burglary. Several studies (Chiricos et al., 1996; Lane and Meeker, 2011; Weitzer and Kubrin, 2004) report that exposure to crime in the media is related to higher reported fear.

REPEAT VICTIMIZATION

Another outcome of the growth of victimization surveys and the development of new data analysis techniques, particularly through the use of computer mapping, is increased interest in repeat victimization, or revictimization. *Repeat victimization* may be defined as the repeated occurrence of crime involving either the same victim or the same location. Even casual observation demonstrates that repeat victimization is common with some crimes. For example, it is not unusual for domestic violence victims to drop charges or refuse to cooperate with the prosecution, despite records of ongoing violent episodes. Sherman (1995) points out that the police often receive repeated calls for service stemming from domestic violence at the same addresses.

In one of the earliest examinations of repeat victimization, Polvi et al. (1990) noted that the risk of being a repeat burglary victim is 12 times higher than expected, and this risk is more pronounced immediately after an initial burglary. This heightened risk persists for approximately three months and then levels off to normal expected levels.

Major victimization surveys, such as the National Crime Victimization Survey (NCVS), the Crime Survey for England and Wales (CSEW)/British Crime

Survey (BCS), and the International Crime Victims Survey (ICVS), demonstrate the existence of repeat victimization. The NCVS provides some insight through its questions dealing with *series victimizations*. "A series victimization is defined as six or more similar but separate crimes which the victim is unable to recall individually or describe in detail to an interviewer" (Bureau of Justice Statistics, 2003). The 2005 NCVS reveals that 4.1 percent of all crimes of violence are series victimizations. Similarly, 3.9 percent of all personal crimes and 0.5 percent of all property crimes fall into the series victimization category (Bureau of Justice Statistics, 2006). Analysis of the BCS also shows that multiple victimization episodes are concentrated among relatively few victims. Ellingworth and associates (1995), using BCS data from 1982 through 1992, point out that approximately one-quarter to one-third of all property crime is committed against people victimized five or more times within a one-year period of time. This means that almost two-thirds of victims are repeat victims. Similarly, approximately 50 percent of personal crimes appear as repeat victimizations (Ellingworth et al., 1995). Data from the 2000 ICVS appear in Table 2.4 and show that 46 percent of sexual crimes and 41 percent of assaults are repeats (Weisel, 2005). Burglary exhibits the lowest level of repeats, but even there, it is 17 percent of offenses.

Another way of demonstrating revictimization using victimization data is to compare prevalence and incidence data. *Prevalence data* refer to the number of individuals who experience victimization over a period of time, whereas *incidence data* represent the total number of offenses reported during the same period. Any point at which the number of incidents exceeds the number of victims would indicate revictimization. Various analyses of survey data demonstrate the often concentrated nature of victimization. Pease (1998) notes that 2 percent of all respondents account for 41 percent of all property crimes, while 1 percent account for 59 percent of the personal crimes. Farrell and Pease (2003) report that 25 percent of all burglaries in Charlotte, North Carolina, are repeat victimizations. Using data on 19 countries from the ICVS, Farrell and Bouloukos (2001) find that more than 40 percent of the sexual assaults and more than 30 percent of all assaults and robberies are repeats.

Thus far, the discussion has implicitly assumed that revictimization involves only the same victims. Revictimization, however, is not restricted in this way. Farrell (2005, 2010) notes that repeats can take a variety of forms. A *near repeat* is one in which a neighbor may be victimized in the same or a similar way as the initial victim (Johnson & Bowers, 2005). A *virtual repeat* involves a follow-up victimization of

TABLE 2.4 Estimates of Repeat Victimization from the ICVS	
Offense	Repeat Offenses (%)
Sexual Assault	46
Assault	41
Robbery	27
Vandalism to Vehicles	25
Theft from Vehicles	21
Vehicle Theft	20
Burglary	17
Source: Weisel (2005).	

a similar person, place, or item, not necessarily nearby (Farrell, 2010; Pease, 1998). In virtual repeats, the emphasis is on the method of offending or the similarity of the targets. Recognition of offenses as a repeat victimization, either as a near or virtual repeat, provides important information for assisting victims.

One problem with identifying repeat victimization involves the impact of short time frames within which repeats may occur. Ellingworth and associates (1995) note that most levels of repeat victimization in the BCS are probably underreported because they rely on repeats only within a one-year time frame, which minimizes the potential for repeats before or after the survey boundaries. The problem of short time frames for repeat victimization is very evident when considering the NCVS. The NCVS reveals significantly lower repeat victimization compared with the ICVS for every category of victimization, including sexual offenses (51 percent repeats in the ICVS; 23 percent in the NCVS), assaults and threats (46 percent ICVS; 26 percent NCVS), and burglary (40 percent ICVS; 18 percent NCVS) (Farrell et al., 2005). The reason for this is the six-month time frame used by the NCVS and the 12-month time frame used by the ICVS. Kleemans (2001) notes that 9 percent of repeat burglaries occur within one month, 30 percent occur within six months, and almost half occur within one year. Thus, the time frame under consideration makes a difference for the finding of repeat victimization.

Beyond documenting the extent of repeat victimization, research also provides information on the time frame of repeats. Pease (1998) notes that a great deal of revictimization tends to occur within a short period of time after the first victimization. Similar results appear in Bowers et al.'s (1998) examination of repeat victimization of nonresidential locations and Johnson et al.'s (1997) burglary study. In both analyses, the risk of repeats remains higher within relatively short periods of time following the initial victimization. Weisel (2005) demonstrates that the time frame for many repeats remains short for a range of offenses (see Table 2.5).

For example, 15 percent of domestic violence repeats take place within one day, and 25 percent occur within five weeks (Lloyd et al., 1994). Similarly, 25 percent of repeat residential burglaries in Tallahassee occur within one week, and 51 percent occur within one month (Robinson, 1998). The information on the time frame of repeats may be useful for the introduction of prevention initiatives.

WEB ACTIVITY

You can read more about repeat victimization and responding to the problem in a guide from the Center for Problem-Oriented Policing at **http://www.popcenter.org/tools/repeat_victimization/.**

Evidence of repeat victimization, victim recidivism, or chronic victimization is not restricted to survey data or to individuals. Efforts to improve police effectiveness and efficiency have prompted the development of various techniques to identify what are known as crime *hot spots*. "Hot spots" are "small places in which the occurrence of crime is so frequent that it is highly predictable" (Sherman, 1995: 36).

TABLE 2.5 Time Frame for Repeat Victimization		
Offense	Proportion of Repeats by Time Period	Where
Domestic Violence	15% within 24 hours	Merseyside, England
	25% within five weeks	
Bank Robbery	33% within three months	England
Residential Burglary	25% within one week	Tallahassee, Florida
	51% within one month	
	11% within one week	Merseyside, England
	33% within one month	
Nonresidential Burglary	17% within one week	Merseyside, England
	43% within one month	
Property Crime at Schools	70% within one month	Merseyside, England

Source: Weisel (2005).

The use of computer mapping has enhanced the ability of most police departments to identify such places. Sherman and associates (1989) noted that all domestic disturbance calls in Minneapolis came from only 9 percent of the places in town, all assaults occurred at 7 percent of the locations, and all burglaries took place at 11 percent of the places. Farrell and Pease (2003) noted that 1 percent of all Charlotte addresses account for 39 percent of all reported burglaries. Similar concentrations of offenses and calls for police service have been found in many other locations (see, e.g., Block & Block, 1995; Spelman, 1995). What is not always demonstrated is whether the calls involve the same victims. While domestic violence calls to the same address probably involve the same victim and offender (Farrell et al., 1995), repeated assault calls to a bar may involve different patrons every time. In either case, the value of the information is in its ability to inform responses to victimization.

Explanations for repeat victimization can generally be divided into two categories: risk heterogeneity and state dependence (Farrell et al., 1995). *Risk heterogeneity*, or a *flag explanation* (Gill & Pease, 1998), suggests that the prior victimization or some other factor identifies the victim or location as an appropriate target for further victimization. As such, subsequent victimizations may be committed by different offenders who are attracted to the target by its apparent vulnerability or some other characteristic. Farrell and associates (1995) use the example of repeated fights at a bar as an indication of risk heterogeneity, where people looking for fights or interested in risky situations are attracted to establishments with a reputation for conflict. Those locations and/or the employees of those bars are then at a higher risk for repeat victimization.

Event dependency, or *boost explanations* (Gill & Pease, 1998), refers to situations in which (usually) the same offender commits another offense based on past experiences with that victim or location. Successful past offending leads to a further attempt against the same target. It is possible under this situation that a new offender commits a follow-up offense as a result of information shared among offenders. In this case, specific information about the target based on a past offense is the key to subsequent actions.

Revictimization information can be useful for developing responses by both potential victims and community agencies. Pease (1998: 3) offers three conclusive findings based on studies of repeat victimization. First, "victimization is the best single predictor of victimization." Second, "when victimization recurs it tends to do so quickly." Finally, offenders take advantage of the opportunities that appear in the first offense. These findings do not mean that every victim will be victimized again in the future. Rather, they indicate that victims may be more vulnerable because of circumstances or lifestyle. Past victimization should be used to assess what factors contributed to the crime and what actions can be taken to mitigate future vulnerability. Just as people use knowledge of the victimization of others as a warning sign, so should a victim take heed. Unfortunately, for many victims, "Lightning *does* strike twice!"

Despite the increased interest in repeat victimization, there are several issues that require more attention. Perhaps the most pressing issue is to identify the extent of such activity. While the evidence shows that there is a great deal of repeat victimization, not all criminal acts are followed by a further act against the same location or individual. Identifying which acts will result in a repeat victimization *prior* to the subsequent act is an elusive task. All of the existing research offers an after-the-fact analysis of the extent of the problem. It is possible, therefore, that interventions targeting past victims may result in a lot of unnecessary effort. On the other hand, such targeting should be more effective than interventions aimed at the general public, many of whom would never become a victim in the first place.

SUMMARY

How much criminal victimization is there in society? One thing that should be evident after working your way through this chapter is that criminologists and victimologists cannot provide an exact answer. However, by using different data sources, they can give some estimates as to the nature and extent of the victimization problem.

No matter which approach a researcher takes when he or she tackles this question, certain systematic problems have the potential to hamper those measurement efforts. The materials in this chapter shed light on what some of these obstacles are, how they impinge upon the data, and what can be done to minimize these intrusions. As you can see, victim surveys are very much like any other consumer product. People are constantly tinkering, updating, and refining these instruments to take advantage of the most current technology available.

SECTION III

Victim-Centered Theory

Victim Blaming

Helen Eigenberg and Tammy Garland

Early systems of justice were quite different from our modern ones and victims had a different role. In fact, one can argue that victims historically played a more significant role in determining "justice." Early systems of justice did not rely upon incarceration as a means of punishment. Prior to the creation of jails and prisons, justice was more often focused on retribution which meant that offenders were punished in proportion to the level of victimization they had caused. As a result, restitution was common. In other words, attempts were made to make the victim "whole again" or to return them, as near as possible, to their previous state as a non-victim. This "eye for an eye" philosophy generally resulted in payments to the victim and his/her family. The development of the American criminal justice system tended to follow another path. Major philosophers of the time, such as Locke and Hobbes, gave rise to the idea of the social contract. These philosophers stressed that crime is a threat to the social order, more so than a harm to individuals. As such, crime, and therefore victimization, became a state matter. This ideology resulted in the development of two related, but separate, justice systems in America. The criminal justice system deals with crimes against the state and the civil system is available to redress harm to individuals. So if one is a victim of robbery, the punishment will likely be incarceration for the crime committed against the state. The victim has little to no say in the charging, conviction, or sentencing process. Instead, he or she is merely part of the evidence. In contrast, victims may take the offender to civil court where damages may be awarded – if the victim has the resources to pursue a civil case and if the offender has any to be awarded to the victim. The structure of the American justice system, then, in large part shifted the focus from harm to victims to harm to the state; thus, it can be argued that victims lost their role in the criminal justice system (although they retain it in the civil system). Thus part of the focus for the victims' rights movement has been to put the victim back in the system.

Ironically, one of the ways that victims re-emerged in the study of crime related to the ways that they contributed to their victimization. Victim blaming, victim facilitation, and victim precipitation are some of the many labels used to examine the concept of shared responsibility for criminal acts. Generally speaking, victim precipitative behaviors are those which cause victims to bring about their own victimization. For example, "a woman who walks alone toward her car on an unlighted street at night causes her own rape as surely as the man who precipitates his car theft by accidentally leaving his car keys in the car ignition or the man who slaps his wife and brings about his own demise" (Franklin & Franklin, 1976). As one might image, this type of approach has caused a great deal of controversy.

Theorizing Victimization

There is historical tendency to place responsibility for victimization on the victim, at least to some degree. Early victimologists, for example, created typologies which classified victims according to their degree of responsibility. von Hentig (1941, 1948) was one of the first victimologists to engage in this process. His work clearly was focused on explaining criminal behavior, but he was one of the first scholars to examine the role of victims in an attempt to understand criminality. He examined the degree to which people were victim prone and argued there were "born victims" just as there were "born criminals." Born victims were self-destructive individuals who solicited the actions of their "predators" (1941:303). He developed a typology based on psychological, social, and biological factors and classified victims according to 13 categories reflecting varying "risk" of victimization. For example, he argued that both the young (children and infants) as well as the elderly were victim prone as were immigrants (because of their lack of familiarity with the language and culture) and minorities (because they were "racially disadvantaged"). Other categories included the "mentally defective" (including insane individuals as well as those addicted to drugs and alcohol), dull normals (individuals with low intelligence), depressed individuals, wanton people (i.e., promiscuous), tormentors (abusive parents), and the "acquisitive" who were greedy individuals. "Lonesome and heartbroken" widows/widowers and the "blocked, exempted or fighting" individuals were who victims of blackmail, extortion and confidence games also were separate categories. Finally, women, as a group, were born victims because they were weak and easy prey. Some of these people represented in his typology indicate groups who are more vulnerable to victimization simply because of who they are and their social status (e.g., the young, elderly, mentally ill, and immigrants). Other groups, however, place themselves in situations that make them vulnerable (e.g., the acquisitive individual or those who fall victim to extortion). von Hentig acknowledged that in some cases victims made "little or no contribution" to their victimization, but he also argued that more often there was a "reciprocal action" between perpetrators and victims. As such, the victim was no longer a passive object, but an active subject in the process of criminalization. In other words, victimization was a process of social interaction. This conclusion led other victimologists to study the process of becoming a victim.

Many victimologists followed von Hentig's example and devised various typologies which categorized the degree of shared responsibility between victims and offenders (Barnes & Teeters, 1959; Fattah, 1967; Karmen, 1980; Lamborn, 1968; Mendelsohn, 1963; Schafer, 1968; Sheley, 1979; Silverman, 1974). Mendelsohn (1956, 1963) is one of the most famous of these early victimologists; he is often referred to as the "father of victimology" because he used that term in an early paper presented at a conference in Bucharest in 1947 (see Knaper & Herbers, 2006). He was Rumanian (and later Israeli) and a practicing attorney who developed an interest in victims because he observed that most of his cases involved pre-existing interpersonal relationships. He coined the terms victimology and victimity which referred to the common characteristics that define all victims (e.g., the things they all share). Given his legal background as a defense attorney, it is not surprising that he established a typology classifying victims based on victim culpability or the degree of guilt that could be attributed to the actions of the victim.

He identified six categories of victim. Completely innocent victims bear no responsibility for their victimization and did nothing to contribute to the act. Victims with minor guilt are those whose inadvertent actions led to victimization. Voluntary victims actually helped create their victimization. Most guilty victims initiate a crime against another person and then end up being victimized instead (e.g., a robber who is murdered). Imaginary victims are delusional and/or fabricate a crime based on personal motivations (e.g., to get someone in trouble for committing a crime that did not exist). While his earlier work focused mainly on categorizing victims based on their role in criminal acts using a narrow view of criminality (e.g., what we would call street crime today), his later scholarship (1976, 1982) significantly broadened this perspective to include victims of work accidents and genocide. This typology identified five types of victims: (1) victims of criminals; (2) victims of one's self (suicide, subconscious impulses, self-destructive behavior); (3) victims of anti-social behavior on the part of the environment (e.g., social oppression, class discrimination, genocide, war crimes); (4) victims of technology (e.g., insufficient testing of a medicine which produces harm) and (5) victims of the natural environment (floods and hurricanes).

In general, Mendelsohn argued the goal of victimology was to find ways to produce fewer victims, thereby introducing the concept of victim prevention, but his views on victimization also allowed for determining the culpability of the victim which contributed to the development of the concept of victim precipitation. Like von Hentig, Mendelsohn clarified that some victims were not directly responsible for their victimization, but he also argued that some victims were guiltier than the offender. This type of thinking was influential in creating a conceptual climate whereby victims began to share responsibility for their victimization.

Merging the work of von Hentig and Mendelsohn, Schafer (1968) based his classification of victims on functional responsibility rather than risk factors. He identified seven types of victims. Schafer's typology categorized victims with regards to responsibility: no responsibility (unrelated, biologically weak, socially weak, and political victims), little responsibility (precipitative victims), and moderate/high responsibility (provocative and self-victimizing victims). Unrelated victims are individuals who are the unfortunate recipient of an offenders' criminal behavior and thus bears no responsibility for the act. Likewise, biologically weak victims (e.g., elderly, young, physically handicapped) and socially weak victims (immigrants and minorities) bear no responsibility for their victimization; they simply are attractive targets due to physical or social characteristics. Similarly, political victims who are victimized because they opposed people and institutions in power also bear no responsibility for their victimization. Provocative victims share some responsibility because the offender is reacting at some level to the behavior of the victim. Precipitative victims also bear some responsibility as they directly place themselves in situations that can result in victimization (e.g., based on

Figure 2.1: Comparisons of Victim Responsibility: von Hentig, Mendelsohn, and Schafer

Level of Response	von Hentig Concept: Victim Prone Individuals	Mendelsohn Concept: Victim Culpability	Schafer Concept: Functional Responsibility
• No Victim Responsibility	• Young/Children • Females • Old/Elderly • Mentally Defective/ Mentally Ill • Immigrants • Minorities • Dull Normals	• Completely Innocent Victims	• Unrelated victims • Biologically Weak Victims • Socially Weak Victims • Political Victims
• Low Victim Responsibility	• Depressed People • Wanton Individuals • Lonesome/Heartbroken • Blocked/Exempted/ Fighting	• Victims with Minor Guilt • Victims as Guilty as the Offender • Victim more Guilty than Offender	• Precipitative Victims
• Moderate/ High Victim Responsibility	• Acquisitive • Tormenter	• Most Guilty Victim	• Provocative Victims • Self-Victimizing
• No Victimization	• Did not address	• Imaginary victim	• Did not address

how they dress or by frequenting certain places); however, self-victimizing individuals are deemed to bear total responsibility for their victimization. These individuals engage in activities such as drug use, prostitution, and gambling; therefore, their participation in "illegal" activities is deemed to make them totally culpable if they are victimized (e.g., the prostitute who gets robbed by her client). Rather than simply being a victim, individuals cause transgressions against them due to negligence or provocation. Schafer's concept of "functional responsibility," therefore, maintained it is the responsibility of the victim to actively prevent their own victimization from occurring (Wallace, 2007). While von Hentig, Mendelsohn, and Schafer all differed in how they classified the level of precipitation caused by the victim, all of them are similar in many respects (see Figure 2.1).

These approaches tend to divide some finite amount of responsibility between victims and offenders. Victims can be fully responsible, completely innocent of precipitation, or somewhere in between. Proponents of this perspective contend that the victim's actions are important and influence the way the criminal justice system responds to the offender as well as the way in which the public views the crime. Opponents argue that victim precipitation results in blaming the victim and diverts attention away from perpetrators and their responsibility for the crime.

The concept of victim blaming, then, is used to help address several important questions about victimization. Who is responsible for the criminal act? Is it the offender, the victim, or both? Is one more responsible than the other? Is it appropriate to examine the role of the victim at all? Do crime prevention efforts require consideration of victims and any role they may play in their victimization? What role does society play in victim blaming? This chapter addresses these issues. It addresses the development of the concept of victim precipitation, discusses problems with the concept of shared responsibility and examines why the approach is so popular.

Development of the Concept of Victim Precipitation

While the concept of victim precipitation was evident in the earliest literature on victimology, the term itself owes its origins to two classic criminological studies. Marvin Wolfgang (1958) first coined the term victim precipitation in his classic work on homicide, and it was further popularized by his student, Menachim Amir, who applied the concept to rape.

Wolfgang examined homicide records in Philadelphia from 1948-1952 and found that victims initially had used physical force against their perpetrators in about one out of every four cases of murder. They may have drawn weapons or physically assaulted the other party who, in turn, then killed the initial aggressor. These cases were deemed to be victim precipitated. Wolfgang also found that these cases often involved victims and offenders who were known to each other and that they had experienced prior altercations with one another. Victims of precipitated homicides were more likely to have been drinking prior to their homicides than victims who had not initiated any violence toward their perpetrators. Most victim precipitated homicides involved male victims, and most of them were murdered by other males. Few women committed homicide, although when women did murder, it was often in response to men who had initiated violence toward them.

Amir (1971) also used Philadelphia police files to analyze rapes reported in 1958 and 1960. He considered a rape to be victim precipitated when males believed that females had consented to sexual acts but then rescinded their original acceptance. According to Amir, victim precipitated rapes were

> those rape situations in which the victim actually, or so it was deemed, agreed to sexual relations but retracted before the act or did not react strongly enough when the suggestion was made by the offender(s). The term applies also to cases in risky situations marred with sexuality, especially when she uses what could be interpreted as indecency in language and gestures, or constitutes what could be taken as an invitation to sexual relations (1971:266).

In other words, it was the offender's interpretation of the events which was crucial to identifying the victim as blameworthy; therefore, a victim's behavior was not as important as the "offender's interpretation of her actions" (1971:20). Thus, if the victim was perceived to be acting provocatively or seductively, or if she had a "bad" reputation, the rape was defined as victim precipitated. This also was the case if she engaged in other "risky" behavior such as drinking, going to bars alone, wearing revealing clothing or hitchhiking. Despite the very broad definition of victim precipitation used in Amir's study and the focus on the offender's interpretation of the victim's acts (rather than her actual behavior), a relatively small proportion of the rapes qualified as victim precipitated: only 19 percent or about one in five rapes. These "victim precipitated rapes" were more likely to involve white females or teenage girls than adult women or women of color, and these victims were more apt to have met their rapist(s) at bars or parties than were women whose rapes which did not involve victim precipitation.

Amir's research was criticized a great deal, in large part, because of his focus on the perpetrator's *interpretations* of the victim's actions. This interpretation rendered the actual behavior of the victim meaningless. For example, a woman could have been held down and raped while she was screaming no, but it would have been a victim-precipitated rape if the offender believed she had originally consented, if she had a reputation for having multiple sexual partners, or if she engaged in any of the other factors which made her culpable according to Amir. As Weis and Borges (1973) note, the "only ingredient necessary for constituting a victim precipitated rape is the offender's imagination" (1973:80).

Amir's work and subsequent theorists who use the concept of victim precipitation also apply the concept in ways that deviate substantively from

Wolfgang's initial conception. Remember that Wolfgang argued that victim precipitation occurred when a victim first initiated violence. These victims first committed or attempted to commit a crime. In other words, they were murdered after they attempted to assault or murder someone else. This logic does not flow in the same way in Amir's study. His victims were not raped after attempting to rape someone else. Thus, the original conceptualization of victim precipitation was altered significantly in ways that most contemporary victimologists fail to consider.

Amir's work also was criticized because of his overly broad generalizations. For example, he concluded that "in a way, the victim is always the cause of the crime" (Amir, 1971:258). These types of statements go way beyond his data and exaggerate the degree of victim precipitation – even when using his own broad definition. Amir, then, was accused of using rape myths to blame victims and giving scientific legitimacy to this practice (see Ward, 1995); however, many other issues also surface when victimology concentrates on the notion of shared responsibility.

Other theories regarding victimization emerged, and many, including lifestyle and routine activities, continue to place blame on the victim. Both lifestyle and routine activities emphasize how "situations and/or contexts carry their own level of risk for victimization" (Schreck & Fisher, 2004:1023). Hindelang, Gottfredson, and Garafolo (1978) determined that one's lifestyle was the major factor in ascertaining the risk for criminal victimization. Social structure, role expectations, demographic characteristics, daily routine, and exposure to certain groups were determinants as to whether an individual would be victimized. Hence, individuals who come into contact with groups of a criminal nature on a regular basis are more likely to be victimized. For example, young persons are more likely to be victimized than older persons due to the disproportionate exposure to those who may be involved in crime and delinquency (Wallace, 2007). This theoretical perspective assumes that people can reduce their risk of victimization by taking less risks such as staying home at night, refraining from public places (especially "dangerous ones"), and staying away from violent situations. It is problematic to assume that one can predict these things, but it also fails to sufficiently account for a variety of victimization experiences especially interpersonal violence. For example, women might avoid date rape and domestic violence if they never engaged in intimate relationships; however, this is not a realistic approach to crime prevention. Furthermore, it implies that victims who engage in "risky" lifestyles are somehow to blame for their victimization.

Similar to lifestyle theory, "the routine activities approach" maintains that the convergence in time and space leads to crime and victimization. In order for victimization to occur, there must be a suitable target, a motivated offender, and the absence of a capable guardian (Cohen & Felson, 1979). Suitable targets present easy access and escape, offer some reward, and generally involve an element of portability (e.g., property that can easily be moved). A motivated offender is one who is easily tempted and/or provoked as well as one who is idle and/or bored. The absence of a capable guardian includes parents, neighbors, authorities and/or friends who might be in a position to thwart victimization. Hence, the risk of victimization increases when an individual's daily routine and activities brings that person and/or his or her property in close proximity with a motivated offender in the absence of a capable guardian (Cohen, Kluegel & Land, 1981; Cohen & Felson, 1979; de Coster, Estes & Mueller, 1999). Although the theory has traditionally been linked to property crimes, especially burglary and robbery, current research has been applied to predatory crimes such as rape, stalking, and sexual harassment (de Coster, Estes & Mueller, 1999; Fisher, Cullen & Turner, 2002; Mustaine & Tewksbury, 1999, 2002). Researchers substantiate routine activities theory by demonstrating the correlation between exposure to risk and actual victimization; therefore, victims can (theoretically) reduce their chances of victimization by making themselves a less convenient target (sometimes referred to as target hardening). This perspective assumes that criminality is a product of rational thought processes as opposed to a series of random events. While victims may be able to make themselves a less attractive target for car theft by taking their keys out of their vehicle, it is less clear how victims of acquaintance rape or domestic violence, for example, could make themselves less vulnerable or that it would make much difference to their offenders if they were not such an "easy" target.

While these approaches have remained popular, they continue to emphasize that victims precipitate their own victimization, at least to some degree. Karmen (2004) further cautions that blaming those who are victimized creates a system which results in stigmatization, which also is counterproductive to the objectives of the criminal justice system.

Problems Associated with the Concept of Victim Precipitation

The concept of victim blaming has many weaknesses. Some of these weaknesses include the use of tautological reasoning, conceptual difficulties, placing undue responsibility on victims, creating culturally legitimate victims, and excusing offenders' behaviors. These problems are briefly reviewed in the following sections.

Tautological Reasoning or Circular Thinking

Historically, criminologists have concentrated on identifying the differences between criminals and those who obey the law. Likewise, victimologists have been concerned with studying the process of victimization to determine if there are differences between victims and non-victims; however, these types of studies have serious methodological flaws. They rely upon samples of victims in order to determine common characteristics which contribute to victimization, although these studies fail to evaluate the degree to which non-victims in the general populations also exhibit similar behaviors. This has resulted in circular reasoning. As Franklin and Franklin (1976) explain:

> The victims' precipitative behaviors lead to the criminal deeds because the victims' behaviors were precipitative. The interrelatedness of the independent and dependent variables "victim precipitation" and "victimization" becomes more apparent when an attempt is made to identify victim precipitation in the absence of victimization. For example, a woman walking alone at night on an unlighted street under present conceptions of victimology can hardly be thought of as engaging in crime precipitative behavior if no criminal act takes place (1976:127-128).

In other words, empirical research has failed to identify any common characteristics that cause one to become a victim other than the process of victimization. The only thing that causes one to be a victim is the process of being victimized and the process of being victimized is the only thing that distinguishes victims from non-victims.

Conceptual Weaknesses

Victim precipitation, by definition, asks whether victims bear some proportion of blame because of their actions. As a result, it creates a continuum whereby victims conceptually can be found to range from totally blameless on one end to fully responsible on the other (Karmen, 2004). Completely innocent victims are not blamed for their victimization and bear no responsibility for their victimization. For example, with respect to property offenses, they took all the actions they could to protect their belongings. They bought and used locking devices, burglar alarms, and other deterrent devices. With respect to crimes of violence, they limited their contact with dangerous people and did not instigate any criminal acts or confrontations with potentially violent people. At the other end of the continuum, victims may be fully accountable and totally responsible for their victimization.

The notion of totally innocent victims is problematic because it implies that all other victims bear some degree of responsibility. With the advantage of 20/20 hindsight, most victims could have "done more" to prevent their victimization which makes the "totally innocent" victim quite rare. It also implies that victims know how to prevent their victimization and ignores that many people in our society face disproportionate risk of victimization. Furthermore, even if it were possible to fully "protect" property, it is even more difficult to image how individuals are supposed to ensure that they refrain from contact with dangerous people. If they were all identified by a scarlet letter, this might be possible. Absent such an identification system, people will clearly associate with individuals without any knowledge that they might be violent. For example, most crimes against women are committed by intimates. How should women conduct themselves to ensure they are not exposed to danger in order to retain their status as totally innocent victims?

The concept of fully responsible victims is also problematic. As Karmen (2004) notes, a victim can only be totally responsible when there is no offender at all. In these cases, victims are not victims but offenders posing as victims for some ulterior motive. For example, a person who has paid someone to steal his/her car and reports it to the police is a criminal masquerading as a victim. The fact that the only totally responsible victim is actually an offender destroys the intellectual integrity of the continuum of victim responsibility. Instead of varying degrees of victimization, the continuum actually represents distinctions between victims and offenders. This conceptual weakness may help explain why the focus of much victimological work has been on creating typologies to classify victims rather than discussing any theoretical rational for a continuum of blame.

Places Undue Responsibility on Victims

The notion of victim precipitation also is problematic because it places an unwarranted level of responsibility on victims to prevent their own victimization and many of these actions would require victims to drastically alter their lives. Victims may be able to prevent their victimization by staying in their houses which have bars on the doors and windows; however, most people have to go out sometime and some people live in neighborhoods where crime is rampant making it difficult to minimize the risk of harm. Furthermore, many battered women are, in fact, imprisoned in their homes with "criminals" who beat them and lack any means to prevent their victimization. And even if it were possible to protect oneself from all victimization, many people do not want to live that way. It may be better to risk a burglary than to feel like one lives in a fortress. It may be preferable to risk being robbed by going out at night rather than feeling restricted in one's freedom to go out in public. Sometimes, risk is incurred because of events beyond the control of individuals. For example, if a woman's car breaks down on the interstate and she does not have a cell phone, she may have to accept a ride from a stranger in order to get assistance (or risk spending the night on the side of the road waiting for someone to help with no guarantee that they are trustworthy either). Thus, in some circumstances, people have no choice but to engage in "risky" behavior.

Creates Culturally Legitimate Victim

Ryan's (1971) classic work describes the process of victim blaming. He contends that victims first must be seen as deficient in some way; e.g., that there is something wrong with them. Victims can be distinguished from non-victims based on their attitudes, behavior, or some basic characteristic. Then these differences are assumed to be the cause of their victimization. If they were not different, they would not be victimized. Victims are then warned that they must change in order to become like the non-victim group if they are to avoid victimization, and if they fail to avoid victimization they are to blame. Finally, some governmental bureaucracy or social service agency is assigned responsibility for dealing with "the problem."

An important part of this process, then, begins with defining groups of people as deficient, because they then become culturally legitimate or deserving victims. In fact, the process of creating legitimate victims is central to many types of crimes. For example, in the Holocaust, definitions of ethnicity were used to demonize Jews and to make it palatable to victimize them. Similarly, gays or lesbians are viewed as legitimate victims of hate crimes because they would be innocent victims if they were heterosexuals. They only need to change their sexual orientation to protect themselves; or at a minimum, go to heroic lengths to ensure that no one knows that they are gay. Prostitutes are blamed for their victimization if they are raped because they engage in sexually risky and promiscuous behavior in the first place. They do not warrant our sympathy or any response by the criminal justice system. The process of creating culturally legitimate victims makes it more acceptable for some types of people to be victimized and society is less willing to use its resources to do anything about it. As Weis and Borges note,

> some victimologists have . . . turned victimology into the art of blaming the victim. If the impression of a "legitimate victim" is created, then part of the burden of guilt is relieved from the perpetrator, and some crimes, like rape for example, can emerge as without either victims or offenders (1971:85).

This process of creating culturally legitimate victims is harmful to victims. They are further traumatized when society engages in victim blaming. Not only must they deal with the consequences of the victimization itself, but they must cope with the added burden of being told that they are, in some part, to blame. It is no wonder then why some victims of crime are reluctant to reveal their victimization to the police and/or researchers conducting victimization surveys. Many victims use silence to protect themselves from the additional victimization that occurs when they are blamed for their own plight.

Excuses Offenders Behavior and Diminishes Responsibility

If, in fact, there is some finite amount of responsibility to be allocated for any crime, then, by definition, offenders escape full responsibility for their acts when victims are blamed. "Attention is focused on the behavior and motives of the victim rather than on the offender" (Scully, 1990:45). The concept of victim precipitation provides a cultural framework which offenders can use to rationalize their behavior (Fattah, 1976; Sykes & Matza, 1957; Scully, 1990; Stanko, 1993). According to offenders, victims, then, ask for or deserve what they get; or at the extreme end of the continuum, they deny any harm whatsoever. For example, Scully's study of convicted rapists demonstrated that these offenders used culturally accepted stereotypes about women to create legitimate victims who were blamed for their own victimization. A couple of quotes from the rapists are quite illustrative. For example, one man convicted of a gang rape stated: "I'm against hurting women. She should have resisted. None of us were the type of person that would use force on a woman. . . . I loved her – like all women" (1990:129). Another serial killer and rapist reported that his victims physically "enjoyed the sex [rape]. Once they got involved, it would be difficult to resist. I was always kind and gentle until I started to kill them" (1990:130). A man who abducted his victim at knifepoint on the street stated "to be honest, we [his family] knew she was a damn whore and whether she screwed 1 or 50 guys didn't matter" (1990:108).

These victim blaming views affect the way that individual offenders excuse their behavior, but because they are culturally derived, their excuses have a staying power that goes individual rationalization. For example, attorneys use these same stereotypes to try to garner sympathy from judges and juries. Likewise, prosecutors can sometimes be wary of initiating cases against victims who appear culpable or who are viewed as culturally legitimate victims. These actions suggest that society, as a whole, is very supportive of the notion of victim precipitation.

Popularity of Victim Precipitation

This brief overview has demonstrated that there are many problems associated with the concept of victim precipitation and that engaging in blaming victims may be harmful to many (most) victims, then is seems logical to ask why it is that we, as a society, continue to endorse these beliefs? There are several possible answers to this question.

First, victim blaming is consistent with another powerful set of societal beliefs involving a just world (Lerner, 1965). Most individuals want to, or in fact do, believe that people get what they deserve in society. In other words, bad things do not happen to good people. This type of thinking also allows people to feel a false sense of security. It implies that everyone has control over their lives and that individuals can prevent victimization if they simply take certain precautions and behave in certain ways. It allows people to avoid the alternative conclusion – that crime is often random and unpredictable, and that victims can do little to prevent it.

Second, victim blaming perspectives allow for, conceptually, the idea of victim prevention. While this may give people a (false) sense of empowerment as individuals, it also may increase the harm done when people are victimized. Imagine a woman who has attended a rape crisis training session and who has taken copious notes about how to stare strangers in the eyes, to always walk assertively, to carry keys between her fingers to use them as a weapon, to scream if she is abducted to get help, and so on and so on. This same woman is abducted by a stranger with a knife in a parking lot and is raped. She is so scared she does not scream or resist in any other physical ways. She may blame her self even more than a woman who had not taken any victim prevention courses if she feels that she failed to take the "appropriate" actions to protect herself.

Third, victim blaming helps answer difficult questions about the motivations of offenders and diverts attention from traditional criminology's inability to prevent crime. Traditional criminology has spent most of this century examining the distinctions between criminals and noncriminals and identifying reasons for criminality, however, it has not made much headway. Thus blaming the victim in some cases is easier to understand than the motivations of the criminal. Furthermore, concentrating on the victims allows us to shift our attention from offenders as a means to prevent crime. The new focus on victims and victim prevention has coincided with the failure of traditional crime prevention techniques. One might argue that the criminal justice system and criminology shifted the focus from offenders to victims out of necessity. Unable to devise strategies to control crime, the attention is shifted to victims and victim prevention. In both instances, however, the focus continues to be on personal accountability and the actions of individuals while social structural examinations remain rare.

Individual level explanations are very popular in the United States. As a society, we tend to endorse the idea that criminals have free will and choose criminality. Victims fail to take sufficient preventative measures and therefore cause their own victimization. Neither explanation examines crime as a social problem rooted in the social structure. For example, poverty causes some offenders to commit crime as a means to secure economic goods necessary for survival. Poverty also makes people more vulnerable to victimization. Poor people are more apt to live in neighborhoods where crime is higher and are less apt to be able to afford security alarms and other types of preventative measures. In other words, both crime and victimization could be prevented by making an effort to reduce poverty. Actions could include changing welfare systems, tax structures, or creating employment opportunities in low income neighborhoods. However, individual level explanations do not require an examination of the social structure.

By failing to examine the social structure, victimology, for the most part, also ignores the ways in which political power affects our understanding of both crime and victimization. For example, a broader definition of victims might challenge social definitions of crime in rather dramatic ways. As Elias notes,

> What if we learned that law enforcement sought to maintain or manage crime, not to prevent or reduce it, or sought social control of certain population groups, not crime control? What if crime waves, media coverage and official crime statistics had little to do with the real victimization level? What if we found our fears and insecurities about crime artificially manipulated for political purposes? Suppose we discovered that most people commit crime, not just certain groups? What if the real career criminals were corporate offenders, not common criminals? What if we found that victims have often been offenders before, and vice versa? What if we discovered that we were as likely to be victimized by a friend or relative as by a stranger (1986:4)?

In other words, victimology has the power to transform our understanding of crime and victimization, although this is not likely to happen unless the field of victimology also changes.

Victimology today tends to concentrate on pitting victims against offenders and ignores the role of social structure. Although victimology, as a field of study, began by examining victims in the broadest sense of the word (e.g., including victims of natural disaster, the Holocaust), contemporary victimology concentrates almost exclusively on victims of street crime (Elias, 1986). Doing so provides Americans with a narrow definition of crime and victimization and creates a "limited social reality of crime" (Elias, 1986:3). Harms such as white-collar crime, consumer fraud, pollution, toxic waste dumping, workplace hazards, police violence, and interpersonal violence by intimates generally fail to be defined as crime. As a result, these victims also fail to be defined as such. The concept of victim precipitation has been central to the study of victimology; however, it has posed many difficulties. Not only does it cause further victimization to some victims who blame themselves or who experience victim blaming by the criminal justice system or others in society, but it affects our very conceptualization of crime and victimization. It keeps us from asking very different questions which might drastically alter our understanding of both crime and victimization.

References

Amir, M. (1971). *Patterns in Forcible Rape.* Chicago: University of Chicago Press.

Barnes, H. & N. Teeters (1943). *New Horizons in Criminology.* New York: Prentice Hall.

Cohen, L.E. & M. Felson (1979). "Social Change and Crime Rate Trends: A Routine Activity Approach." *American Sociological Review*, 44, 588-608.

Cohen, L.E., J.R. Kluegel & K.C. Land (1981). "Social Inequality and Criminal Victimization." *American Sociological Review*, 46, 505-524.

De Coster, S., S.B. Estes & C.W. Mueller (1999). "Routine Activities and Sexual Harassment in the Workplace." *Work and Occupations*, 26(1), 21-49.

Doerner, W.G. & S.P. Lab (2008). *Victimology,* Fifth Edition. Newark, NJ: LexisNexis/Matthew Bender.

Elias, R. (1986). *The Politics of Victimization: Victims, Victimology and Human Rights*. New York: Oxford.

Fattah, E. (1976). "The Use of the Victim as an Agent of Self-legitimization: Toward a Dynamic Explanation of Criminal Behavior." In E.Viano (ed.) *Victims and Society* (pp. 105-129). Washington, DC: Visage.

Fisher, B.S., F.T. Cullen & M.G. Turner (2002). "Being Pursued: Stalking Victimization in a National Study of College Women." *Criminology and Public Policy*, 1, 257-308.

Franklin, C. & A. Franklin (1976). "Victimology Revisited." *Criminology*, 14, 125-136.

Hindelang, M.J., M.R. Gottfredson & J. Garofalo (1978). *Victims of Personal Crime: An Empirical Foundation for Theory of Personal Victimization*. Cambridge, MA: Ballinger.

Karmen, A. (2004). *Crime Victims*, Fifth Edition. New York: Wadsworth.

Karmen, A. (1980). "Auto Theft: Beyond Victim Blaming." *Victimology*, 5, 161-174.

Knaper, M. & I. Hurbers (2006). "The Victim and Victimology." *Tilburg Research: Victim Empowerment*, 491, 22-23.

Lamborn, L. (1968). "Toward a Victim Orientation in Criminal Theory." *Rutgers Law Review*, 22, 733-768.

Mendelsohn, B. (1982). "Socio-analytic Introduction to Research in a General Victimological and Criminological Perspective." In H. Schneider (ed.) *The Victim in International Perspective*. New York: Walter de Gruyter.

Mendelsohn, B. (1976). "Victimology and Contemporary Society's Trends." *Victimology*, 1, 8-28.

Mustaine, E.E. & R. Tewksbury (2002). "Sexual Assault of College Women: A Feminist Interpretation of a Routine Activities Analysis." *Criminal Justice Review*, 27, 89-123.

Mustaine, E.E. & R. Tewksbury (1999). "A Routine Activity Theory Explanation for Women's Stalking Victimizations." *Violence against Women*, 5(1), 43-62.

Schafer, S. (1968). *The Victim and His Criminal*. New York: Random House.

Schreck, C.J. & B.S. Fisher (2004). "Specifying the Influence of Family and Peers on Violent Victimization: Extending Routine Activities and Lifestyles Theories." *Journal of Interpersonal Violence*, 19, 1021-1041.

Scully, D. (1990). *Understanding Sexual Violence: A Study of Convicted Rapists*. Boston: Unwin Hyman.

Sheley, J. (1979). *Understanding Crime: Concepts, Issues, and Decisions*. Belmont, CA: Wadsworth.

Stanko, B. (1993). *Intimate Intrusions: Women's Experiences of Male Violence*. Boston: Unwin Hyman.

Silverman, R. (1974). "Victim Precipitation: An Examination of the Concept." In I. Drapkin and E. Viano (ed.) *Victimology: A New Focus* (pp. 99-110). Lexington, MA: Heath.

von Hentig, H. (1948). *The Criminal and His Victim: Studies in the Sociobiology of Crime.* New Haven, CT: Yale University Press.

von Hentig, H. (1941). "Remarks on the Interaction of Perpetrator and Victim." *Journal of Criminal Law and Criminology*, 72, 742-762.

Wallace, H. (2007). *Victimology: Legal, Psychological, and Social Perspectives*, Second Edition. Boston: Pearson.

Ward, C. (1995). *Attitudes toward Rape: Feminist and Social Psychological Perspectives.* Thousand Oaks, CA: Sage.

Weis, C. & S. Borges (1973). "Victimology and the Case of the Legitimate Victim." In L. Schultz (ed.) *Rape Victimology* (pp. 91-141). Springfield, IL: Charles C Thomas.

Wolfgang, M. (1958). *Patterns in Criminal Homicide.* Philadelphia: University of Pennsylvania Press.

SECTION IV

Types and Impact of Crime Victimization

CHILD MALTREATMENT

by William G. Doerner and Steven P. Lab

INTRODUCTION

One of the sadder experiences children endure is victimizations perpetrated by family members. Some parents routinely beat their offspring; others deny them food and affection. Still others sexually molest children. Until recently, these victims had no special legal safeguards. Many states placed the welfare of children under "cruelty to animals" provisions. Fortunately, the diligent efforts of child advocacy groups have changed that picture. As Box 10.1 illustrates, child maltreatment has become a prominent national concern.

Research in the area of child maltreatment has revolved around three questions. First, how widespread or prevalent are child abuse and neglect? Second, what are the correlates of child maltreatment? Third, what causes people to engage in this type of behavior? In addition to these concerns, this chapter probes what is meant by child abuse and neglect, what child abuse laws cover, and some strategies people have suggested to combat this problem.

THE HISTORICAL STATUS OF CHILDREN

Child maltreatment is not of recent vintage. For most of history, children were looked at as family property. The ancient Romans believed that the father was endowed with the power of *patriae potestas* (Thomas, 1972). In other words, fathers had the right to sell, kill, or allow their progeny to continue to live. The ancient Greeks, especially the Spartans, practiced infanticide and abandonment of physically deformed newborns (deMause, 1974). The story of Oedipus Rex is testimony to the fact that these practices were accepted among both the lower and higher classes in society. Biblical stories also depict instances of child abuse, such as Abraham's aborted sacrifice of his son Isaac and King Herod's slaughter of the innocents. Other accounts of inhumane treatment have persisted through the ages. Fairy tales and literary stories chronicle the abuse and suffering that some young characters endured (Schiavone, 2016). Children were treated no differently from other property owned by the father (Whitehead & Lab, 2015).

 WEB ACTIVITY

The American Humane Association has expanded its mission to include the protection of children. For more details, visit the website at **http://www.americanhumane.org/.**

Why were children treated in such ways? Both emotional and economic factors help explain this high degree of indifference toward children. First, life expectancy was very short. The majority of infants died during the first year of life. Therefore, emotional attachments to newborns were avoided as a defense mechanism against the highly probable death of the infant. Second, families simply could not bear the burden of feeding and caring for another member. Children, because they could not work in the fields and contribute to the household, represented a drain on the already limited family resources.

This status was especially true for female offspring who would need a dowry in order to find a suitable husband.

Children who survived the first few years of life quickly found themselves thrust into the position of being "little adults" (Aries, 1962). There was no status of "childhood" as we know it today. As "little adults," children took part in all adult activities. They were expected to go to work and help support themselves. They received no formal education. Rather, schooling often entailed being sold into apprenticeship in order to bring money into the family and to provide a skill for the child.

This situation persisted into the Industrial Revolution. At that time, the severe economic competition for labor was fulfilled by exposing children to long and arduous work hours under unsafe conditions. The identification of "childhood" as a distinct station in life began to emerge slowly. Infant mortality showed signs of diminishing. Clergy, educators, and other child advocates stepped forward. As the statuses of "child" and "adolescence" emerged, there was a concurrent rise in concern over the treatment of children (Davis et al., 2004). Society started to realize that youths needed to be handled differently from adults. Local school boards have become enmeshed in long debates over the merits and utility of corporal punishment. Today, there is a concerted effort to ban the application of corporal punishment in schools in the U.S.A., and 31 states now prohibit such disciplinary actions (Center for Effective Discipline, 2016a). In addition, organizations such as the American Academy of Pediatrics (2012), the American Psychological Association (1976), the American Academy of Child and Adolescent Psychiatry (2012), and the United Nations Committee on the Rights of the Child (2016) have taken a formal stance against corporal punishment. At the last count, over 100 countries have outlawed corporal punishment of children in schools (Center for Effective Discipline, 2016b). At the same time, Florida courts view corporal punishment as a parental privilege and place disciplinary measures outside the scope of child maltreatment statutes (*Kama v. State*, 1987; *Raford v. State*, 2002; *Wilson v. State*, 1999). In other words, it is not possible for a parent to commit a simple battery against his or her child when administering physical punishment. Of course, if disciplinary measures exceed the level of good taste, then felony charges may be appropriate.

While the acceptance of maltreatment waned, it did not disappear. The privacy of the home and the assumed sanctity of parental authority allowed much to take place out of sight. What happened within the protected confines of the home was considered to fall beyond the purview of society.

THE DISCOVERY OF CHILD MALTREATMENT

Until relatively recently, child abuse was not easy to detect. John Caffey, a pediatric radiologist, published a study in 1946 outlining bone damage of mysterious origin that he found in some of his young patients. While not accusing parents of being the direct source of these injuries, Caffey (1946) noted that some parental explanations of various accidents were preposterous. Caffey's discovery prompted other physicians to conduct similar investigations. These researchers also stopped short of blaming parents for the intentional infliction of the observed injuries. Eventually, Caffey (1957) came to suspect that parents were responsible for this "unspecified trauma." However, this accusation still did not clarify whether the injuries were intentional or accidental.

The first public denunciation of parents as intentional abusers of their offspring appeared in the early 1960s. In a groundbreaking publication, Kempe et al. (1962) abandoned the term *unspecified trauma* and introduced a new phrase, *the battered child syndrome*. Kempe's radiological research team (1962: 107) applied this new terminology to "young children who have received serious physical abuse, generally from a parent or foster parent."

This discovery launched a movement aimed at eradicating this new-found concern. Before detailing those efforts, though, two questions arise. First, why did it take so long to discover child abuse, especially because it is such a serious problem? Second, why did radiologists, and not some other medical group, such as pediatricians, discover this phenomenon?

 WEB ACTIVITY

The legacy of Dr. C. Henry Kempe continues through the work of The Kempe Foundation for the Prevention and Treatment of Child Abuse and Neglect. Visit the website at **http://www.kempe.org.**

UNDERSTANDING THE DISCOVERY OF CHILD MALTREATMENT

Four obstacles impeded the recognition of these injured children as victims of abuse (Pfohl, 1977). First, although emergency room physicians dealt with the physical aftermath of brutal beatings, they did not understand what they saw. Second, physicians were unable to bring themselves to realize that parents would beat their children or inflict such severe wounds deliberately. A third hurdle was the confidential doctor–patient relationship. Physicians generally regarded the parent, not the child, as their client. Disclosing confidential information to the authorities would violate ethical standards. Such action could subject the physician to civil liability and professional censure. Finally, testifying in court would place physicians in the awkward position of having to defend their medical expertise and diagnosis to laypersons.

Providing courtroom testimony can be a daunting experience for people who work in the medical field. For one thing, *gray cases* (instances where ambiguous patient details, implausible caregiver explanations, and conflicting observations can cloud a conclusion) represent a formidable challenge to the accuracy of a physician's diagnostic skills when assessing whether maltreatment is the root cause of the patient's condition (Chaiyachati et al., 2016; Ryznar et al., 2015). Then, if the case does find its way into the court system, attending physicians face a second round of acrimonious scrutiny. A lawyer, while questioning the physician's expert witness testimony, might resort to the tactic of framing his or her query in legal, rather than medical, terms. For instance, if the examining attorney asks whether the physician reached a conclusion based on "reasonable medical certainty," the parties have just entered a confusing arena. Quite often, medical personnel lack a precise understanding of what this legal standard entails because it is not a medical term (Dias et al., 2015). At the same time, lawyers may not appreciate the extent to which they have muddled the medical complexities (Myers, 2015). As one observer explains, "doctors and lawyers do not speak the same language, work in different disciplinary frameworks, and have different end goals" (Narang, 2015: 232). As a result, it is no small wonder that medical personnel do not relish being placed under a legal microscope.

Concerning the question of why radiologists were the discoverers, Pfohl (1977) explains that radiologists differed from physicians in four important ways. First, radiologists examine X-rays, not people. They can be more objective because they have no direct contact with the patient. Second, the goal of radiology is to discover new diagnostic categories, whereas direct care providers simply identify a condition and place it into a logical, already existing category. Third, the doctor–patient relationship was not a stumbling block because the patient is the person who is being X-rayed. The fourth and most important point deals with the issue of professional control.

Pediatric radiology was a peripheral medical specialty during the 1950s. It lacked professional prestige. Instead of dealing directly with patients, radiologists conducted research alone in isolated laboratories. This separation from patients also meant that radiologists did not make glamorous life-or-death decisions. As a result, child abuse offered a unique opportunity for this marginal branch to become more integrated into the mainstream medical profession. After all, it involved the clinical task of diagnosis. Making the correct assessment could spell the difference between life and death for a young patient.

The term *battered child syndrome* was born. Adding the word "syndrome" after the term *battered child* created a new medical diagnostic category. These facts, coupled with the advances of other professions whose goal was to "cure" abusers through therapy, elevated the discovery of child abuse to prominence. Child abuse became an integral component of medical parlance.

A SURVEY OF CHILD MALTREATMENT LAWS

Immediately after the "discovery" of child abuse, state legislatures raced to enact new laws. A wave of legislative adjustments followed in the late 1960s and early 1970s. The task was to respond to aspects that were overlooked in the hasty lawmaking process. Except for some minor tinkering, maltreatment statutes have remained largely intact since that time. The passage of a federal law dealing with child abuse and neglect brought greater standardization to state statutes.

Although abuse and neglect fall under the broad and more encompassing term of *maltreatment*, they are two distinct phenomena. *Abuse* is the commission of an act upon the child, while *neglect* refers to the omission of a caretaker function.

To gain a more thorough understanding of child maltreatment laws, our analysis focuses upon a limited range of topics. First, we review the statutory definitions of abuse and neglect. Next, we direct our attention to provisions governing who should report such incidents, what the report should contain, and the central register. Finally, the discussion concludes by pointing out some problem areas that remain.

Statutory Definitions

Most state laws define abuse and neglect in very general terms. The purpose behind this approach is to encourage the reporting of as many suspected cases as possible. By casting out a broad net, the hope is to uncover instances of maltreatment that may otherwise go undetected. Critics, though, charge that such an expansive definition invites excessive governmental intervention.

Abuse generally refers to any non-accidental infliction of injury that seriously impairs a child's physical or mental health. Most statutory definitions outlaw sexual abuse, sexual exploitation, pornography, and juvenile prostitution. Some jurisdictions make it a point to exclude reasonable disciplinary measures such as controlled spanking of a child by a parent, guardian, or custodian. Although corporal punishment is a common corrective method in this country, there is the fear that it could lead to maltreatment. Most states fail to define emotional abuse explicitly, although virtually every state includes the term in its provisions.

Neglect is the withholding of life's essentials. These necessary ingredients include food, clothing, shelter, and medical treatment. Some states recognize that parents may hold religious beliefs that prohibit them from seeking medical care. They place such persons outside the scope of the neglect definition. However, if the child's condition involves a life-threatening situation or serious disability, the courts will not hesitate to intervene and order the administration of appropriate medical treatment. Some statutes also mention such offenses as failure to make child support payments, alcoholic or substance-dependent parents who cannot supervise their offspring properly, permitting a child to be habitually truant from school, and family abandonment.

The federal "Child Abuse Prevention and Treatment Act" (42 U.S.C. 5101, *et seq.*) captures the essence of these statutory details. It defines child maltreatment in terms of three components. First, the act or failure to take appropriate action must produce an unacceptable risk of serious physical or emotional harm, death, sexual abuse, or exploitation. Second, the target of this maltreatment is a child, usually a person under the age of 18. Finally, the perpetrator is a parent or caretaker who bears responsibility for the child's welfare and well-being.

As one might imagine, there are a variety of behaviors that fall under the rubric of child maltreatment. Box 10.2 attempts to capture the breadth of these activities by displaying the major types of child maltreatment along with definitions and examples for each category. Box 10.3 lists a less common, but just as harmful, behavior.

The Reporter

A significant element of child abuse laws is the mandatory reporting provisions. Any person who witnesses or learns of a child maltreatment incident has the obligation to report the occurrence to the authorities. Anyone who knowingly fails to make such a report may risk a criminal penalty. In addition, it is

---

BOX 10.2 MAJOR TYPES OF CHILD ABUSE AND NEGLECT

Physical abuse is nonaccidental physical injury (ranging from minor bruises to severe fractures or death) as a result of punching, beating, kicking, biting, shaking, throwing, stabbing, choking, hitting (with a hand, stick, strap, or other object), burning, or otherwise harming a child, that is inflicted by a parent, caregiver, or other person who has responsibility for the child. Such injury is considered abuse regardless of whether the caregiver intended to hurt the child. Physical discipline, such as spanking or paddling, is not considered abuse as long as it is reasonable and causes no bodily injury to the child.

Neglect is the failure of a parent, guardian, or other caregiver to provide for a child's basic needs. Neglect may be:

- Physical (e.g., failure to provide necessary food or shelter, or lack of appropriate supervision)

- Medical (e.g., failure to provide necessary medical or mental health treatment)

- Educational (e.g., failure to educate a child or attend to special education needs)

- Emotional (e.g., inattention to a child's emotional needs, failure to provide psychological care, or permitting the child to use alcohol or other drugs)

Sexual abuse includes activities by a parent or caregiver such as fondling a child's genitals, penetration, incest, rape, sodomy, indecent exposure, and exploitation through prostitution or the production of pornographic materials.

Emotional abuse (or psychological abuse) is a pattern of behavior that impairs a child's emotional development or sense of self-worth. This may include constant criticism, threats, or rejection, as well as withholding love, support, or guidance. Emotional abuse is often difficult to prove and, therefore, child protective services may not be able to intervene without evidence of harm or mental injury to the child. Emotional abuse is almost always present when other forms are identified.

Abandonment is now defined in many States as a form of neglect. In general, a child is considered to be abandoned when the parent's identity or whereabouts are unknown, the child has been left alone in circumstances where the child suffers serious harm, or the parent has failed to maintain contact with the child or provide reasonable support for a specified period of time.

Substance abuse is an element of the definition of child abuse or neglect in many States. Circumstances that are considered abuse or neglect in some States include:

- Prenatal exposure of a child to harm due to the mother's use of an illegal drug or other substance;

- Manufacture of methamphetamine in the presence of a child;

- Selling, distributing, or giving illegal drugs or alcohol to a child; and,

- Use of a controlled substance by a caregiver that impairs the caregiver's ability to adequately care for the child.

Source: Child Welfare Information Gateway (2013a).

What is "Shaken Baby Syndrome?"

Shaken baby syndrome is a type of inflicted traumatic brain injury that happens when a baby is violently shaken. A baby has weak neck muscles and a large, heavy head. Shaking makes the fragile brain bounce back and forth inside the skull and causes bruising, swelling, and bleeding, which can lead to permanent, severe brain damage or death. The characteristic injuries of shaken baby syndrome are subdural hemorrhages (bleeding in the brain), retinal hemorrhages (bleeding in the retina), damage to the spinal cord and neck, and fractures of the ribs and bones. These injuries may not be immediately noticeable. Symptoms of shaken baby syndrome include extreme irritability, lethargy, poor feeding, breathing problems, convulsions, vomiting, and pale or bluish skin. Shaken baby injuries usually occur in children younger than 2-years-old, but may be seen in children up to the age of 5.

What is the prognosis?

In comparison with accidental traumatic brain injury in infants, shaken baby injuries have a much worse prognosis. Damage to the retina of the eye can cause blindness. The majority of infants who survive severe shaking will have some form of neurological or mental disability, such as cerebral palsy or mental retardation, which may not be fully apparent before 6 years of age. Children with shaken baby syndrome may require lifelong medical care.

Source: National Institute of Neurological Disorders and Stroke (2015).

---

common for state laws to designate members of certain professions as mandatory reporters. According to one review of state child maltreatment laws (Child Welfare Information Gateway, 2016a), those persons typically required to report suspected cases of maltreatment include the following:

- Social workers;
- Teachers, principals, and other school personnel;
- Physicians, nurses, and other health care providers;
- Counselors, therapists, and mental health professionals;
- Childcare providers;
- Medical examiners or coroners;
- Law enforcement officers.

As already mentioned, medical personnel championed the early battle against child maltreatment. However, physicians were initially very reluctant to report suspected cases of abuse or neglect. In fact, when states were drafting their original child abuse laws, the American Medical Association opposed any provision that required doctors to report suspicious cases (No Author, 1964). One reason for this stance was a fear of legal and professional repercussions.

Most states normally regard doctor–patient interaction as a *privileged relationship*. A privileged relationship means there is an inviolable, non-intrudable bond between two parties. The physician cannot reveal any information gathered in that confidential capacity without first obtaining the patient's consent.

Should a doctor break that trust, he or she could face a civil lawsuit and professional censure. Some other privileged discussions are conversations attorneys hold with their clients and the confessions ministers hear from their penitents.

Because the traditional doctor–patient privileged relationship could hinder physician reporting of suspected abuse and neglect, many states created an exemption. Today, the doctor–patient privileged relationship does not exist in child maltreatment cases. In addition, states have extended this protection by granting *legislative immunity* to any person who makes a child maltreatment report in *good faith*. That is, if a person contacts the authorities out of genuine concern for the child's well-being, he or she cannot be sued if the allegation turns out to be false. However, the obstacles of identifying, understanding, diagnosing, and then dealing with child protective services are still challenging steps for attending physicians today.

The Report

State statutes require that reporters contact authorities about alleged maltreatment as quickly as possible. Some states stipulate that the initial disclosure can be an oral statement, followed a short time later by a written report. The purpose of an oral report is to avoid any cumbersome bureaucratic delays when a child is at risk. The written report must include the victim's name, parents' identity, address, and nature of the injuries. It should also contain color photographs and X-rays, if possible. It must also indicate whether there are other siblings in jeopardy. Box 10.4 details some of the observations that are useful in trying to establish whether an abusive or neglectful situation exists.

One area of intense legislative debate in some jurisdictions was the issue of to whom to submit the report. Most statutes designate a public social service agency as the primary recipient of child abuse and neglect reports. However, such an arrangement is not satisfactory, for at least three reasons. First, most social service agencies conduct their business on a nine-to-five, Monday through Friday schedule. Lack of availability and the inability to research family records at night, on weekends, or on holidays become key concerns. One way to circumvent this difficulty is to establish a 24-hour telephone hotline. People who are worried about a child's situation can contact the hotline at any time and on any day of the week to file a confidential report. The counselor will ask a series of questions, gather all the pertinent information, and compile it on an intake form. Figure 10.1 displays the form used by the Florida Abuse Hotline. The counselor will determine whether an immediate intervention or a routine investigation is warranted and notify either law enforcement or child protective services.

BOX 10.4 SOME INDICATORS OF CHILD MALTREATMENT

Consider the possibility of physical abuse when the child:

- Has unexplained burns, bites, bruises, broken bones, or black eyes.
- Has fading bruises or other marks noticeable after an absence from school.
- Seems frightened of the parents and protests or cries when it is time to go home.
- Shrinks at the approach of adults.
- Reports injury by a parent or another adult caregiver.
- Abuses animals or pets.

Consider the possibility of neglect when the child:

- Is frequently absent from school.
- Begs or steals food or money.
- Lacks needed medical or dental care, immunizations, or glasses.
- Is consistently dirty and has severe body odor.
- Lacks sufficient clothing for the weather.
- Abuses alcohol or other drugs.
- States that there is no one at home to provide care.

Consider the possibility of sexual abuse when the child:

- Has difficulty walking or sitting.
- Suddenly refuses to change for gym or to participate in physical activities.

- Reports nightmares or bedwetting.
- Experiences a sudden change in appetite.
- Demonstrates bizarre, sophisticated, or unusual sexual knowledge or behavior.
- Becomes pregnant or contracts a venereal disease, particularly if under age 14.
- Runs away.
- Reports sexual abuse by a parent or another adult caregiver.

Consider the possibility of emotional maltreatment when the child:

- Shows extremes in behavior, such as overly compliant or demanding behavior, extreme passivity, or aggression.
- Is either inappropriately adult (e.g., parenting other children) or inappropriately infantile (e.g., frequently rocking or head-banging).
- Is delayed in physical or emotional development.
- Has attempted suicide.
- Reports a lack of attachment to the parent.

Source: Constructed by the authors, from the Child Welfare Information Gateway (2013a).

Second, although search-and-seizure guidelines empower the police to make warrantless entries into houses or other structures if an emergency exists, such lawful powers do not extend automatically to non-sworn personnel acting as governmental agents.

Third, it is not uncommon for the perpetrator to be present when the child protective services worker arrives. Because of the potential explosiveness involved and possible violence directed against the social worker, many states also include the police as an appropriate agency to handle child maltreatment reports (Cross et al., 2005). The offender's presence may fuel antagonisms. For example, if the child is in danger, the investigator may place the minor in *protective custody*. In this situation, the worker terminates parental custody for the time being, removes the child from the home, and places him or her in foster care for safekeeping pending judicial review at a later date. In addition to arousing parental anger, this step can stir up resentments within the child. As one victim told the U.S. Attorney General's Task Force (1984: 15):

> Why should I have been taken out of my home? I was the victim. I had [done] nothing. I did nothing wrong. My father should have been taken out, not me.

THE CENTRAL REGISTER

A critical component of child maltreatment laws is the establishment of a central register. A *central register* is a depository that stores records of all allegations of child abuse and neglect. Register users can index cases by the child's name, parent's name, and perpetrator's name. While many states have had such a tool for some time, a federal hotline now exists.

 WEB ACTIVITY

The National Resource Center for Permanency and Family Connections houses information regarding state child abuse registries. You can locate that website at **http://www.nrcpfc.org/.**

The purpose of this record-keeping system is to help in the diagnosis by tracking relevant case histories. In the past, some enterprising abusers skirted detection by taking the child to a different hospital or a new doctor every time the child needed medical attention. This strategy usually succeeded because the attending physician lacked access to any previous medical records. With the central register, chronic abusers have a more difficult time eluding detection.

Some Trouble Spots

Although child abuse and neglect laws have undergone much revision, some gaps remain. One troublesome area revolves around definitional aspects. Most states have an expansive construction of what constitutes abuse and neglect. They cast as wide a net as possible in the hope that valid cases of maltreatment do not go undetected. However, not everyone views maltreatment in the same way. Social workers and police officers, for example, may regard instances of maltreatment as being more serious than do doctors and lawyers (Giovannoni & Becerra, 1979; Saunders, 1988). Even teachers (Webster et al., 2005) and pediatricians (Levi et al., 2006) disagree among themselves as to how to categorize cases. Differences also exist among groups such as police, mental health therapists, and child protection services workers (Cross et al., 2005; Deisz et al., 1996; Everson et al., 1996). These divergent definitions can strain already scarce resources by compelling a small staff to investigate a large number of allegations. For example, four out of every five reports alleging child maltreatment during 2014 turned out to be unfounded or unsubstantiated (Child Welfare Information Gateway, 2016b: 20). In other words, the caseworker was unable to confirm that maltreatment had taken place. Such a high rate of unfounded allegations is a source of concern that scarce resources are being diverted away from children who really do need attention (Melton, 2005).

A second problem is that not all states place the same degree of emphasis on child maltreatment. Designated violations range from misdemeanors in some states to felonies in others. Even though the U.S.A. does have a national data collection system in place for child abuse and neglect, it may be that variations in state reports stem from differing definitions (Whitaker et al., 2005).

A related issue is the level of proof required to initiate a social service intervention. Most child protective services regard the "proof beyond a reasonable doubt" standard, the criterion for a criminal court conviction, as being far too rigid. The fear is that too many children in need of help would go unserved if this legalistic criterion is invoked. Similarly, the "probable cause" standard police officers must use when making an arrest is also considered overly restrictive. As a result, many states rely on a much more lenient threshold of "some credible evidence" to identify circumstances that trigger official action (Cross & Casanueva, 2009).

A fourth difficulty involves the lack of reporting. Despite statutory protection, many professionals are still reluctant to report suspected instances of maltreatment. Some develop *countertransference*—a sense of guilt, shame, or anxiety that leads to non-reporting (Pollak & Levy, 1988). Others either waiver in their initial assessment that the situation is serious, or they fear that an interruption in an ongoing treatment program would halt any progress already made (Kalichman et al., 1990; Willis & Wells, 1988; Zellman, 1990a, 1990b).

Finally, the issue of training has not received sufficient attention. Teachers, for example, spend a lot of time in direct contact with children. One might think that teacher preparation courses and state licensing requirements would devote detailed attention to the topic of child abuse and neglect. Perhaps one solution would be for legislation to require specific instruction to all workers whose occupational duties involve routine contact with children (Crenshaw et al., 1995; Lamond, 1989; U.S. Attorney General's Task Force, 1984).

THE CHILD WELFARE SYSTEM

Once a report of child maltreatment is initiated, the child welfare system moves into action. Much like the criminal justice system, the child welfare system is a conglomeration of numerous public and private entities as opposed to a unified model. Some of the system's responsibilities include investigative duties, foster care, medical services,

 WEB ACTIVITY

The State of Virginia now requires applicants seeking or renewing a teacher's license to first complete a training module on how to recognize and intervene when suspicions of child maltreatment arise. You can find those training materials at **http://www.doe.virginia.gov/teaching/ licensure/child_abuse_training.shtml.**

mental health treatment, substance abuse counseling, employment assistance, and welfare options. All of these activities are united by the same goal of protecting the best interests of the child.

Figure 10.2 is a diagram of the child welfare system. Upon receipt of a child maltreatment allegation, Child Protective Services (CPS) conducts an evaluation of the information. *Screening* takes place at this point. If it appears that the conditions in the report do not constitute abuse or neglect, the case is removed from the system. On the other hand, if the case merits a closer look, a *referral* is made and the file is routed for further processing. In 2014, CPS handled 3.6 million allegations, of which 39 percent were screened out and 61 percent were screened in (Child Welfare Information Gateway, 2016b: 8).

The second stage, the investigation, may take place immediately if the circumstances warrant, or—if there is no danger to the child—shortly thereafter. As mentioned earlier, the child may be removed from the household and placed in *protective custody* if his or her safety is imperiled. The CPS investigator will interview family members, will make a risk assessment, and may contact other parties, such as doctors, teachers, and neighbors. Once the CPS worker has gathered all the information possible, the case will be marked as "unsubstantiated" or "substantiated." An *unsubstantiated* disposition means the allegation is unfounded and the case is closed. In other words, there is not enough evidence to support the claim that the child was maltreated or is at risk of being maltreated. A *substantiated* disposition means that the CPS investigation concurred that maltreatment had occurred or is taking place or that the child's well-being is at risk. Child maltreatment statistics for 2014 in the U.S.A. reveal that 3.9 million children were monitored, and approximately one out of every five was substantiated as a maltreatment case (Child Welfare Information Gateway, 2016b: 20).

The third stage involves processing substantiated cases. If the situation involved a one-time incident and the child is not at any further risk, the case may be terminated. Sometimes, the determination may be that unfavorable conditions exist and that the family and/or child may benefit from receiving some type of social services. In other instances, CPS may route the case to the juvenile dependency court for formal handling. In 2014, 2.9 million children received some type of social service after the CPS investigation was concluded, and more than 147,000 victims were placed in foster care (Child Welfare Information Gateway, 2016b: 77–78).

THE EXTENT OF CHILD MALTREATMENT

Measuring child maltreatment is very difficult. These acts usually take place out of the public eye. As a result, it is a very difficult offense to detect. The neighbors rarely see it, and the police have a hard time discovering it. When it is

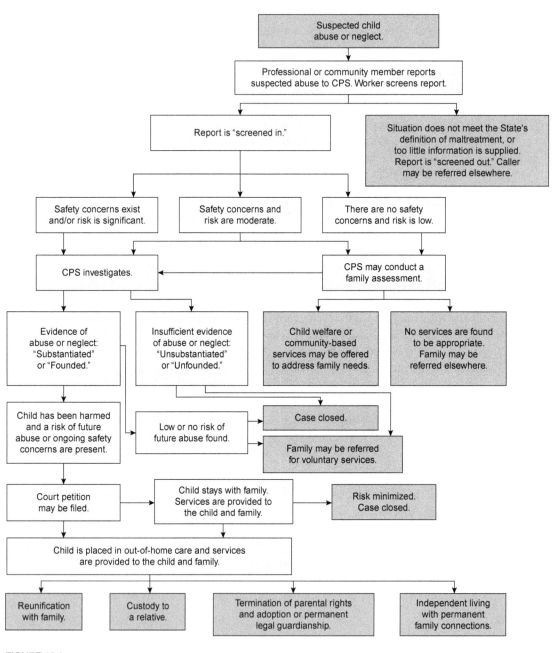

FIGURE 10.2
The Child Welfare System

Source: Child Welfare Information Gateway (2013b: 9).

detected, the victim may be too young to explain what happened. As a result, nobody really knows how pervasive child abuse is.

 WEB ACTIVITY

The Child Welfare Information Gateway, an arm of the U.S. Department of Health and Human Services, houses a wealth of information about child abuse and neglect. You can access this collection at **https://www.childwelfare.gov/.**

Although the incidence of child maltreatment remains elusive, the National Child Abuse and Neglect Data System (Child Welfare Information Gateway, 2016b) estimates that 702,000 children were victims of abuse and neglect in 2014. Sadly, 1,546 or 2.1 of every 100,000 American children, died from maltreatment in 2014 (Child Welfare Information Gateway, 2016b: 51). In other words, four to five children die from maltreatment every day in this country. In terms of age, 44 percent of the fatalities involved infants in their first year of life and another 38 percent were aged 4 or younger (Child Welfare Information Gateway, 2016b: 60). By way of comparison, the *Uniform Crime Reports* listed 177 murder victims in 2014 as infants. Another 283 homicide victims came from the 1- to 4-year-old age bracket, while an additional 83 criminal homicide victims were between the ages of 5 and 8 (Federal Bureau of Investigation, 2015b).

Most observers would agree that these numbers underestimate the true extent of child fatalities due to maltreatment. One review team examined medical examiner records in North Carolina for 1985 to 1994. They contended that child abuse statistics actually underestimate the true number of child homicide cases by 60 percent (Herman-Giddens et al., 1999). A similar investigation in Colorado showed that half the maltreatment deaths between 1990 and 1998 were misclassified (Crume et al., 2002). A national review illustrates how inconsistent coding might mask the underlying cause of death. Klevens and Leeb (2010) determined that many cases labeled as malnutrition actually stemmed from the infliction of head trauma. To combat this problem, all the states in this country now employ *child fatality review teams* (Douglas & Cunningham, 2008). These groups combine the expertise of child protective services workers, law enforcement officers, coroners and medical examiners, health care workers, prosecutors, and others to investigate child deaths to determine whether maltreatment was involved. Some signs that may suggest abuse or neglect include severe head trauma, the shaken baby syndrome (see Box 10.3), injuries to the abdomen or thorax areas, scalding, drowning, suffocation, poisoning, and chronic neglect. Over the years, these review teams have issued recommendations regarding such aspects as educational campaigns to increase awareness, training, protocols for law enforcement officers and coroners to follow during death investigations and autopsies, highlighting common risk factors, and increasing

 WEB ACTIVITY

The National Center for Child Death Review is an important resource in the effort to combat child maltreatment. Its website is available at **http://www.childdeathreview.org/.**

interagency coordination (Douglas & Cunningham, 2008; Palusci et al., 2010; Palusci & Covington, 2014).

The Children's Bureau, housed in the U.S. Department of Health and Human Services, compiles yearly figures on child maltreatment in the U.S.A. based on information provided by state child protective service agencies. According to the best available estimates, authorities received reports involving 3.6 million referrals, covering 702,000 children alleged to be maltreatment victims in 2014. However, investigators were able to substantiate the allegations in fewer than 20 percent of the cases (Child Welfare Information Gateway, 2016b). A *substantiated allegation* means that sufficient evidence existed to confirm the reporting person's suspicions. In other words, the case did involve child maltreatment.

It is important to realize that child maltreatment figures may not reflect actual changes in the level of maltreatment. It is possible that a heightened awareness of child abuse has led to greater reporting of maltreatment by the public, more intensive investigative efforts, and better methods for tabulating the data by interested agencies. Given the historical treatment and place of children in society, it is very likely that the growing numbers are the result of better counting rather than a rampant escalation of abusive incidents. Figure 10.3 contains a visual depiction of the different types of substantiated maltreatment involved in cases handled during 2014. As you can see, neglect tops the list.

Box 10.5 lists some child maltreatment statistics. As alarming as these statistics may be, the reader should bear one thing in mind: no one yet has compiled an accurate count of the number of crippling injuries or the physical and mental

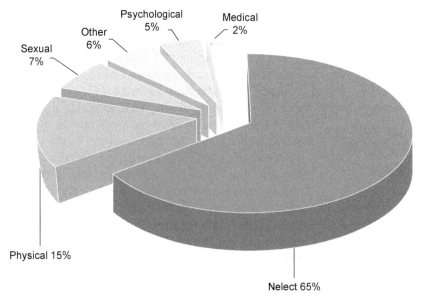

FIGURE 10.3
Types of Maltreatment Victims, 2014

Source: Compiled by the authors, from the Child Welfare Information Gateway (2016b: 42–43).

retardation cases that stem from this kind of violence. All that we can do at this point is to make ballpark estimates of what suffering our children endure.

One way to grasp the impact of child maltreatment is to look at the monetary costs associated with this type of victimization. In Chapter 3, we explained that victims sustain a host of direct and indirect costs as a result of being victimized. Direct costs pertain to the immediate consequences. These outlays include expenditures for physical health problems and mental health problems as well as expenses incurred by the child welfare, law enforcement, and judicial sectors. Indirect costs refer to long-term or secondary effects. This category includes special education, extended health costs, subsequent juvenile delinquency, future adult criminality, and lost productivity from the labor force.

Another helpful distinction is to separate child maltreatment statistics into prevalence and incidence reports. When applying this approach to the costs associated with child maltreatment, *prevalence* estimates tally the expenses that occur over a period of time, while *incidence* estimates calculate the lifetime costs. All told, one model puts the lifetime costs of child abuse and neglect cases that emerge each year at about $124 billion in 2010 dollars (Fang et al., 2012). Another estimate is that child maltreatment drains $220 million every day from the national economy (Gelles & Perlman, 2012).

A WORD OF CAUTION REGARDING OFFICIAL MALTREATMENT STATISTICS

Many people think of child abuse victims as being infants or small children. Quite often, however, the data source itself can influence what one finds.

Clinical studies, which are based on counseling records, usually reveal that the very young are victims. Yet surveys show that child maltreatment spans all ages. Survey data generally record a high proportion of non-white victims, whereas clinical studies do not. This relationship probably reflects differential accessibility. Many African Americans, due to their impoverished status, are unable to afford private therapy.

A common finding in family violence research is the relationship between child maltreatment and social class. Reliance upon official records usually shows that maltreatment cases are concentrated at the lower end of the social class spectrum. It is possible that lower class people resort to violence more often to resolve misunderstandings (Gelles, 1973; Wolfgang & Ferracuti, 1967). At the same time, official abuse and neglect statistics contain an inherent slant. Because members of the lower class come under the watchful eyes of service providers more often, higher rates of detected maltreatment and other problematic conditions should come as no surprise. In other words, it is entirely possible that child maltreatment is just as prevalent in the middle and upper classes as it is in the lower class. "Surveillance bias" may be responsible for this so-called "empirical regularity." As Chaffin and Bard (2006: 301) explain, *surveillance bias* "refers to any increased, systematic outcome-related scrutiny that may exist for some individuals or groups but not others." With respect to families that have been flagged for child abuse or neglect intervention, surveillance bias means that "service participants may be more likely to be reported for maltreatment than comparable nonservice participants because they are subject to greater scrutiny by virtue of interacting with service providers and service systems" (Chaffin & Bard, 2006: 301–302). The critical difference is that members of the middle and upper classes have the advantage of more resources. As a result, they can escape monitoring, while those of the lower class are not so fortunate. Given this orientation, Gelles (1975, 1980) recommends that attention be focused more upon the "gatekeepers"—the system personnel who have the power to confer the label of child maltreatment. One should keep these admonitions in mind when reading profiles such as the one in Box 10.6.

At least one researcher has taken this suggestion to heart. Handelman (1979) investigated a variety of alleged maltreatment cases that were referred to a social service agency for official investigation. Taking an organizational approach, Handelman showed how agency emphasis upon certain carefully selected details influenced the

BOX 10.6 WHO COMMITS THESE ACTS?

There is no single profile of a perpetrator of fatal child abuse, although certain characteristics reappear in many studies. Frequently, the perpetrator is:

- a young adult in his or her mid-20s;
- without a high school diploma;
- living at or below the poverty level;
- depressed;
- may have difficulty coping with stressful situations.

Source: Child Welfare Information Gateway (2015).

degree of intervention required in each case. In other words, the imposition of the label "child abuse" depended on the presence or absence of certain cues. They included the social worker's interpretation of what constitutes abuse and neglect, the client's amenability to accepting the label of child abuse, and the caseload the worker was currently handling.

The defi nitional ambiguity surrounding child abuse and neglect, coupled with bureaucratic mandates, may infl uence the offi cial designation of problem families as abusive families. On the other hand, the system may overlook and discard actual cases of child abuse because the workload is suffi ciently high to keep all agency workers fruitfully occupied. [...]

Legal Reform

Participation in criminal justice system proceedings can be a traumatic experience for children. In fact, the American Bar Association requires attorneys to consider the child's well-being carefully before deciding whether the victim should testify in court (Khoury, 2011). However, victim testimony is a crucial component in an adversarial system of justice. Without a victim's account, most cases are simply not prosecutable. As a result, some jurisdictions employ victim counselors to help combat the emotional upheaval which victims incur and to sustain victim credibility by increasing cognitive recall. The content of these disclosures may fall under the protection of victim counsel or privilege laws in some states. Box 10.12 contains provisions that allow Florida judges to close the courtroom and to allow a hearsay exception when dealing with child abuse cases.

Any reform effort must weigh victim trauma against the defendant's constitutional rights. The defendant has the right to confront and to cross-examine witnesses under the Fourteenth Amendment of the United States Constitution.

BOX 10.12 FLORIDA TRIAL GUIDELINES INVOLVING CHILD VICTIMS AND CHILD WITNESSES

Closing the Courtroom

If the victim of a sex offense is testifying concerning that offense in any civil or criminal trial, the court shall clear the courtroom of all persons upon the request of the victim, regardless of the victim's age or mental capacity, except that parties to the cause and their immediate families or guardians, attorneys and their secretaries, officers of the court, jurors, newspaper reporters or broadcasters, court reporters, and, at the request of the victim, victim or witness advocates designated by the state attorney may remain in the courtroom.

Hearsay Exception; Statement of Child Victim

Unless the source of information or the method or circumstances by which the statement is reported indicates a lack of trustworthiness, an out-of-court statement made by a child victim with a physical, mental, emotional, or developmental age of 16 or less describing any act of child abuse or neglect, any act of sexual abuse against a child, the offense of child abuse, the offense of aggravated child abuse, or any offense involving an unlawful sexual act, contact, intrusion, or penetration performed in the presence of, with, by, or on the declarant child, not otherwise admissible, is admissible in evidence in any civil or criminal proceeding if:

1. The court finds in a hearing conducted outside the presence of the jury that the time, content, and circumstances of the statement provide sufficient safeguards of reliability. In making its determination, the court may consider the mental and physical age and maturity of the child, the nature and duration of the abuse or offense, the relationship of the child to the offender, the reliability of the assertion, the reliability of the child victim, and any other factor deemed appropriate; and

2. The child either:

   a. Testifies; or

   b. Is unavailable as a witness, provided that there is other corroborative evidence of the abuse or offense. Unavailability shall include a finding by the court that the child's participation in the trial or proceeding would result in a substantial likelihood of severe emotional or mental harm.

Source: Florida Statutes, 2016, § 918.16(2); § 90.803(23)(a).

Back in Chapter 9, when we were exploring intimate partner violence, we introduced the U.S. Supreme Court decisions *Crawford v. Washington* (2004) and *Giles v. California* (2008). *Crawford* dealt with the admissibility of testimonial statements when the declarant was unavailable, and *Giles* involved forfeiture by wrongdoing when the defendant caused the declarant to be unavailable to testify in court. How these cases will impact child abuse cases in which the victim is too afraid to testify and how they affect the admissibility of CAC-videotaped interviews is starting to unfold.

There is the right to a public trial under the Sixth Amendment, and the public has the right to access the proceedings under the First Amendment. The difficulty, then, becomes one of balancing victim trauma induced by system participation against the defendant's interests. As we stressed in Chapter 1, this is the criminal's, not the victim's, justice system.

Some states in this country relax the hearsay rule when the following circumstances are present: a child victim is under a certain age, he or she is involved in a child abuse case, and the trustworthiness of a statement made out of court and not under oath can be established. The *hearsay rule* disallows statements made by a third party because the court cannot evaluate that person's credibility and, thus, the defense is unable to impeach that testimony. Judges waive the hearsay rule only under very narrow circumstances.

Another mechanism to reduce victim trauma is the use of *in camera* proceedings (Brancatelli, 2009). One such effort has been to allow child victims to testify outside the courtroom in less formal, less threatening surroundings, such as the children's advocacy center discussed earlier in this chapter. This practice allows the judge to interview a child in private and to videotape the testimony for the trial. An example of a state statute allowing for this practice is reproduced in Box 10.13.

 WEB ACTIVITY

The National Association of Counsel for Children devotes its effort to educating judges and lawyers who work in the best interests of the child. See its website at **http://www.naccchildlaw.org/**, which contains a wealth of information.

Although the use of *in camera* proceedings is innovative, it has encountered certain legal objections. First, some defendants have argued that such proceedings violate their constitutional right to confront and cross-examine witnesses. These complaints have been quashed by allowing the defense counsel to attend the out-of-court questioning. In addition, the courts have ruled that the defendant does not have to be physically present in the same room with the witness. A suitable alternative arrangement is to have the defendant view witness testimony from another location via closed circuit television.

A second objection deals with the right of the public to have access to the trial. Sufficient precedent exists that the public has limited access to observe judicial proceedings without jeopardizing the legal process. A similar third objection

BOX 10.13 AN EXAMPLE OF A STATUTE ALLOWING VIDEOTAPING OF TESTIMONY IN CHILD SEXUAL ABUSE CASES

(1) On motion and hearing in camera and a finding that there is a substantial likelihood that a victim or witness who is under the age of 18 or who has an intellectual disability as defined in s. 393.063 would suffer at least moderate emotional or mental harm due to the presence of the defendant if such victim or witness is required to testify in open court, or is unavailable as defined in s. 90.804(1), the trial court may order the videotaping of the testimony of the victim or witness in a case, whether civil or criminal in nature, in which videotaped testimony is to be used at trial in lieu of trial testimony in open court.

(4) The defendant and the defendant's counsel must be present at the videotaping, unless the defendant has waived this right. The court may require the defendant to view the testimony from outside the presence of the child or the person who has an intellectual disability by means of a two-way mirror or another similar method that ensures that the defendant can observe and hear the testimony of the victim or witness in person, but that the victim or witness cannot hear or see the defendant. The defendant and the attorney for the defendant may communicate by any appropriate private method.

Source: Florida Statutes, 2016, § 92.53.

deals with the defendant's right to a public trial. Precedence is mixed on this point. After reviewing a variety of cases, Melton (1980: 282) concluded that "embarrassment and emotional trauma to witnesses simply do not permit a trial judge to close his courtroom to the entire public." While *in camera* proceedings may avoid the inducement of unnecessary trauma, not all courts have reached a definitive conclusion about the conditions under which it is permissible.

Perhaps Vandervort (2006: 1415) captured this dilemma in the following remarks:

> Videotaping has often been opposed by prosecutors and urged by defense advocates. This has largely been a quixotic debate that has taken place in a vacuum with advocates for either side advancing their perceived interests and without consideration of how other investigative methods and tools might complement the use of videotaping. Moreover, the broader community's interests have been largely absent from this debate. Our findings suggest that, at least when used as part of a carefully thought-out investigative protocol, videotaping has a deleterious impact upon defendants' interests and a very positive impact on prosecutors' efforts to successfully prosecute child sexual abuse cases.

SUMMARY

It has taken our society a long time to recognize that child maltreatment exists. Once discovered, states implemented laws forbidding the victimization of children. Maltreatment, however, tends to take place behind closed doors. It often involves victims who are unable to defend themselves, making detection difficult. While reporting laws aim to remedy this dilemma, they have had a boomerang effect. About three-quarters of all child maltreatment complaints are graded as unfounded or unsubstantiated.

Other coping strategies have surfaced. Together, they suggest that the eradication of child abuse and neglect is everybody's responsibility. One way to place this mandate into perspective is to realize that somewhere in this country another child probably died from maltreatment during the time it took you to read this chapter.

Link: https://www.acf.hhs.gov/cb/resource/child-maltreatment-2016

INTIMATE PARTNER VIOLENCE

by William G. Doerner and Steven P. Lab

INTRODUCTION

When one thinks of crime and criminals, the image which most often comes to mind is that of stranger-to-stranger violations. In actuality, however, you are more likely to be killed or beaten by a person you know than by a total stranger. Furthermore, the violent offender is probably not just a passing acquaintance or somebody you nod to at the grocery store. It is more than likely that that person will be an immediate family member or someone with whom you share a very close personal relationship.

Every day, hundreds of husbands brutalize their wives. Much of this violence is hidden from the public eye. It frequently takes place in private, behind closed doors, where no one can see the physical infliction or hear the anguished pleas for help. In addition, if people should hear the muffled sounds of a beating, many would not intervene, based on the belief that "a man's home is his castle."

It is only recently that we have come to realize the amount of human suffering that takes place within families. Gradually, this internal domestic strife is becoming more exposed to public view. Society is finally starting to recognize the problem of intimate partner violence (IPV) as a major public health hazard. More than one-third of the non-fatal violent incidents experienced by men and women from 2002 through 2011 involved altercations with an intimate partner (Catalano, 2013). Similarly, information available from the FBI *Supplementary Homicide Reports* leads to the conclusion that female homicide victims, when compared to male homicide victims, are much more likely to be killed by an intimate partner (Catalano, 2013).

This chapter deals with violence between husbands and wives or other conjugal cohabitants. We look at the pervasiveness of this problem and at the types of statutory provisions that govern these behaviors. We also examine how academicians account for IPV. As you will see, the IPV problem has dropped into the laps of law enforcement personnel, and they have assumed responsibility as first responders. The primary reason why the police deal with IPV is that no other public agency operates seven days a week, 24 hours a day, 365 days a year. Because they did not anticipate these tasks as the dawning problem became more pervasive, law enforcement agencies often lacked the resources and skills required to deal with this form of violence. Despite this shortcoming, police departments and the rest of the justice community continue to look for ways to combat this social problem.

A BRIEF HISTORY OF INTIMATE PARTNER VIOLENCE

The domination of men over women has strong historical roots. Early Roman law treated women as the property of their husbands, a custom reinforced by biblical passages, Christianity, English common law, and the mores of

American colonists (Dobash & Dobash, 1977–1978, 1979; Edwards, 1989; Pleck, 1989). As property, women were subject to the control of their fathers or husbands, who held the power of life and death over them.

Women have held no legal standing throughout most of history. Any harm committed against a woman was viewed as an offense against the father or husband, not against her. Consequently, it was the male "owner" who sought vengeance or compensation for his loss. At the same time, a female could not be a culpable party. The father or the husband was the one held responsible for any injurious action by his woman. Buzawa and Buzawa (1990) point out that husbands or fathers were expected to punish women. In fact, many Western cultures proscribed official punishment of women in their legal codes.

The legal movement in this country to restrict wife beating can be divided into roughly three stages. The first period occurred in the mid-1600s, when the Puritans in Massachusetts enacted laws against wife beating and family violence (Pleck, 1989). Pleck points out, however, that these laws were rarely enforced. This laxity was due, in large part, to the strong belief in family privacy and the acceptance of physical force by the husband as a valid form of discipline.

A second upswing in concern over IPV appeared in the late 1800s, when states began passing laws restricting family violence. Worries over immigration, rising crime, the use of alcohol, and other factors prompted the passage of laws restricting family conflict and allowing for outside intervention (Pleck, 1989). Some states even mandated public flogging as a punishment for beating women. As with the earlier movement, however, these laws and punishments were seldom enforced (Pleck, 1989).

While these protective actions were evolving, some nineteenth-century state supreme court decisions continued to condone wife beating. However, husbands were advised that physical chastisement should not exceed the boundaries of good taste (Dobash & Dobash, 1977–1978; Pleck, 1979). It is important to note that it was not until the early part of the twentieth century that women in the U.S.A. gained *suffrage*, the right to vote (see Box 9.1).

The fate of the Equal Rights Amendment (ERA) is another example of the diminished status held by women. The first Equal Rights Amendment was proposed on December 23, 1923. However, it languished in Congress for years and never got out of committee. Another version of the ERA was approved by the House in 1971 and by the Senate in 1972. The text was very simple. It read, "Equality of rights under the law shall not be denied or abridged by the United States or by any State on account of sex" (U.S. Statutes at Large, 1972). However, this effort eventually failed because only 35 out of the necessary 38 states had ratified the ERA when the time for consideration expired. More recently, a resolution extending the deadline for approving the ERA was introduced on May 7, 2015 in the Senate (Congressional Record, 2015b) and is currently under consideration. The point remains, though, that women have a lesser status than men and have encountered strong resistance to achieving parity.

The third stage of interest in IPV is the one currently in effect. The 1960s saw the beginning of general social unrest and demands for equality. Concerns over rape, intimate partner abuse, and family violence became rallying cries for the emerging women's movement. Calls for greater police intervention into domestic violence replaced family privacy issues. It was during this time that physicians and social workers became vocal about family violence and brought these problems to the attention of society (Pleck, 1989). Remarkably, not a single research article in the *Journal of Marriage and the Family*, a premiere scholarly outlet in this area, addressed the issue of family violence prior to 1969 (Wardell et al., 1983). Reflecting on the historical paucity of interest in IPV, Dobash and Dobash (1977–1978: 427) pointed out that:

 WEB ACTIVITY

You can track the progress of the federal Equal Rights Amendment by accessing the website maintained by the Alice Paul Institute at **http://equalrightsamendment.org/.**

[W]ife-beating is not, in the strictest sense of the words, a "deviant," "aberrant," or "pathological" act. Rather, it is a form of behavior which has existed for centuries as an acceptable, and, indeed, a desirable part of a patriarchal family system within a patriarchal society, and much of the ideology and many of the institutional arrangements which support the patriarchy through the subordination, domination and control of women are still reflected in our culture and our social institutions.

Perhaps the greatest breakthrough for interest in IPV was the publication in 1984 of the Minneapolis Experiment, which evaluated the effectiveness of arresting abusive husbands. This research, which will be discussed in more detail later in this chapter, generated a great deal of policy change, spawned widespread debate in the academic community, and prompted a series of replications.

The renewed interest in IPV has gone relatively unabated. While some feminist scholars lament that research involving violence against women continues to be housed in specialized and separate disciplinary silos (Basile, 2009; Ford, 2009; Jordan, 2009), IPV continues to be a leading issue within the larger framework and growth of victimology. The criminal's justice system has adapted by altering different policies and procedures for dealing with abusive offenders and their victims. Academic interest has also kept pace. A casual inspection of most library holdings will uncover a large selection of materials dealing with IPV.

 WEB ACTIVITY

Presidential Proclamations are one tool to draw attention to an existing social problem, give it official recognition, and chronicle some efforts intended to remedy the issue. You can read such a recent declaration by looking at **https://www.whitehouse.gov/the-press-office/2015/09/30/presidential-proclamation-national-domestic-violence-awareness-month.**

THE EXTENT OF INTIMATE PARTNER VIOLENCE

Estimates of how often IPV occurs show some variation from one study to the next. Sometimes the definitions researchers employ are responsible for these differences. Despite these apparent differences, victimologists would agree that there are several types of IPV. As Box 9.2 shows, there are at least five major forms of IPV. They include physical abuse, sexual abuse, emotional abuse, economic abuse, and psychological abuse.

One well-known survey instrument, the Conflict Tactics Scale (CTS), is an unofficial measure used frequently to assess the extent of marital violence. The CTS represents a range of responses to conflict, extending from non-violent to violent actions. Respondents are asked to indicate how often each response was resorted to in the past year. Using the original version of the

An activist participating in a Walk a Mile in Her Shoes® event at the University of Southern Indiana in Evansville, Indiana, holds a cutout that represents a woman who died from intimate partner violence. Walk a Mile in Her Shoes® asks men and women to walk in high-heeled shoes to protest rape, sexual assault, and gender violence.

CREDIT: AP Photo/*The Evansville Courier & Press*, Molly Bartels

BOX 9.2 TYPES OF DOMESTIC VIOLENCE

We define domestic violence as a pattern of abusive behavior in any relationship that is used by one partner to gain or maintain power and control over another intimate partner. Domestic violence can be physical, sexual, emotional, economic, or psychological actions or threats of actions that influence another person. This includes any behaviors that intimidate, manipulate, humiliate, isolate, frighten, terrorize, coerce, threaten, blame, hurt, injure, or wound someone.

- **Physical Abuse:** Hitting, slapping, shoving, grabbing, pinching, biting, hair-pulling, etc. are types of physical abuse. This type of abuse also includes denying a partner medical care or forcing alcohol and/or drug use upon him or her.

- **Sexual Abuse:** Coercing or attempting to coerce any sexual contact or behavior without consent. Sexual abuse includes, but is certainly not limited to, marital rape, attacks on sexual parts of the body, forcing sex after physical violence has occurred, or treating one in a sexually demeaning manner.

- **Emotional Abuse:** Undermining an individual's sense of self-worth and/or self-esteem is abusive. This may include, but is not limited to, constant criticism, diminishing one's abilities, name-calling, or damaging one's relationship with his or her children.

- **Economic Abuse:** Is defined as making or attempting to make an individual financially dependent by maintaining total control over financial resources, withholding one's access to money, or forbidding one's attendance at school or employment.

- **Psychological Abuse:** Elements of psychological abuse include—but are not limited to—causing fear by intimidation; threatening physical harm to self, partner, children, or partner's family or friends; destruction of pets and property; and forcing isolation from family, friends, or school and/or work.

Source: Office on Violence Against Women (2015).

CTS, Straus and colleagues (1980) found that 16 percent of the subjects reported at least one violent episode within the previous year. More than a quarter of these people acknowledged participating in at least one violent confrontation with their partner during the marriage.

While the CTS enjoyed wide usage when it was introduced, it had some limitations (Dobash et al., 1992). First, only one member of a household was typically surveyed. This shortcoming meant that there were no comparative data against which to gauge the responses. Lack of validation is especially problematic because husbands tend to see less violence than do wives (Browning & Dutton, 1986). Second, these data were limited in terms of assessing the degree of conflict. There was no indication as to the kind of object used in various categories, the number of times an act occurred during each instance, the degree of force used, or differences in the strength of the combatants (Frieze & Browne, 1989). Third, there was no information on the severity of the actual harm, if any, inflicted. Finally, there was rarely any information gathered on the length of the marriage, age of the parties, family socioeconomic conditions, or other demographic characteristics.

Despite these shortcomings, the CTS carried at least three benefits (Schafer, 1996). First, reliance upon a standardized protocol makes it much easier to compare results from one project to the next and to develop a continuous body of knowledge. Second, using a standardized questionnaire may serve as a tool to minimize subject memory decay. As discussed in Chapter 2, recall problems are a source of constant worry for survey researchers. Finally, using a standardized set of questions over many different settings makes refinements and improvements possible.

These considerations prompted Straus and his associates to produce more refined versions of the instrument (Straus et al., 1996; Straus & Douglas, 2004). The revised scale includes more items pertaining to abuse, documents psychological abuse, delves into different forms of sexual violence, and includes outcome measures such as injury. Efforts at establishing the reliability, validity, and applicability of this revised protocol continue. In fact, at least one observer (Langhinrichsen-Rohling, 2005) considers the creation of the CTS and its ensuing development as the most fertile advance in IPV research.

Gelles and Straus (1988) claim that approximately 25 percent of all couples will experience abuse during their lifetimes. As one research team succinctly explained, "the percentage of women who will experience partner violence victimization is far greater than the percentage of women who experience breast cancer" (Logan et al., 2006: 177).

IPV figures, whether official or self-reported, undercount the actual level of abuse and are subject to a great deal of speculation. One reason for inaccuracy may be that many studies fail to register the number of times violence occurs in a relationship, opting instead to simply count whether any abuse has occurred. Looking at the number of times abuse occurred, Straus (1978) reported an average of three altercations a year.

 WEB ACTIVITY

Many researchers have used the Revised Conflict Tactics Scale (CTS2). You may view a copy of this instrument at **http://fluidsurveys.com/s/conflict-tactics/?ef.**

Another problem is that many studies refer only to married couples. Studies of courtship patterns reveal that violence between dating partners is a common occurrence (Katz et al., 2012; Sikes et al., 2012). Apparently, some people view this period as a "training ground" for marital interaction. In addition, researchers tend to overlook the amount of violence that occurs between same-sex couples (Lockhart et al., 1994).

Finally, reconciling disparate research results is often difficult due to differences in study design. Besides using different definitions of abuse, the data sources also vary (such as police records, social service agencies, single-city surveys, or estimates by "experts"). As a result, researchers suspect that the actual number of IPV cases is close to 50 percent of all couples (Feld & Straus, 1989). The inescapable conclusion generated from these and other projects is that IPV is an all-too-frequent act. See Box 9.3 for a way to assess whether abuse is taking place in a relationship.

With the redesign of the *National Crime Victimization Survey* (NCVS) discussed earlier in Chapter 2 comes more detailed information regarding IPV. The term *intimate partner violence* includes physical episodes involving current or former spouses, boyfriends, and girlfriends (Catalano, 2015). Figure 9.1 displays reported episodes from 1994 through 2011. While female victimization rates show a decline over the years, the gap between the female and male victimization rates remains pronounced. Females are more likely than males to experience harm at the hands of their intimates. Eighty-five percent of victims of intimate partner violence during this period were female (Catalano, 2013: 12).

The recognition of IPV as a public health issue prompted the Centers for Disease Control and Prevention to sponsor *The National Intimate Partner and Sexual Violence Survey* (NISVS) in 2010. Lifetime estimates of IPV indicate that one out of every three women and one out of every four men in this country will become victims of some form of IPV during their lifetimes (Breiding et al., 2014: 9–10). Approximately 7 million women and 5.7 million men reported experiencing sexual battery, physical violence, and/or stalking by an intimate partner within the previous year alone. We will touch upon the consequences and ramifications that accompany a problem of this magnitude throughout the remainder of this chapter.

 WEB ACTIVITY

If you are interested in learning more about *The National Intimate Partner and Sexual Violence Survey*, go to **http:// www.cdc.gov/violenceprevention/ nisvs/.**

Any discussion of IPV must recognize that these incidents have the potential to escalate into lethal confrontations. The Federal Bureau of Investigation (2015a) advises that 14,249 homicides occurred throughout the

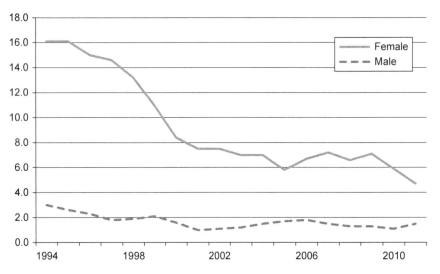

FIGURE 9.1
**Intimate Partner
Violence Rates, per
1,000, by Sex,
1994–2011**

Source: Adapted from
Catalano (2015: 12).

nation in 2014. The *Supplementary Homicide Reports* (Federal Bureau of Investigation, 2015c), which contain a rich array of data, has information available on 11,961 of these cases. Tabulations based on these files reveal that 79 percent of the victims knew their assailants, while 21 percent were murdered by strangers. As the reader can see, homicide victims are more likely to expire from injuries they sustain at the hands of people whom they know rather than complete strangers. This tidbit is exactly what we learned in Chapter 1 from Wolfgang's (1958) classic study of homicide in Philadelphia.

IPV is not restricted to husbands hurting their wives. Sometimes, women batter their mates. When the idea of women striking their mates was first introduced (Steinmetz, 1977–1978, 1978b), some commentators dismissed this notion as a "red herring" or a misleading distortion of the real problem (Fields & Kirchner, 1978). The idea of *sexual symmetry*, that women are equally as violent as their partners, overlooks the degree to which serious injuries are inflicted, whether the act was initiated in self-defense, and the intensity of the response (Dobash et al., 1992). People who adhere to the family violence perspective would welcome greater attention to this and other related topics. However, those who endorse a strict feminist viewpoint would reject this call because it ignores the imbalanced relationship between gender and power (Stalans & Lurigio, 1995). Perhaps the best summary of this situation came when Henning and colleagues (2006: 6) wrote:

> Those arguing that IPV is a gendered crime with female victims and male offenders will highlight the fact that most of the women in our sample were primary victims. People arguing that women are just as violent as men and that the criminal justice system is biased against

males will point to the "female batterers" we identified. Our opinion is that both pieces of information are important and must be acknowledged for the field to advance beyond the highly polarized debate that continues to fuel a growing backlash against domestic violence initiatives.

Part of the reason behind using the more expansive term *intimate partner violence*, as opposed to *spouse abuse*, is the growing recognition that violence also occurs within same-sex relationships. Some writers have concluded that violence between same-sex couples takes place at about the same rate as it does in heterosexual pairings or even higher (Aulivola, 2004; Finneran & Stephenson, 2012; McClennen, 2005; Messinger, 2011; Stanley et al., 2006). Instead of painting the issue of spouse abuse along gender lines where women are victims and men are the aggressors, the suggestion these observers make is to recast the issue in terms of intimate partner violence and focus upon violence within primary relationships.

Women sometimes strike back at their assailants. Research over the past three decades shows that approximately three-quarters of the homicides involving a male partner death were preceded by instances of IPV perpetrated upon the female partner (Campbell et al., 2007: 247). The fact that these women were IPV victims has led lawyers to raise the *battered woman syndrome* as a self-defense explanation, a concept we will delve into later in this chapter. The argument is that these women were so traumatized by previous beatings that they simply seized the opportunity to kill their assailants to prevent any further victimization episodes. In any event, situations such as those typified here caused one author to remark, "A man's home may be his castle, but a woman's home too often is her dungeon" (Costa, 1984: 8). [...]

Learned Helplessness

According to Lenore Walker (1979), many battered women suffer from the syndrome which she identifies as *learned helplessness*. The idea of learned helplessness centers upon three components. The first is the information a person has about what is going to happen. The second aspect is the knowledge or perception about what will happen. This component usually comes from past experiences (or lack thereof). The third component is the person's behavior toward the event that takes place. Some people believe they cannot influence or control what is about to happen to them. As these perceptions mount and grow more overwhelming, the victim comes to believe she is helpless to alter her environment. In other words, she develops a belief that she is not in charge of the world around her and that she cannot change the flow of events. As a result, the victim becomes helpless in her struggle and may appear apathetic to some viewers.

The idea of learned helplessness follows from sociocultural explanations of the relative place of males and females in society. Some professionals contend that battered partners remain in destructive relationships for economic reasons. IPV victims may lack the monetary resources that would enable them to depart. They may have no place to go. They may not be able to support themselves financially. They may have young children to support. They lack marketable job skills. In short, the circumstances are such that some victims are unable to exert control over themselves or their environments. The perceived, or actual, inability to support oneself or gain employment may be an outcome of the historical role of women in society.

The Cycle of Violence as Backdrop

As Chapter 3 explained, contributing to a sense of helplessness is the reality that battered women are not beaten every minute of the day. Instead, there is a *cycle of violence*, which gradually builds their feelings of being powerless and unable to alter their plight. Walker sees this cycle as consisting of three distinct stages: (1) the tension-building phase; (2) the battering episode; and (3) the reconciliation period.

The *tension-building phase* may be accompanied by minor assaults. During this period, the woman believes she can deflect her husband's bullying. She may calm the situation by conceding to his wishes or by staying out of his way. Her goal is not to prevent the battering behavior but to avoid it. She becomes grateful that small displays of abusive behavior are not as serious as what they could be. Sometimes, she may even make excuses for the man's behavior. Her general perception is that these incidents are isolated events that will end once the irritant is removed. Thus, she is able to rationalize these outbursts.

The second part of the cycle, the *battering episode*, is the culmination of the frustrations experienced in the first stage. At this point, the man is out of control and acts in a rage. As Walker (1979: 55) explains:

> He starts out wanting to teach the woman a lesson, not intending to inflict any particular injury on her, and stops when he feels she has learned her lesson. By this time, however, she has generally been very severely beaten.

A common rationalization regarding these volatile outbursts is the man's claim that he did not fully realize what he was doing because he had been drinking. This *disinhibition* account acts to transfer responsibility away from the abuser and to characterize alcohol as the real culprit. In other words, the alcohol weakened the man's normal behavioral restraints, thus triggering atypical and uncontrollable violence, sometimes with even more severe consequences (Graham et al., 2011). However, the evidence for how alcohol works as a cause of IPV is unclear (Eckhardt et al., 2015). This fact has prompted some researchers to conclude that although "there is more than a 'kernel of truth' in the drunken bum theory of wife beating, the findings also provide the basis for demythologizing this stereotype" (Kantor & Straus, 1987: 224). One counselor probably had the best handle on this situation when he stated, "While I can't say drinking is the cause of domestic abuse, it definitely pours gasoline on the fire" (Healey et al., 1998: 6).

The final phase is the *reconciliation period*. Here the batterer transforms himself into a very apologetic, tender, and loving character. Pleas for forgiveness and promises of a better future often cloud the anger and fear the victim has experienced at the hands of her partner. As Walker (1979: 58) puts it:

> The batterer truly believes he will never again hurt the woman he loves; he believes he can control himself from now on. He also believes he has taught her such a lesson that she will never again behave in such a manner, and so he will not be tempted to beat her.

It is not uncommon for the batterer to shower the victim with tokens of affection during this period. A bouquet of flowers may appear unannounced. Declarations of love abound. There may be many little thoughtful things, reminiscent of romantic days gone by, to prove the insistence of a loving relationship. However, the cycle-of-violence perspective implies that this period too will pass.

As the couple's relationship proceeds through this cycle again and again, the wife's physical and psychological well-being become compromised. As the Power and Control Wheel contained in Figure 9.2 shows, numerous practices trap the victim in this environment. She may assess her marriage as a failure but not be able to take any remedial steps. There may be strong religious beliefs (Sharp, 2014), family pressures, and other social considerations that prevent action. Postponement of any resolution to the beatings permits the cycle to continue without any end in sight (Eisikovits, 1996). The woman is trapped; she simply learns to live with the violent spasms that characterize the relationship. The learned helplessness perspective centers on the emotional dependency that develops during an intimate relationship. As society expects, the woman becomes more enthralled with her husband. Simultaneously, an economic dependency also surfaces within the household (Sanders, 2015). One writer (Pagelow, 1984: 313) sizes up the situation quite neatly:

> When a woman leaves her abuser, her economic standard of living very likely takes a drastic drop. If she has dependent children, she must take into consideration the lives and welfare of her children, who have roughly one chance out of two of dropping below the poverty level (two out of three for minority children). Is it any wonder that many battered women remain with their abusers for many years, sometimes until the children have grown up and left home?

POLICE INTERVENTION

The first point at which society typically becomes involved in domestic disputes is when a police officer is summoned to an abusive episode. More than likely, this incident is not the first time that the couple has engaged in a violent confrontation with each other. Historically, officers who respond to a call involving IPV have had a variety of alternatives at their disposal: making an arrest, counseling the parties, referring the couple to professional counseling, threatening to make an arrest, separating the parties, or advising the victim to sign a formal complaint. This part of the chapter explores some of these options and their limits.

 WEB ACTIVITY

The Duluth Model is a leading tool for helping us understand and erase domestic violence. For a fuller understanding of this problem, visit the website at **http://www.theduluthmodel.org/**.

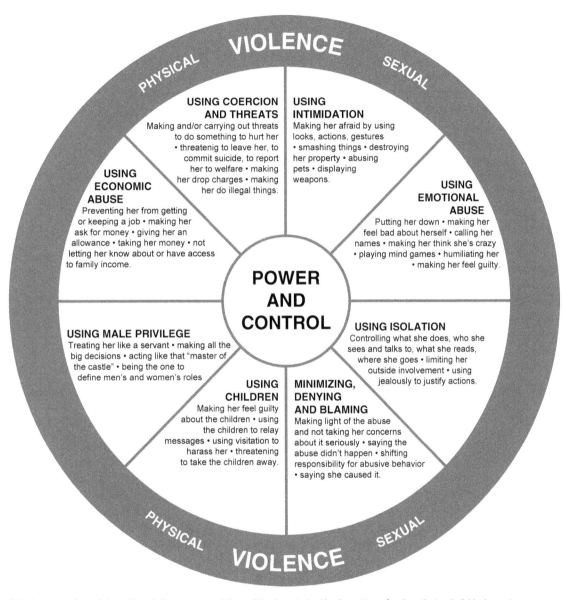

The Power and Control Wheel shows the words "VIOLENCE" and "PHYSICAL" and "SEXUAL" around the outer rim, with sections describing:

USING COERCION AND THREATS
Making and/or carrying out threats to do something to hurt her • threatenig to leave her, to commit suicide, to report her to welfare • making her drop charges • making her do illegal things.

USING INTIMIDATION
Making her afraid by using looks, actions, gestures • smashing things • destroying her property • abusing pets • displaying weapons.

USING EMOTIONAL ABUSE
Putting her down • making her feel bad about herself • calling her names • making her think she's crazy • playing mind games • humiliating her • making her feel guilty.

USING ECONOMIC ABUSE
Preventing her from getting or keeping a job • making her ask for money • giving her an allowance • taking her money • not letting her know about or have access to family income.

POWER AND CONTROL

USING ISOLATION
Controlling what she does, who she sees and talks to, what she reads, where she goes • limiting her outside involvement • using jealously to justify actions.

USING MALE PRIVILEGE
Treating her like a servant • making all the big decisions • acting like that "master of the castle" • being the one to define men's and women's roles

USING CHILDREN
Making her feel guilty about the children • using the children to relay messages • using visitation to harass her • threatening to take the children away.

MINIMIZING, DENYING AND BLAMING
Making light of the abuse and not taking her concerns about it seriously • saying the abuse didn't happen • shifting responsibility for abusive behavior • saying she caused it.

Battering is one form of domestic or intimate partner violence. It is characterized by the pattern of actions that an individual uses to intentionally control or dominate his intimate partner. That is why the words "power and control" are in the center of the wheel. A batterer systematically uses threats, intimidation, and coercion to instill fear in his partner. These behaviors are the spokes of the wheel. Physical and sexual violence holds it all together—this violence is the rim of the wheel.

FIGURE 9.2
The Power and Control Wheel

Source: Domestic Abuse Intervention Programs (n.d.).

The Arrest Option

While one of the more awesome powers entrusted to police officers is that of arrest, there are several restrictions that limit its utility. The first consideration is the distinction between reasonable suspicion and probable cause. *Reasonable suspicion* permits an officer to intrude into a situation to investigate whether a crime has been committed, is being committed, or is about to occur. Probable cause, on the other hand, is more stringent. *Probable cause* means that the facts and circumstances are sufficiently strong enough to make the officer conclude that the accused is the one who committed the crime under investigation. If probable cause is present, the officer can make a legitimate or lawful arrest. If probable cause is absent, the arrest lacks proper foundation. There is not a lawful custodial situation. Any officer who willfully violates this provision may be the subject of a series of administrative, criminal, and civil penalties.

A second major consideration lies in the distinction between a misdemeanor and a felony offense. The general rule of thumb is that an officer may make a lawful arrest for a felony offense, either with or without an arrest warrant, as long as probable cause exists. In a misdemeanor case, though, an officer can make a *warrantless arrest* only if the transgression has taken place in his or her presence. This restriction, called the *misdemeanor rule*, can hamper effective police intervention, particularly in situations in which many offenses are misdemeanors, such as IPV.

One recommendation issued by the U.S. Attorney General's Task Force (1984) called for states to revise their provisions concerning arrests in family violence. The "Violence Against Women Act of 1994" reiterated this position by linking receipt of certain federal funds with revisions to state laws that created an exception to the misdemeanor rule in domestic violence situations. As a result, the states have responded by relaxing the misdemeanor rule in IPV situations (Zeoli et al., 2011). In other words, an officer can now make a legitimate warrantless arrest even though he or she did not observe the crime being committed. The probable cause element, though, has not changed. It still remains the essential ingredient in the decision to take an individual into custody.

 WEB ACTIVITY

The International Association of Chiefs of Police, in conjunction with the U.S. Department of Justice Office on Violence Against Women, has produced a training package to help officers address intimate partner violence. You can see the materials by going to **http://www.theiacp.org/Police-Response-to-Violence-Against-Women.**

Another important determinant in how the police handle a domestic disturbance is whether the suspect is at the scene when the police arrive. If the abuser has left the premises, the officer may not be able to make an immediate arrest. At this point, the officer must assess the extent of injury to the victim. If the injuries are serious and require medical attention, then more than likely the crime is an aggravated battery, which is a felony in most jurisdictions. This classification means the officer can initiate a warrantless arrest. However, if the injuries are minor or non-visible, then it might be difficult to establish that a crime took place. If probable cause is lacking or if the misdemeanor rule is in effect, then the officer is powerless to make a legitimate warrantless arrest. The only thing that will enable the police to arrest the abuser is if the victim signs an affidavit, and that process usually takes some time.

An *affidavit* is an official complaint in which the victim outlines the details of the offense and swears under oath that the individual named in the accusation is the offender. The completion of this legal document and the issuance of a warrant by a judge give the police proper authority to arrest the suspect on a misdemeanor charge.

Should the suspect be present at the scene when the officers arrive, an evaluation of the arrest option is in order. Bear in mind that if the state legislature has not made IPV an exception to the usual misdemeanor rule, then the officer cannot arrest the abuser for a misdemeanor without observing a violation first-hand. However, if the elements for a felony offense fit, the officer may have probable cause for an immediate arrest.

Non-Arrest Options

If an arrest is not possible, or if the officer elects not to pursue the arrest option immediately, a variety of other options are at the officer's disposal. The officer may engage in a *mediation* effort. Ideally, this choice involves talking with each party privately to learn each participant's version of what took place. The officer may suggest one or more ways in which to handle disputes of this nature in the future. Alternatively, he or she may try to extract a promise from the disputants that they will not engage in another confrontation after the officer leaves. The officer then exits, in the belief (or hope) that accord has been re-established.

In other instances, the officer may suggest the couple contact a minister, a counselor, or some other social service agency. The problem with this *referral* option is:

> that it depends upon the efforts of the citizen for initial contact with the agency to which he is referred. Many of those involved in domestic disturbances are prevented from seeking assistance by their own fear, ignorance, or lack of initiative.
>
> (Parnas, 1967: 934–935)

As one psychologist adroitly recognizes, "Regardless of the potential danger, the parties have the Constitutional right to refuse help" (Bard, 1980: 114). In other words, the police are powerless to compel individuals to seek family counseling—even if this recourse is in the best interests of the couple.

Another common tactic is to either threaten or cajole the parties into peaceful behavior. As one veteran commented, "What can a police officer tell a person who has been married 20–25 years! You just have to be a good con artist" (Parnas, 1967: 948). Usually this option comes with the reminder that a return visit by the police will trigger the arrest of either one or both parties.

Perhaps the most typical response is to separate the combatants. Officers do not have the legal authority to order an inhabitant out of his or her own house. However, one prevalent strategy is to request that the perpetrator leave for a "cooling-off" period. Sometimes the request may go unheeded or the occupant may assert the right to remain on the premises. In this situation, the officer might try to regain the upper hand by reminding the uncooperative party of the dire consequences of an arrest. Confronted with a hostile subject and a lack of legitimate alternatives, the officer may enlist the help of the woman. The officer may even offer to drive the woman to a relative's house or to place her and the children, if any, in a domestic violence shelter for the evening. [...]

Legislative Reform

Many state legislatures have responded to the problem of IPV with reforms on several fronts. As noted earlier, one popular approach has been to relax the misdemeanor rule. To bypass this restriction, some state legislatures have declared IPV to be an exception to the usual misdemeanor rule. This legislative maneuver removes the "in the presence of an officer" requirement. As a result, a police officer may make a bona fi de warrantless arrest for a misdemeanor even though he or she did not witness the violation itself. [...]

BOX 9.4 AN EXAMPLE OF LAW ENFORCEMENT POLICY GUIDELINES REGARDING DOMESTIC VIOLENCE ARRESTS

A. Whenever a deputy determines upon probable cause that an act of domestic violence has been committed, the deputy may arrest the person suspected of its commission and charge such person with the appropriate crime. The decision to arrest and charge shall not require the consent of the victim or consideration of the relationship of the parties. Deputies shall notify their supervisor whenever they decide not to make an arrest upon determining that probable cause exists to believe an act of domestic violence has occurred. The reasons for this decision must be documented and articulated in an offense report.

B. Factors which should not be considered in determining whether an arrest will be made include:

1. Marital status, sexual orientation, race, religion, profession, age, disability, cultural, social or political position or socioeconomic status of either party;

2. Ownership, tenancy rights of either party or the fact the incident occurred in a private place;

3. Victim's request that an arrest not be made;

4. Belief that the victim will not cooperate with criminal prosecution or that the arrest may not lead to a conviction;

5. Verbal assurances that the abuse will stop;

6. The fact that the suspect has left the scene;

7. Disposition of previous police calls involving the same victim or suspect;

8. Denial by either party that the abuse occurred when there is evidence of domestic abuse;

9. Lack of a court order restraining or restricting the suspect;

10. Concern about reprisals or restricting the suspect;

11. Adverse financial consequences that might result from arrest;

12. Chemical dependency or intoxication of the parties;

13. Assumptions as to the tolerance of violence by cultural, ethnic, religious, racial or occupational groups;

14. Absence of visible injury or complaints of injury;

15. Presence of children or the immediate dependency of children on the suspect.

C. The deputies making an arrest should inform the arrestee that domestic is a crime and that the State of Florida, not the victim, is responsible for the prosecution. The responding deputies shall not initiate discussion of or accept a complaint withdrawal, or have the victim sign a waiver of prosecution form.

D. The agency shall discourage dual arrests in order to avoid arresting the victim. Where there are allegations that each party assaulted the other, the deputy shall determine whether there is sufficient evidence to conclude that one of the parties is the primary aggressor.

E. Deputies shall not threaten, suggest or otherwise indicate the possible arrest of all parties of the removal of the children from the home, with the intent of discouraging requests for intervention by law enforcement by any party.

F. If no arrest is made, the victim shall be so informed and be notified that he/she can request to have the case reviewed by the State Attorney's Office.

Source: Leon County Sheriff's Office (2014).

Another legislative remedy that gives police officers an immediate response aims to provide safe temporary housing. One fear victims harbor is that the arrested party will return home from jail and embark upon a revengeful rampage. The only alternative available to many women, and one that is often suggested by responding police officers, is to pack their belongings and move their children to a temporary location where they can hide. However, many people do not have the resources to pursue this option. Some are poor; others live too far away from family and friends .

Some social service groups have responded by establishing *refuge houses* or *domestic violence shelters*. The purpose of these places is to provide the battered woman a safe haven where she can live until she decides what to do about the abusive marital situation. The location of these refuge houses remains a well-guarded secret to ensure safety from angry partners who might appear on the premises for retaliation. More recently, some shelters have begun publicizing their presence in an effort to mobilize greater public support (Belluck, 1997). No matter which approach is taken, these havens require considerable finances for housing, furniture, food, clothing, upkeep, and staffi ng. As Box 9.5 shows, these escalating costs have prompted some state legislatures to mandate sur-charges on marriage licenses and divorce settlements to underwrite IPV centers.

 A number of other legislative changes have taken place. Florida police officers who are investigating an incident involving IPV are required by state law to file a written report even if there is no arrest in the matter (Florida Statutes, 2016, § 741.29). That report must contain an explanation of why no arrest was made. In addition, offi cers must give IPV victims a brochure regarding their rights and remedies and document that action in the written report. Unfortunately, though, some officers fi nd ways to circumvent the mandate to fi le a written report when dealing with IPV cases (Cerulli et al., 2015).

Other changes are directed at the judiciary. In Florida, persons arrested on a charge of domestic violence are not entitled to bail; they must remain in jail for a mandatory fi rst appearance hearing before a judge, who then makes a bail decision (Florida Statutes, 2016, § 741.2901(3)). In addition, there is a mini-mum mandatory fi ve-day jail sentence for anyone convicted of domestic violence (Florida Statutes, 2016, § 741.283). Furthermore, any person con-victed of domestic violence in Florida is automatically placed on probation for one year and must attend a batterer's intervention program (Florida Statutes, 2016, § 741.281). [...]

Prosecutorial and Judicial Action

While most attention has been paid to the actions of the police in IPV cases, the victim may also turn directly to the court through the office of the prosecutor. While it is true, then, that not all cases reach the court through an initial police arrest, victims bring few cases (IPV or otherwise) to the prosecutor. The police remain the largest "supplier" of cases for the court.

Evidence exists that there is a high level of attrition in domestic violence cases once they reach the prosecutorial stage. Buzawa and Buzawa (1990) identify a number of reasons for this attrition. First, victims see that there are both immediate and potential costs involved in going through with a case. Among these costs are the possibility of retaliation by the accused, lost time from work, lost income from the accused, and lack of companionship. Second, many victims change their minds about prosecuting after filing charges. They may no longer see the action as important enough to prosecute or may simply lose interest in the case. Third, victims may feel guilty and assume some of the blame for the abusive act. Fourth, some victims may be using the court for purposes other than to prosecute the offender. Some participants may be looking to benefit from *therapeutic jurisprudence*, the healing and sense of empowerment one may gain from moving forward with the case (Cattaneo et al., 2013). They may be trying to teach the accused a lesson, gain revenge, or confirm their own status as a victim, or they may have other reasons that do not require completion of prosecution (Eisikovits, 1996; Fischer & Rose, 1995; Gondolf et al., 1994; Smith, 2000). […]

Each of these reasons for case attrition can contribute to yet another factor—pressure by the prosecutor or state attorney to drop the charges. Based on prior experiences of victims failing to carry through with charges, prosecutors are reluctant to prepare and begin proceedings when they feel it is likely that the victim may withdraw at a later date. Prosecutors, therefore, often influence victims to drop charges by suggesting that the victim was an active participant in the abuse situation. The lack of a clear victim makes a case more difficult to prosecute.

Despite claims that prosecutors often summarily dismiss domestic violence cases, evidence from different jurisdictions reveals that prosecutors make decisions on the basis of case merit more than on the type of case. For example, Schmidt and Steury (1989) note that in cases in which charges were not brought, 45 percent were a result of the fact that victims did not wish to pursue the case, and another 30 percent of the cases rested on questionable legal grounds. Only 14 percent of the cases were deemed not important enough to pursue. Similarly, Sigler and colleagues (1990), in a statewide survey of judges and prosecutors, found that the failure to prosecute was due primarily to victims recanting their testimony or a lack of evidence. The most important factor uncovered in the literature is the level of cooperation by the victim. A lack of cooperation often leads to dismissals or a failure to bring charges (Elliott, 1989).

This discussion on whether to prosecute presupposes that such an intervention will make a difference. There have been few studies regarding the impact of prosecution in domestic violence cases. Elliott (1989), in a review of such studies, notes that court actions tend to have little impact upon subsequent violence. This conclusion is echoed in studies which show that no one court sanction is more effective in reducing recidivism or promoting victim satisfaction (Davis et al., 2008; Gross et al., 2000; Klein & Crowe, 2008; Klein & Tobin, 2008). In fact, evidence is mounting that court-ordered mandatory counseling generally has minimal, if any, impact upon subsequent domestic violence (Labriola et al., 2007). However, it does appear that one subgroup—those men who attend most or all sessions—have much more to lose if they are rearrested and so they refrain from repeat IPV (Brame et al., 2015; Feder & Dugan, 2002; Gordon & Moriarty, 2003). The most notable instance in which prosecution reduces violence is in cases where past violence was less common and not as serious. These conclusions, however, are drawn from few studies, and much more research is needed before suggesting any significant policy changes.

Besides filing criminal charges against an abusive partner, there is the possibility of taking civil action against the offender. Unfortunately, a woman who has made the decision to leave her partner is usually too destitute to pay the attorney fees and filing costs associated with divorce or other civil petitions. Some states now provide a simplified mechanism to secure an *injunction*, or what some people call a *restraining order* or a *protection order*, against the abuser.

Another way to paint the purpose of an injunction is to return to Walker's cycle of violence thesis. An injunction or a judicial non-contact order informs the batterer not to communicate with the victim during the interim following arraignment and completion of the criminal proceedings. In other words, the purpose of an injunction is to interrupt the cycle of violence and allow the victim an opportunity to contemplate an effective exit from the relationship. An injunction is also one way to strengthen the no-drop policy that many prosecutors utilize to compel victim testimony at trial.

Under these provisions, the clerk of the court supplies a preprinted, fill-in-the-blank form to request an injunction or court protection order against the violent party. The clerk also explains how to complete the form. He or she can waive the filing fees if the victim is unable to pay court costs. The clerk also assists in the preparation of these materials. The judge can issue a temporary restraining order on an *ex parte* basis. In other words, the offender does not have to be present in order for the judge to take official action. Any violation of a protective order can constitute either a contempt-of-court charge or a separate criminal violation, and any law enforcement officer may then arrest the offender, which is a significant repercussion for men who do not want others to know about their behavior (Eisikovits, 1996; Fischer & Rose, 1995; Sorenson & Shen, 2005; U.S. Department of Justice, 2002; Wallace & Kelty, 1995). In fact, the federal "Violence Against Women Act" requires judges to enforce injunctions that have been issued outside their states (Eigenberg et al., 2003).

Despite these protections, less than half of the women who secure a temporary restraining order go on to obtain a permanent, final order (Zoellner et al., 2000). Perhaps the process of filing and getting a permanent (as compared to a temporary) court order remains too cumbersome and tedious for these victims (Durfee, 2009; Logan et al., 2005). Another possibility is that the experience of obtaining a restraining order may dissuade some women from seeking further formal action. Women may become wary and noncommittal if they encounter court personnel who are intimidating, condescending, non-supportive, or overly bureaucratic (Bell et al., 2011; Lucken et al., 2015; Wan, 2000). However, there is some evidence that a legislative commitment to combat domestic violence can pay dividends. There are some indications that injunction or protective order provisions substantially reduce IPV violence, although the possibility of ineffective enforcement

WEB ACTIVITY

The Florida Supreme Court has established a template, or a fill-in-the-blank form, which domestic violence victims can use to file for a protective order prohibiting domestic violence. You can view the instructions and a copy of that form by visiting **http://www.flcourts. org/core/fileparse.php/539/urlt/980a. pdf.**

and subsequent stalking does emerge as a valid victim concern (Diviney et al., 2009; Dugan, 2003; Kothari et al., 2012; Logan & Walker, 2009a, 2010a). One study projected that IPV injunctions produce an annual saving of $85 million (costs borne by the justice system, health care services, employers, etc.) for Kentucky taxpayers (Logan et al., 2012: 1148).

There are a number of other proposals aimed at improving the prosecutorial and judicial responses to domestic violence. One such idea has been the introduction of victim advocates into the prosecutor's office and the courtroom. The availability of such individuals can help demystify the court process, provide support to the victim, and assist in the successful prosecution of the case. Closely related to this change is the appointment of specific attorneys to handle domestic violence cases and the use of "vertical adjudication," whereby a single prosecutor handles the case from start to finish (Durfee, 2009; Visher et al., 2007: 4). In one jurisdiction, having investigating officers take digital photographs of victims' injuries and preserving this evidence resulted in more guilty pleas, a greater number of convictions, and longer sentences (Garcia, 2003). Pre-trial domestic violation probation units educate arrested persons about their bond conditions, especially if there is a no-contact-with-victim order, and verify that suspects have acquired alternative living arrangements (Visher et al., 2007). Finally, many jurisdictions have sought to de-emphasize punishment in domestic violence cases and to promote treatment for both the offender and the victim.

Another strategy has entailed efforts to curtail dropping domestic violence cases at the prosecutorial level. As one veteran prosecutor explains (Long, 2008: 21):

WEB ACTIVITY

The American Bar Association has established a Commission on Domestic and Sexual Violence that serves as a clearinghouse. You can access these resources at **http://www.americanbar.org/groups/ domestic_violence.html.**

> Experienced domestic violence prosecutors understand . . . . domestic violence victims often stay with their abusers, regularly minimize their abuse, recant, request the dismissal of charges against their batterers, refuse to testify for the prosecution, or testify on behalf of their batterers.

Such "no-drop" or mandatory prosecution policies, like the guidelines that appear in Box 9.6, seek to force victims to carry through with the case and have the state assume the burden of the prosecution (Buzawa & Buzawa, 1990; Davis & Smith, 1995). The thinking behind these no-drop policies is to let the offender know that it is the state, not the victim, pursuing the case and to make abusers accountable for their actions (Berliner, 2003). This practice also extends the time an IPV case is involved in the courts and keeps the batterer under formal scrutiny for a longer period of time, usually extending from post-arrest release from jail through case disposition (Peterson & Dixon, 2005). Critics, though, question the advisability of coercing victims into prosecution without a fuller understanding of the ramifications (Flemming, 2003; Ford, 2003; Humphries, 2002). Despite the appearance of being harsh remedies, almost two-thirds of IPV victims who sought refuge in battered women's shelters favored mandatory arrest (Novisky & Peralta, 2015) and mandatory prosecution policies (Smith, 2000).

WEB ACTIVITY

AEquitas: The Prosecutors' Resource on Violence Against Women is dedicated to improving justice for women. Its resources may be accessed at **http://www.aequitasresource.org/**.

As recent U.S. Supreme Court cases illustrate, some evidentiary risks or hurdles can accompany a no-drop policy. Among other things, the Sixth Amendment to the U.S. Constitution guarantees defendants the right to confront and cross-examine their accusers. However, when the victim declines to testify or refuses to appear in court, the defendant does not have the opportunity to impeach the witness. Typically, the state is not able to proceed in such instances without relying on hearsay evidence. However, one exception to hearsay is *forfeiture by wrongdoing*. If the defendant impedes the prosecution by threatening, intimidating, or actually harming the victim, then he or she forfeits any Sixth Amendment protections against statements made outside the courtroom. As the U.S. Supreme Court explained, "one who obtains the absence of a witness by wrongdoing forfeits the constitutional right to confrontation" (*Davis v. Washington*, 2006, p. 18).

COORDINATING SYSTEM APPROACHES

Instead of thinking that any single agency can have a major impact on IPV, it is more reasonable to assume that coordinated efforts of several agencies will be more effective. Coupling arrest with aggressive prosecution, for example, may reduce subsequent offending more than arrest alone. Indeed, one criticism of the Minneapolis Experiment and its replications was the lack of information on what happened to the offender following the arrest. Unfortunately, relatively few analyses look at broader-based system approaches.

Tolman and Weisz (1995) reported on one coordinated arrest and prosecution program in Illinois. DuPage County instituted a program that included a pro-arrest policy as well as prosecution based on complaints signed by the police when victims refused to do so. While officers can sign complaints in many jurisdictions, it is not very common, because the refusal of victims to sign generally signifies a future lack of cooperation with the prosecution. In the DuPage program, the prosecution actively worked to gain victim participation in the case. Analyzing 690 domestic abuse cases, Tolman and Weisz (1995) found the highest recidivism levels in cases of arrests with no convictions. Conversely, arrests ending in conviction displayed the lowest recidivism rates. The authors argue that this system approach is more effective than individual agency initiatives.

Another cooperative arrangement holding potential for stemming IPV entails coupling victim or social service agencies with the criminal justice system (Ahmad & Mullings, 1999; Spence-Diehl & Potocky-Tripodi, 2001). The use or inclusion of victim or social service agencies has become increasingly common in recent years. Many police departments will call upon specially trained individuals to assist in responding to IPV or sexual assault cases. Similarly, prosecuting attorneys often rely on victim advocates and social service agencies to help guide victims through legal proceedings, encourage victims to carry through with a prosecution, and conduct danger assessments. Concern for the ongoing safety of IPV victims has prompted some jurisdictions to evaluate the volatility of the victim's situation. While there are several standardized protocols currently in use (Campbell et al., 2003, 2009), they typically rely on themes similar to those that appear in Box 9.7. In fact, some evidence suggests that this attention enhances victim cooperation immensely (Dawson & Dinovitzer, 2001).

A recent effort in Milwaukee provides a good illustration that the "go-it-alone" approach often invites failure. Prosecutors in that city unilaterally decided to accept more IPV cases for court action by relaxing the emphasis on victim cooperation. However, there was no corresponding effort to enlist the help of other members of

 WEB ACTIVITY

For a fuller look at lethality assessment programs and how they work, visit **http://www.dcjs.virginia.gov/ research/documents/Lethality_ Assess_Report_FINAL.pdf** as well as **https://www.dangerassessment.org/.**

BOX 9.7 PROMINENT RISK FACTORS IN AN IPV DANGER OR LETHALITY ASSESSMENT

- Is there a history of domestic violence?
- Does the perpetrator have obsessive or possessive thoughts?
- Has the perpetrator threatened to kill the victim?
- Does the perpetrator feel betrayed by the victim?
- Is the victim attempting to separate from the perpetrator?
- Have there been prior calls to the police?
- Is there increasing drug or alcohol use by the perpetrator?
- What is the prior criminal history of the perpetrator?
- Is the perpetrator depressed?
- Does the perpetrator have specific "fantasies" of homicide or suicide?

- Does the perpetrator have access to or a fascination with weapons?
- Has the perpetrator abused animals/pets?
- Has the perpetrator demonstrated rage or hostile behavior toward police or others?
- Has there been an increase in the frequency or severity of the violence (whether documented or not)?
- Has the perpetrator been violent toward children?
- Has there been strangulation involved and how often?
- Is there a history of stalking behavior?

Source: State of Nevada Advisory Council for Prosecuting Attorneys (2006).

the criminal justice system. Police officers did not receive any training or instruction on how to improve evidence-gathering at crime scenes, victim advocates were not prepared for the increased number of clients, court resources were not increased to handle an expanding docket, and the prosecution staff did not grow. As Davis and colleagues (2003: 279) termed it, this situation "was a recipe for disaster." The flood of case filings resulted in substantial delays from start to finish, a rise in pre-trial repeat offenses, lower conviction rates, and enormous victim dissatisfaction. These misguided experiences led the authors to warn that "good intentions do not always result in good public policy" (Davis et al., 2003: 280).

Relatively little empirical research has been conducted looking at the use of victim advocates and social service agencies. In one report, Davis and Taylor (1997) analyzed the impact of a program that combined the police with social workers in New York City. This program, the Domestic Violence Intervention Education Project (DVIEP), involved crisis response teams in two main functions. One was to follow up on IPV calls handled by routine patrol. The second function involved educating the public about family violence and invoking system response. The authors were able to make random assignments of IPV cases to either the DVIEP program or normal police intervention. Similarly, the education program was randomly assigned to different households. Unfortunately, the evaluation showed no impact upon subsequent self-reports of IPV or upon the seriousness of subsequent abuse. On the other hand, the project significantly increased the willingness of respondents to call for police assistance (Davis & Taylor, 1997). It would appear that the project had its greatest impact upon altering the amenability of victims to recognize their victimization as a problem and one that required some form of intervention. What is missing from the evaluation is any assessment of the quality of the intervention, especially across cases, and the extent to which the program prompted other positive responses on the part of the victims.

More attention needs to be paid to systemic responses to IPV. These efforts are not uncommon. Unfortunately, few have undergone rigorous evaluation, leaving the programs with little more than faith in their abilities. It would be advantageous to know what type of cooperative intervention works best and in what settings each is most appropriate. As Miller (2006: 1125) explains:

> [A] single solution, such as a single domestic violence intervention program or a mandatory arrest, prosecution, and counseling program for known abusers, is untenable. We know that not all IPV abusers should be arrested. And we know that some abusers, if not incapacitated, will continue a pattern of intimate terrorism that will result in severe, chronic, or permanent injury or death. Imagine a highly curable illness (e.g., bronchitis) that affects 19% of the women in the general

population and a different type of illness (e.g., a mutated flu virus) that can threaten the lives of 2% of the women. Are those numbers big enough to warrant therapeutic or preventive strategies? Are they different enough to warrant different responses?

OTHER RESPONSES

Besides making legislative changes that allow greater police action, such as relaxing the misdemeanor rule, most jurisdictions have responded to IPV by enacting laws aimed at threatening behavior and situations. Perhaps the most notable of these efforts is the growth of anti-stalking laws, outlawing gun possession by domestic violators, court-ordered mandatory counseling for convicted batterers, granting clemency to battered women convicted of killing their partners, the installation of a national hotline, and impaneling fatality review teams.

Stalking Laws

While the word "stalking" may bring an immediate picture to mind, there is no single accepted definition of what the term means. According to Wright and colleagues (1997: 487), *stalking* "is the act of following, viewing, communicating with, or moving threateningly or menacingly toward another person." The inclusion of "viewing" and "communicating with" in the definition may surprise some readers. These kinds of actions, however, can create a great deal of anxiety and fear, especially if they are part of a repeated pattern or coupled with other activities.

The NCVS recently conducted a *Supplemental Victimization Survey* that explored stalking experiences (Catalano, 2012). In addition to the components of inducing fear in the victim and taking place on multiple occasions, the survey focused on the following unwanted behaviors:

- making unwanted phone calls.
- sending unsolicited or unwanted letters or emails.
- following or spying on the victim.
- showing up at places without a legitimate reason.
- waiting at places for the victim.
- leaving unwanted items, presents, or flowers.
- posting information or spreading rumors about the victim on the Internet, in a public place, or by word of mouth.

The combination of action with both fear and repetition may be seen in Florida's stalking statute, shown in Box 9.8.

The three key features of most anti-stalking codes are the existence of threatening behavior, criminal intent by the offender, and repetition in the activity.

1. As used in this section, the term:

    a. "Harass" means to engage in a course of conduct directed at a specific person that causes substantial emotional distress in such person and serves no legitimate purpose.

    b. "Course of conduct" means a pattern of conduct composed of a series of acts over a period of time, however short, evidencing a continuity of purpose. The term does not include constitutionally protected activity such as picketing or other organized protests.

    c. "Credible threat" means a verbal or nonverbal threat, or a combination of the two, including threats delivered by electronic communication or implied by a pattern of conduct, which places the person who is the target of the threat in reasonable fear for his or her safety or the safety of his or her family members or individuals closely associated with the person, and which is made with the apparent ability to carry out the threat to cause such harm. It is not necessary to prove that the person making the threat had the intent to actually carry out the threat. The present incarceration of the person making the threat is not a bar to prosecution under this section.

    d. "Cyberstalk" means to engage in a course of conduct to communicate, or to cause to be communicated, words, images, or language by or through the use of electronic mail or electronic communication, directed at a specific person, causing substantial emotional distress to that person and serving no legitimate purpose.

Source: Florida Statutes, 2016, § 784.048.

These three factors are important because there is no other law violation involved in most instances. For example, in the absence of an anti-stalking code, simply following someone around is not illegal, even though it may be construed as harassment (Sheridan et al., 2001). In fact, some professions, such as private investigation or journalism, typically require one person to follow another. Determining threat or criminal intent is not easy. The usual standard, however, involves recognizing what a "reasonable person" would fear or find acceptable. The requirement for repeated action or a pattern of activity also helps outline what constitutes stalking. It is important, therefore, for legislation to allow for the distinction between different types of "following" behavior. One example of this evolving notion would be the phenomenon of *cyberstalking*, which refers to harassment conducted via the Internet, email, spyware, cell phones, global positioning systems, or other means of electronic communication (Southworth et al., 2007).

As far as IPV goes, stalking often takes place once the victim has decided to end the "cycle of violence." As mentioned earlier, the cycle of violence progresses through three distinct stages: the tension-building phase, the battering episode, and the reconciliation period. However, once the woman is determined to abandon the abusive relationship, the male partner may be at a loss as to how best to regain control over her. When the mollifying behaviors that worked so well before fizzle out, the male may resort to stalking activity or threats in an effort to thwart her escape and re-establish control over the victim (DeKeseredy et al., 2006; Edwards & Gidycz, 2014; Logan & Walker, 2009b, 2010b; Melton, 2007a, 2007b; Norris et al., 2011; Roberts, 2005). This behavior is so common that Logan and Walker (2009b) resort to the term *partner stalking.*

Many state codes have been challenged on a number of fronts. The most strenuous objections have focused on the perceived ambiguity and extensive breadth of the statutes (Bjerregaard, 1996; Sohn, 1994; Thomas, 1997). For example, critics have charged that terminology such as "repeatedly" and "intent to cause emotional distress" is too vague, thus rendering the statutes unconstitutional. Other challenges attack provisions that outlaw such things as "contacting another person . . . . without the consent of the other person" or "following" another person. The contention is that this wording is so broad that it criminalizes constitutionally protected behaviors. In almost every case, the courts have rejected these arguments and upheld the constitutionality of stalking laws.

Penalties for stalking depend on past violations as well as the extent of any injury or threat. Misdemeanor violations typically allow for a jail term of up to one year. Felony violations, however, can carry substantial penalties, particularly if there are aggravating circumstances, such as the use of a weapon, the violation of a restraining order, or a prior conviction. These penalties may include imprisonment or fines of $10,000 or more. It is also possible that stalking may constitute a violent crime for purposes of "three-strikes" laws in some states, resulting in life sentences without parole.

 WEB ACTIVITY

The Stalking Resource Center, maintained by the National Center for Victims of Crime, offers a wide range of information about stalking that you can find at **http://www.victimsofcrime. org/our-programs/stalking-resource-center.**

Despite the growth of stalking legislation, research on the topic is still in the formative stage. Many discussions point to media accounts of well-known, spectacular stalking incidents, typically involving celebrities or politicians, or actions resulting in murder (Hickey, 2016; Marquez & Scalora, 2011). Much more common is stalking of women by ex-husbands or ex-boyfriends. Information gleaned from the *National Intimate Partner and Sexual Violence Survey* estimates that one out of six women "have experienced stalking during their lifetimes that made them feel very fearful or made them believe that they or someone close to them would be harmed or killed" (Breiding et al., 2014: 6). More pointedly, the *Supplemental Victimization Survey* to the NCVS estimates that 5.3 million adults in this country are the victims of stalking or harassment every year, with 70 percent of these perpetrators being intimate partners or friends and acquaintances (Catalano, 2015). Interestingly, most victims are reluctant to notify the authorities about their experiences (Menard & Cox, 2016).

The extent to which stalking laws will impact the level of domestic abuse is unknown at this time. Most statutes are too new to have undergone extensive impact analysis. It is unclear, for example, to what extent these laws are being used by victims and enforced by the police and the courts. The fact that the statutes have withstood constitutional challenges suggests that they should receive attention as a legitimate tool in the fight against IPV.

The Lautenberg Amendment

Congress passed a bill, introduced by Senator Frank R. Lautenberg, that banned gun ownership by any person ever convicted of a misdemeanor domestic violence charge (see Box 9.9). This amendment to the "Gun Control Act of 1968" took effect on September 30, 1996. A number of states followed this federal strategy by either changing their own IPV statutes to prohibit abusers from possessing firearms or including similar language in the provisions of a restraining order (Nathan, 2000).

The goal behind this initiative is to combat violence against women. IPV homicides made up 16 percent of all homicides committed in this country between 1980 and 2008. More than two-thirds of the murder victims killed by current or former spouses died from gunshot wounds (Cooper & Smith, 2011). As Box 9.10 shows, a greater awareness of the explosive nature of IPV situations has prompted the authorities to become more meticulous about seizing firearms when appropriate.

Opposition to this initiative formed very quickly, and a flurry of outcries soon crystallized. Opponents argued that extending a weapons ban to persons *ever*

BOX 9.9 AN EXCERPT FROM THE LAUTENBERG AMENDMENT

(g) It shall be unlawful for any person–

    (8) who is subject to a court order that–

    (A) was issued after a hearing of which such person received actual notice, and at which such person had an opportunity to participate;

    (B) restrains such person from harassing, stalking, or threatening an intimate partner of such person or child of such intimate partner or person, or engaging in other conduct that would place an intimate partner in reasonable fear of bodily injury to the partner or child; and

    (C) (i) includes a finding that such person represents a credible threat to the physical safety of such intimate partner or child; or

    (ii) by its terms explicitly prohibits the use, attempted use, or threatened use of physical force against such intimate partner or child that would reasonably be expected to cause bodily injury; or

    (9) who has been convicted in any court of a misdemeanor crime of domestic violence, to ship or transport in interstate or foreign commerce, or possess in or affecting commerce, any firearm or ammunition; or to receive any firearm or ammunition which has been shipped or transported in interstate or foreign commerce.

Source: 18 U.S.C. § 922.

---

convicted of domestic violence was nothing more than an *ex post facto* law and patently unconstitutional. In other words, additional penalties were being applied to cases that were already concluded and to situations in which individuals had already completed their sentences. Proponents maintained that the critics were wrong: the new laws made possession of a weapon by convicted IPV offenders after the passage date a completely new charge. Because the language outlawed a new behavior, it did not violate the prohibition against *ex post facto* laws.

Observers also noted that the weapons ban meant that law enforcement officers and members of the military with IPV histories fell under these provisions. These persons could not perform essential job functions if they were not allowed to carry a firearm. Efforts to gain a public interest exemption for these groups have failed (Nathan, 2000).

A Supreme Court decision (*U.S. v. Hayes*, 2009) lends further support to the weapons ban. Hayes was convicted in 1994, prior to this federal law taking effect, of misdemeanor battery on his wife. However, West Virginia did not have a specific domestic violence statute on the books at that time. Hence, Hayes was convicted under the generic battery statute. In 2004, officers determined that Hayes kept a rifle and several other firearms in his house. The officers arrested Hayes, and he was convicted of violating the federal weapons ban. Hayes appealed his conviction, maintaining that his 1994 conviction was not a qualifying offense because West Virginia did not have a specific domestic violence statute at that time. After analyzing the circumstances and determining that Hayes had committed a simple battery on his spouse, the Supreme Court rejected his argument and upheld his conviction.

Finally, others contended that these provisions violated the equal protection clause because harsher penalties were being exacted from misdemeanants than from felons (Nelson, 1999). In other words, convicted felons could petition to have their civil rights restored. If successful, they could lawfully possess a firearm. No corresponding reinstatement procedure exists for misdemeanants. To date, the Lautenberg Amendment has survived these and other challenges. [...]

⊕ WEB ACTIVITY

The State of Florida Attorney General partners with the Florida Coalition Against Domestic Violence to produce the annual report written by the Statewide Domestic Violence Fatality Review Team. You can find more details about this initiative at **http://fcadv.org/department-children-and-families-and-florida-coalition-against-domestic-violence-create-statewide-do.**

SUMMARY

Intimate partner violence is gaining broad recognition as a pressing social problem. People who profess to love one another hurt each other regularly. Abusive behavior appears to be almost an integral part of these relationships. It may be very difficult for an outsider to comprehend why anyone would tolerate being victimized repeatedly in this way. However, as the learned helplessness perspective explains, many people are trapped into staying in an abusive relationship. Fleeing from the abuser is not always a viable option.

Some people look to the criminal's justice system—particularly the police—to provide effective relief to IPV victims. While police folklore holds that non-intervention is a more suitable stance, the Minneapolis Experiment suggested otherwise. That study reported less intimate partner violence after the police took the abuser into custody. While there are some doubts over the wisdom of basing public policy on the outcome of a single study, many law enforcement agencies reacted almost immediately. They instituted policies that instructed officers to make an arrest for IPV whenever possible. More recent studies, however, suggest that these policies may have been implemented too hastily. The more prudent path for the criminal justice system to pursue in IPV matters is to retain an open mind and be willing to try different approaches as research and practice dictate. As Davis and Smith (1995: 551) explain:

> We have come a long way in changing how the criminal justice system responds to domestic violence cases. Significant reforms have included mandatory arrest policies, no-drop prosecution practices, civil restraining orders, and batterer treatment programs. Unfortunately, research findings on these reforms have not been encouraging, and it is unclear whether these reforms are making victims safer from harm or changing batterers' violent behavior. [...]

Elder Abuse, Neglect, and Exploitation

by Lawrence A. Frolik and Linda S. Whitton

Did You Know?

- Most abusers are people close to the victim—usually family members or caregivers.
- Most communities have agencies and programs to help abuse victims.
- Keeping vulnerable seniors connected to their communities with home visits and phone calls can reduce or prevent elder abuse.
- Your identity will be protected if you report suspected elder abuse.

"Elder abuse," as that term is used in the law, applies to more than just physical and psychological harm; it also includes neglect and financial exploitation. Many factors make it difficult to track how often elder abuse, neglect, and exploitation occur. Even though there is no central reporting system, the National Committee for the Prevention of Elder Abuse estimates that 4 6 percent of all elderly are abused. In the past, elder abuse was frequently hidden or dismissed as uncommon, but today government and social service agencies acknowledge that elder abuse, neglect, and exploitation occur frequently. This chapter looks at the nature and causes of elder abuse, the circumstances in which it often occurs, and what you can do if you, or someone you know, are victimized or in danger of becoming a victim.

What Are Abuse, Neglect, and Exploitation?

Abuse, neglect, and exploitation form the trio of what is usually just called elder abuse. Abuse can be conduct or statements that injure or threaten the physical or psychological well-being of an older person. Even onetime physical assaults, if harmful enough, are considered elder abuse. Inappropriate restraint of a person is a form of physical abuse. For example, a caregiver who ties an older person in bed for hours so that he or she will not get up unassisted and fall is committing an act of elder abuse. Nonconsensual sexual contact of any kind is also a form of physical abuse.

Psychological abuse, even though it may leave no physical injury, is no less serious than physical abuse. It can range from threatening to abandon the older person, or to put him in a nursing home, to threatening physical force if the person does not cooperate in daily tasks such as eating, bathing, and taking medication. Even repeated insults and shouting are a form of psychological abuse because they undermine the victim's sense of self-worth and security.

"Exploitation" is the term frequently used to describe financial abuse—that is, the misuse or theft of another person's property and money. Blatant forms of financial abuse include using the victim's ATM card without permission to withdraw money, or using the victim's power of attorney to steal the victim's property or money from bank accounts. More subtle forms of financial exploitation can occur when the abuser has close and frequent contact with the victim—such as where a relative caregiver shares the same home with the victim. The caregiver may be able to slowly siphon off the older person's assets. This can be accomplished by taking more than a fair share of that person's monthly retirement or Social Security benefits for the common household expenses or by spending the older person's money for the benefit of other family members. Abusive family members who pay for expensive vacations, houses, or automobiles with the elderly relative's money may justify the expenditures on the grounds that the money will be theirs someday anyway, or that the elderly victim is also benefiting from the expenditures.

Abusive acts often contain elements that are physical, psychological, and financial. For example, a family member may bring an elderly relative to his home for a "visit" and then seek permanent guardianship over that relative, arguing that he or she is no longer able to handle personal care and financial decisions. Using guardianship as a means to control the older person and his or her assets can be a form of legal "kidnapping" when that individual is not in a psychological position to freely object to the arrangement. Threats of nursing home placement or emotional abandonment may pressure the older person into going along with the arrangement. Domineering family members have also been known to cut off communication between elderly relatives and other family members or friends. The increasing frequency of adult children fighting over their parents and their parents' assets has prompted some elder advocates to call these guardianships "will contests while the person is still alive."

Unlike acts of physical, psychological, and financial abuse, which involve intentional threats or conduct, neglect is a failure to act that puts the older victim at risk. For example, it is elder neglect when a caregiver fails to provide essential medicine, food, or shelter to an older person. Liability for neglect is based on a legal "duty" to act. That duty is usually based on a contract when the neglect occurs in a nursing home or at the hands of someone hired to provide home care.

Neglect by family members who have volunteered to care for an elderly person at home may be more difficult to prove. No family member, with the exception of a spouse, has a duty to provide care to another adult. However, once that responsibility has been accepted and the vulnerable person has become dependent on that care, most states recognize that the volunteer caregiver has a duty to continue that care or to seek out an alternative caregiver. For example, Adam begins to provide daily help to his 88-year-old grandfather, Grant, who lives next door and must use a wheelchair. Having let Grant become dependent on his care, Adam cannot simply go on an extended vacation without making some provision for Grant's care while he is gone.

Most state statutes that deal with protection of vulnerable older persons also include "self-neglect" as a basis for protective legal intervention. This intervention may take the form of voluntary acceptance of protective services such as home-delivered meals or housekeeping assistance or involuntary measures such as guardianship. Appropriate protective intervention depends on the degree of self-neglect and the ability of the vulnerable adult to make rational decisions. Although self-neglect is often listed as a type of elder abuse that will trigger protective intervention, it is really not abuse in the technical sense. Rather, self-neglect is a descriptive term for a person's inability to care for herself or to make appropriate arrangements for such care.

Where Does Elder Abuse Occur?

Elder abuse occurs both in institutional settings, such as nursing homes, assisted living facilities, and board and care homes, and in noninstitutional settings, such as the victim's home or the home of a caregiver. Although the impact on the victim is essentially the same in either setting, where the abuse occurs is relevant to answering questions about how to effectively help victims and how to prevent the abuse from happening again. Whether in an institutional or noninstitutional setting, abuse occurs more frequently to seniors who are dependent and isolated.

Institutional Settings
Abuse in an institutional setting is usually perpetrated by individual employees. Physically abusive acts may include hitting uncooperative residents and using excessive physical restraints or drugs to keep residents contained and less demanding of staff time. Sexual assault is another form of physical abuse that can occur in institutional settings.

Neglect in an institutional setting usually takes the form of inadequate attention to resident needs, such as not responding to call buttons, providing substandard care, or failing to provide a decent emotional atmosphere of safety and concern for the older person's well-being. Signs of neglect in nursing homes range from residents who have infected bedsores due to lack of proper repositioning in their beds to residents who suffer severe weight loss and kidney failure from dehydration and inadequate assistance with eating.

Although residents are discouraged from keeping cash in their rooms, financial exploitation still occurs in an institutional setting. Financial abuse includes not only theft of whatever petty cash the resident might keep in the room, but also theft of residents' personal belongings, such as jewelry, radios, and televisions. As a result, the freedom to enjoy one's jewelry and other valuables can be compromised by the need to protect property from theft while residents are sleeping or out of their rooms for meals and activities.

Abuse and neglect are more common in institutions that serve the poor because such institutions often cannot afford to hire quality employees or to provide decent care. Undertrained, overworked, and poorly supervised employees too often lash out at the residents. Financially stressed institutions may cut corners on the amount of staff and other services in order to meet budget. The isolation and dependency of the residents and their lack of housing alternatives leave them no choice but to endure these unsatisfactory living conditions.

Even institutions that serve the middle class frequently have too few staff, pay low wages, and provide inadequate training. One of the primary reasons for this is inadequate public funding for those residents who have run out of money to pay for their own care. Medicaid, a hybrid program financed by both the federal and state governments, is the sole source of payment for a majority of nursing home residents. Unfortunately, the Medicaid reimbursement rates pay only about 70 percent of the actual cost of such residents' care, leaving nursing homes to find creative ways to balance their budgets.

Noninstitutional Settings

Abuse in a noninstitutional setting usually happens at the hands of a caregiver, often a family member. Because incidents of slapping or yelling at the victim often occur in the privacy of the victim's home or home of the caregiver, the victim's friends or other family members may be unaware that it is happening. Some victims put up with the abuse for fear they will lose the caregiver or that the caregiver—often an adult child—will get into trouble with the law. Other victims are too isolated or too physically or mentally incapacitated to seek help.

Some abuse occurs when caregivers fail to understand the older person's medical needs. For example, Judy is caring for her elderly aunt May, who suffers from diabetes. Judy does not understand the importance of diet in controlling Aunt May's diabetes and so fails to provide a proper diet or to monitor what Aunt May eats. Other abuse is just very negligent caregiving. It may range from failing to seek medical attention soon enough for the older person to more intentional abuse, such as leaving bedridden persons to lie in their own waste or refusing to feed them by hand because it is "too much work."

Financial exploitation by caregivers is fairly common and difficult to uncover. Some caregivers enter into the relationship specifically to financially exploit the victim. Often the victim is not even aware of the exploitation. For example, when the caregiver lives with the victim, it is easy to commingle funds and use the older person's money for the caregiver's support. The elderly victim may be lonely or depressed and believe that flattering attention by a caregiver or a "new best friend" is genuine. In such circumstances, the victim can be manipulated into making gifts or giving the abuser access to the victim's bank accounts and other property.

Causes of Abuse, Neglect, and Exploitation

Some who abuse the elderly are persons who have the specific, bad intent to exploit or injure their victims. They select the elderly as victims because they are available, vulnerable, and less likely to report the abuse. Others—usually family members—believe that they are entitled to use the victim's property and money as "payment" for caregiving or as part of the inheritance that will eventually be theirs. In other cases, caregivers simply become so frustrated with their duties and so angry with the older person that they lash out from the fatigue of caring for someone who may be uncooperative or even physically and verbally abusive to the caregiver. To be sure, the stress of caregiving can lead to despair, anger, and resentment, but abuse is never a proper response. Caregivers should seek available social services and other forms of support that will lessen their burden.

Studies have found that some abuse is revenge motivated—adult children retaliating against their older parents for abuse committed against them as children. Other abusers consider violence a normal and acceptable way of responding to someone who is uncooperative or burdensome. Many abusers suffer from alcohol or drug dependency and financially exploit the elder person to obtain money for their addiction. Caregivers who are financially dependent upon the older person may subconsciously resent their dependency and respond by abusing, neglecting, or exploiting the older person. For others, abuse is a way of gaining control and satisfying an emotional need to dominate the victim.

Solutions

Area Agencies on Aging and Adult Protective Services
Every state has enacted laws designed to protect the elderly from abuse, neglect, and exploitation. The federal government contributes limited funds to

129

states to help combat the problem. Federal grants are made to each state's agency on aging, which in turn provides money to local Area Agencies on Aging (AAAs). The state agency on aging serves as a general coordinator of all services and programs related to the assistance of elderly people within the state. The local AAAs supervise the actual delivery of services, usually at the county level.

The Older Americans Act Amendments of 1987 require state agencies on aging to assess the need for elder abuse prevention services and to create a state plan to prevent elder abuse within the state (Pub. L. No. 100-175, §144, 101 Stat. 926, 948-50 [1987]). Unfortunately, the federal funding to prevent elder abuse has never been sufficient, which explains in part why the problem is still so prevalent. Despite the lack of adequate funding, states have enacted adult protective services statutes as a means of establishing a comprehensive response to the problem of elder abuse. The statutes define elder abuse, provide ways to uncover it, establish the guidelines for protective interventions, and create punishments for the abusers.

All the statutes define elder abuse as physical harm. Some include the infliction of mental anguish or psychological injury, although that is sometimes limited to psychological abuse that is severe enough to require medical attention. A few states recognize unreasonable confinement as elder abuse, as well as neglect that rises to the level of a failure to provide for basic needs, including food, shelter, and care for physical and mental health. Self-neglect can be the basis for an investigation if the individual's personal safety is an issue. Financial exploitation is also included as abuse and is generally defined as the illegal or improper use of an elderly individual's resources or property for the benefit of the exploiter or another.

Many of the adult protective services laws require reporting of suspected abuse by professionals, such as health care personnel, social service providers, law enforcement officers, social workers, physicians, and nurses. To encourage nonmandatory reporting, all states guarantee to protect the identity of abuse reporters, although a few states permit limited disclosure of the reporter's identity under special circumstances. All states' statutes provide for some sort of initial investigation when a report of alleged abuse is received. The investigation will be carried out by a state or county agency. A few states require that the local law enforcement agency investigate elder abuse complaints.

After an investigation is completed, or if the older person requests assistance, the protective services agency is supposed to take the steps necessary to terminate the abuse and to meet the older individual's care needs. Usually, protective services include several types of assistance, such as a visiting nurse or home health aid, Meals-on-Wheels, light housekeeping, and legal assistance if necessary. The older person who is believed to be at risk for abuse, neglect, or exploitation must voluntarily accept assistance. If the person does not agree and adult protective services believes that the person is no longer capable of engaging in self-care or making rational decisions about needed care, adult protective services has authority to seek a temporary court order for emergency protective intervention and, when necessary, involuntary guardianship over the person.

Self-neglect often triggers services that the individual may not want. For example, Elaine, age 85, is found in poor condition living in her home, with a dozen or more cats, rotted food and trash all over the house, and no heat. Under many state adult protective services statutes, a state could force its way into the home, remove the animals, and either force Elaine to take care of herself or move her into a facility with supportive services, such as a nursing home.

The involvement of adult protective services can also lead to help for overstressed caregivers who may be well intentioned but who have snapped under the pressure of their caregiving responsibilities. If investigation reveals that the alleged abuser is generally a good caregiver but in need of support and a break, adult protective services may be able to arrange counseling and education for the caregiver as well as regular respite care for the vulnerable elder. Such services provide the caregiver with emotional support as well as periodic relief from caregiving so that the caregiver can attend to his or her own needs.

Criminal and Civil Law Remedies

Most elder abuse is also a crime under various state laws, including laws that criminalize assault and battery, theft, and extortion. In addition, a number of states have enacted statutes that specifically criminalize abuse of the elderly. Unfortunately, in many cases the abused older person will not report the crime out of a sense of loyalty if the abuser is a family member or caregiver or out of fear of retaliation by the abuser. Even if the abuse is reported, the criminal justice system may not respond quickly enough to protect the older person.

Another avenue for relief is a civil suit asking for a restraining or protective order against the abuser. Every state has special restraining orders and protective orders that can be invoked in the case of intrafamily abuse. These statutes, generally referred to as Domestic Violence Acts, permit the victim to obtain a court order forbidding contact between the abuser and the victim and requiring the abuser to leave the victim's household. Unfortunately, some of these statutes can be used only against a spouse. Even a protective order is not a guarantee that the violence or abuse will stop. If the abuser is also the older person's live-in caregiver, the older person may have no alternative other than moving to a nursing home for needed care. A surprising number of elderly would rather endure abusive or neglectful care than move into a nursing home.

Special Solutions for Abuse in an Institutional Setting

If abuse occurs in an institutional setting, there are several state offices whose responsibility it is to investigate complaints and find solutions. The local long-term care ombudsman is responsible for investigating reports of abuse in nursing homes and other residential care facilities (see Chapter 7 for more information about the Long-Term Care Ombudsman program). Although the long-term care ombudsman does not have direct authority to bring civil or criminal penalties against the nursing home or the abusive employee, the ombudsman often works with the nursing home to address and correct abuse problems. In very serious situations, including those involving a pattern of abuse, the ombudsman may assist the state agency that supervises nursing homes (often the state Department of Health or the state Department of Family and Social Services) and the state attorney general's office to pursue civil fines and criminal charges against abusers and the facilities in which abuse has occurred.

The victim, or someone who suspects that a resident has been victimized, may also make a complaint directly to the state regulatory agency for nursing homes or the state attorney general's office. State attorney general's offices have Medicaid fraud and control units that are required to investigate and prosecute patient fraud, abuse, and neglect in facilities that participate in Medicaid.

Community Programs

In addition to government offices that have a responsibility for investigating and addressing elder abuse, many communities have developed cooperative partnerships among seniors, law enforcement, and social service agencies for the purpose of preventing and redressing elder abuse. One such partnership is called Triad. The Triad concept was developed through the collaboration of AARP, the International Association of Chiefs of Police, and the National Sheriffs' Association. Each Triad is formed at the community level and comprises senior citizens, law enforcement agencies, and community groups that provide elder support and protection services.

Triads sponsor both educational programs and assistance in the community to help seniors avoid becoming the victims of elder abuse. Examples of such programs include the following:

- programs on how to avoid criminal victimization
- information on the latest fraud schemes and scams
- guidelines for dealing with telephone solicitations and door-to-door salespeople
- home security information and inspections
- Adopt-a-Senior visits for shut-ins
- safe shopping day programs that provide senior transportation to local grocers

- safe walks programs that arrange transportation to safe locations where seniors can enjoy weekly walking and exercise
- telephone reassurance programs

The success of these and other community-based programs has demonstrated that greater public awareness about the elder abuse problem, education of seniors, and services that keep seniors connected to their communities are essential components in preventing and reducing the incidence of elder abuse.

For More Information

AARP (202-434-AARP)
(http://www.aarp.org)

Find information about how communities can develop programs to fight fraud and abuse.

Eldercare Locator (800-677-1116)
(http://www.eldercare.gov)

Find information about local programs and services, including home-delivered meals, adult day care, caregiver support services, and legal assistance.

National Association of Triads (NATI) (800-424-7827)
(http://www.nationaltriad.org)

Find advice and technical assistance for local Triads.

National Domestic Violence Hotline (800-799-SAFE)
(http://www.ndvh.org)

Find local domestic violence shelters, other emergency shelters, legal aid programs, and social service programs.

National Committee for the Prevention of Elder Abuse
(http://www.preventelderabuse.org)

Find information and links to resources for elder abuse victims as well as for community groups and professionals who would like to improve programs and services for the prevention of crime and abuse against elders.

Female Sex Offenders – Does Anyone Really Get Hurt?

Amie R. Schiedegger

In recent years attention has finally been given to the problem of female sex offenders. Most often when one thinks of a stereotypical "sex offender" one envisions a male perpetrator. For some, the thought of a female sex offender is almost impossible to imagine. Except for perhaps prostitution, it is difficult to think of a crime for which a female is thought of as the most likely perpetrator. Although a "benefit of the doubt" such as this might seem harmless on its face, upon closer examination one can begin to see how harmful this presumption can be. Assuming females are not or cannot be sex offenders is harmful to their victims, society, and even the offender who knows her behavior is wrong and needs help to stop offending. The assumption that women are not or cannot sexually victimize others hinders our full understanding of human behavior and criminal behavior specifically.

In this chapter the author discusses relevant research relating to female sex offenders. Included is a discussion of the obstacles related to defining, researching, and understanding the problem. To fully examine the issue at hand, gender roles, sexual scripts, legal definitions of sexual offenses, and attitudes towards female offenders are explored.

After evaluating the perpetrator side of the crime equation, attention shifts to the plight of victims of female sex offenders. The short- and long-term impact sexual victimization can have on an individual and the responses they often encounter from professional services are discussed. It is important to remember that victims of female sex offenders are a diverse population. Victims differ by age, gender, and relationship to the offender. Each of these variables is discusses within this reading. To illustrate the double standard between female sex offenders and male sex offenders, the problem of sexual misconduct between female teacher and adolescent male students is explored.

Finally, the chapter concludes with a brief discussion of the cycle of victimization and offending.

Female Sex Offenders

In comparison to their male counterparts, female sex offenders are severely under researched, underreported, and misunderstood. The terms "female" and "sex offender" do not seem to coincide with our mental images of either a "female" or a "sex offender". The female sex offender violates both her gender role expectations and sexual scripts. These two terms are crucial to understand, as they are but two of the reasons female sex offenders have been thought of as merely an aberration of little significance (O'Hagan, 1989) rather than a legitimate social problem. Also, the legal definitions of various sex offenses hinder researchers' abilities to gather accurate statistics about female sex offenders and the judicial system from adequately prosecuting female offenders. Below is a discussion of these variables and the impact they have on understanding female sex offenders.

Before exploring some of the variables that hamper the study of female sex offenders, it should be pointed out that researchers, however flawed or limited in their scope or methodology, have been able to provide some insight into the typical characteristics of a female sex offender. Generally speaking, the typical female sex offender is 20-30 years old, white, victimizes acquaintances or relatives under the age of 13, and is equally as likely to victimize males as females (Vandiver, 2006; Vandiver & Kercher, 2004; Vandiver & Walker, 2002; Lewis & Stanley, 2000; Nathan & Ward, 2002).

Gender and Sexual Scripts

Gender roles and sexual scripts are social constructs. Both consist of sets of behavioral expectations based on categorizing behaviors as "naturally" masculine or feminine (Rothenberg, 1998). Gender roles include expected likes and dislikes, as will as, public and private behaviors based solely on one's sex (biological category). Gender roles are imposed upon us early in life. Shortly after birth, males and females are color-coded into "masculine" blue and "feminine" pink. Thus, the cycle of gender expectations begins. Everything from acceptable toy choices and play behaviors to school performance and career choices are influenced by gender role expectations. The key to understanding the importance of gender roles is in acknowledging that these roles are falsely assumed to be the "natural" behaviors and preferences for females and males. It logically follows then, that behaviors and preferences that do not adhere to assigned gender roles are presumed to be "unnatural." As a gender, females are expected to be loving, nurturing, protective, passive, and even helpless in many situations (Rothenberg, 1998).

Sex offending violates each of these gender roles and is thus unnatural for the female offender, perhaps even more so than for the male sex offender who is not expected to have these same gender qualities (Denov, 2003).

Similar to gender roles, sexual scripts are socially constructed expectations of human behavior. Sexual scripts relate specifically to acceptable sexual behaviors and desires for females and males (Denov, 2001; Mendel, 1995; Byers, 1996). For example, traditional sexual scripts portray males as sexually assertive, persuasive, and even coercive by nature. Female scripts, on the contrary, assume females are naturally sexually passive, reluctant, and protective against unwanted sexual advances. Even wanted sexual encounters are expected to contain an element of restraint or reservation for females. Female sex offenders clearly violate female sexual scripts. Their actions are not sexually passive, reluctant, or protective in nature and thus violate the "natural" sexual inclination and society's assigned expectations of female sexual behavior.

Legal Definitions of Sexual Offenses

The biases generated by both gender role expectations and sexual scripts have impacted the legal definition of sexual offenses. Historically sexually based offenses have been written using gendered language that assumes a male is the perpetrator and a female is the victim (Garland, 2005). The language used in some criminal statutes includes wording such as; he, penis, and ejaculation relating to the offender and; she, vagina, and penetration relating to the victim. Females were incapable of committing some sexual offenses because the definition of the crime excluded them as perpetrators.

Current trends have brought this injustice to light and many states have redefined sexual offenses to include gender-neutral language (Denov, 2003). Some states have adopted language acknowledging the perpetrator as; he/she, the offender, or simply they. Similarly, the use of the words she or female have been excluded from the definition of some crimes and replaced with terms such as "the victim" or any of the gender neutral terms listed above in reference to the injured party. Making such changes results in a more accurate and realistic justice system in relation to sexual offenses. Changing the language of criminal statutes results in the ability for females to be charged with sexual offenses and also for males to be acknowledged as the victim of such offences.

Although changes have occurred in some states and for some offenses, one glaring error exists in the federal definition of forcible rape. Forcible rape is classified as a Part I offense within the Uniform Crime Report (UCR) which is compiled by the Federal Bureau of Investigations (FBI) each year. It is beyond the scope of this chapter to discuss all of the shortcomings of the UCR. However, evaluating the definition of *forcible rape* used by the federal government illustrates one major flaw in the UCR. Differing definitions of crimes from state to state and the federal government results in inaccurate statistics for many crimes, including forcible rape.

The definition of forcible rape used by the FBI is "the carnal knowledge of a female forcibly and against her will. Assaults and attempts to commit rape by force or threat of force are also included..." (FBI, 2006). Sexual attacks on males are recorded as aggravated assaults or lumped into the generic category "sex offenses" depending on the circumstances and the extent of injuries. As reported in the 2006 UCR, 224 females were arrested for forcible rape in 2005. By definition then, the female offenders had to have victimized other females to be classified as forcible rape. For all other sexual offenses, other than forcible rape and prostitution, 5,508 females were arrested in 2005. As one can surmise, definitional differences and limitations for sex offenses, including forcible rape, results in underreporting female sex offending, within official statistics.

Despite the limitations and shortcomings of forcible rape and sexual offense laws, there is little doubt that males commit the vast majority of sexual offenses (Denov, 2003; Snyder, 2000; FBI, 2006). Researchers consistently find rates of only 1-6 percent of all sexual offenses committed by females (FBI, 2002; Snyder, 2000; Home Office, 2001; Canadian Center for Justice Statistics, 2001). This is not to say female sex offending is not an important issue merely because it appears to be a rare phenomenon. As discussed below, victims of female sex offenders can suffer in a variety of ways from their victimization. For some victims the fact the offender was a female is additionally damaging.

Victims of Female Sex Offenders

Victims of sexual offenses regardless of age, sex, or relationship to the offender consistently underreport victimization. Fear of reprisal and embarrassment are two common reasons victims give for not reporting sexual victimization to authorities, parents, or friends. When victims do report sexual assaults, the accusation is often met with a process of "victim blaming" thus victimizing the individual again. For the victims of female sex offenders these variables can be magnified by the fact the assailant was a female. Below is a discussion of some of the effects of victimization, victim blaming responses by professionals and non-professionals, and a look at a specific group of offenders and victims who are rapidly gaining national attention, female teachers and adolescent male students.

Effects of Victimization

Much of the harm caused by female sex offenders is related to the gender role expectations and sexual scripts of males and females discussed above.

Because females are suppose to be loving, nurturing, and protective, violating these assumptions can result in an even greater sense of harm for the victim. Researchers have found that victims of female perpetrated sexual abuse report an even greater sense of shame, damage, and suffering than victims of male offenders (Denov, 2003; Elliott, 1993; Rosencrans, 1997). In Rosencrans' (1997) study of women and men who reported being sexually abused by their mothers, 80 percent viewed the abuse as the "most hidden" aspect of their lives. Only 3 percent of the women, and none of the men, told anyone about the abuse. Male victims of female sexual abuse can suffer from the conflict between their male sexual scripts and gender expectations and those of the female perpetrator. Often times males report questioning their masculinity after being victimized by the "weaker" sex (Struckman-Johnson & Struckman-Johnson, 1994). Because some males experience erections and ejaculation during an assault, they might question if the experience wasn't wanted sexual activity rather than an assault (Walker, Archer & Davies, 2005). On the contrary, Redmond, Kosten, and Reiser (1983) report erections can be a common involuntary response during times of intense pain, anxiety, panic, and/or fear. One could presume that during a sexual assault these might be the very emotions a male is experiencing and not sexual enjoyment. It is important to remember that female sex offenders can force or coerce their victims into a range of sexual activities other than intercourse such as kissing, genital touching, fellatio, or cunnilingus. For many of these behaviors no outward displays of arousal exist for female or male victims. Walker, Archer, and Davies (2005) report the long-term effects of sexual assault to include anxiety, depression, anger, feelings of vulnerability, loss of self-esteem, and self-blame. Such responses to sexual victimization are consistent throughout the volumes of research about both female and male victims of rape and sexual abuse.

Victim Blaming

Victim blaming is a process by which the victim of a crime is held responsible for their victimization, to some degree. Because of the long-held belief that females cannot or do not sexually victimize others, victim blaming helps one to explain the behavior as something the offender might not have done were it not for the behaviors of the victim. Victim blaming for female sex offenders occurs most often when the victim is male. Davies, Pollard, and Archer (2006) presented research subjects with scenarios of sexual assaults in which the victim and perpetrator's sex and sexual orientation varied. The greatest amount of victim blaming occurred when the victim was a heterosexual male sexually assaulted by a female. The researchers concluded that study participants did not consider sexual assaults to be as traumatic for male victims when the perpetrator was a member of the sex to which he was normally attracted. In addition, such victims were perceived as having done something to provoke the assault or not enough to stop it. After all, male sexual scripts assert that men are always ready, and willing, to have sex and should thus enjoy sex with a willing female. Davies, Pollard, and Archer (2006) reported that one male participant in their study wrote that this scenario was "Every man's fantasy" (2006:287) thus how could it be bad. These findings were in keeping with prior research in which participants thought male victims of sexual assault by females were more likely to have encouraged the episode and to have derived pleasure from it (Smith, Pine & Hawley, 1988).

Victim blaming is not limited to hypothetical scenarios presented to college students solely for research purposes. Victim blaming occurs within social services, law enforcement, and therapeutic environments as well. The difference between the aforementioned research and the helping professions listed above is that each of the above is charged with assisting victims and/or investigating and arresting female offenders. By applying traditional sexual scripts of women as incapable of sexually victimizing others, these professions dismiss the harm that is caused to the victim. Researchers have shown ambivalence towards allegations of female sexual abuse by social workers, law enforcement officers, and psychiatrists (Denov, 2003). Cases involving female perpetrators are less likely to result in investigation, arrest or prosecution by both law enforcement and social services. Nelson (1994) recounts the crass attitude and remarks of a police officer when asked why a female babysitter accused of sexually abusing a 5-year-old boy was not charged. The officer's response, "I wish that someone that looked like her had sexually abused me when I was a kid...the kid's mother is overreacting because someone popped her kid's cherry. Hell, it's every guy's dream" (1994:74). Note that the officer was talking about a 5-year-old victim. Even psychologists were found to perceive boys having sex with an adult woman as a "coming of age" experience rather than abuse (Richey-Suttles & Remer, 1997; Denov, 2001 & 2003; Hatherton & Beardsall, 1998). Clearly a double standard exists between male and female sex offenders and that double standard carries over to how victims are perceived and treated. Would a 5-year-old girl be perceived as "coming of age" if an adult male sexually abused her?

Female Teachers and Adolescent Male Student Victims

The problem of inappropriate sexual behaviors between educational personnel and students is not new. Teachers, coaches, administrators, classroom aids, bus drivers, janitors, and even cafeteria workers have been accused and/or convicted of a variety of sexual offenses against students. Although all of these types of abuse warrant thorough research and discussion, this section focuses only on adult female and adolescent male sexual abuse. It is within this dynamic that sexual scripts, victim blaming, and professional and public dismissal of the harm caused by female sex offenders can be illustrated best.

One of the first cases to garner national attention about the problem of female teacher and male student sexual abuse was that of 35-year-old, sixth-grade teacher, Mary Kay Letourneau and 13-year-old Vili Fualaau. The nation was shocked to learn of the ongoing sexual "relationship" between the married mother of four and her former student. At the time of the trial, Letourneau was pregnant with Fualaau's child. Letourneau plead guilty to second-degree rape of a child and was sentenced to six months in jail and three years of sexual deviance treatment. One additional condition of her sentence was that she was to have no contact with the victim for the rest of her life (Stennis, 2006).

Many were outraged by the leniency shown by the court in this case. If the victim had been female and the offender male would the sentence have been the same? Would the situation have been referred to as a "relationship"? The saga continued when, within two weeks of being released from jail, police found Letourneau and Fualaau parked together in a car. Having violated the conditions of her parole, Letourneau was sent to prison to serve the remaining 89 months of her original sentence. Before turning 18-years-old Fualaau fathered a second child with Letourneau. After her release from prison, the 42-year-old Letourneau and 21-year-old Fualaau married. However, before they could get married Fualaau had to petition the court to remove the 1997 sentence banning them from having contact.

Additional examples of female teacher and male student abuse include the case of 33-year-old Gwen Cardozo and 17-year-old Victor Gomez. As a result of a plea agreement Cardozo was sentenced to probation, sex offender registration, and no contact with the victim. Two months after the plea agreement was made, a shotgun brandishing Gomez forced his way into Cordozo's apartment, knowingly violating the court's restraining order. Was this the act of a "jealous lover" or a "scorned victim"? Because Gomez was 18-years-old at the time of the incident, he then faced charges for his actions.

Rebecca Boicelli, like Letourneau before her, conceived a child by a 16-year-old former student. While on maternity leave, police investigated sexual abuse allegations about the teacher. After the birth of her child, Boicelli was hired to teach in a nearby school district. Neither the school board nor the police told her new employer about the sexual abuse investigation (Irvine & Tanner, 2007).

In 2004 Debra Lafave, a 23-year-old reading teacher was charged with criminal sexual conduct with a minor after allegedly having sexual relations with a 14-year-old student. The abuse reportedly occurred at her home, at school, and in her vehicle. In 2005 Lafave rejected a plea agreement opting to go to trial on the charges. Her attorney claimed there was no abuse because Lafave suffered from a mental disorder and the boy pursued his teacher.

One of the most recent cases to garner national attention is that of 25-year-old Kelsey Peterson and a 13-year-old former student. Peterson was the student's math teacher when he was 11 years old. Rumors of inappropriate conduct between the two surfaced in August 2007. In an all too typical response to this type of situation, Peterson's principle gave her a verbal warning about alleged behaviors. After receiving the warning, Paterson told the boy he had to stay away from her. Within a month, the two were communicating again. By October 2007 police were investigating allegations of sexual contact between the two. In letters found in Peterson's apartment, the boy professed his love for her and stated their relationship was not just about sex. Peterson was placed on paid leave October 25, 2007 pending the outcome of the investigation. The next day, the two left the Nebraska town in which they lived and traveled to Mexico. Police in Baja, California captured the couple one week later. The boy told authorities the couple had sex twice. As a result, Peterson faces federal charges of crossing state lines to have sex with a minor in addition to state charges in Nebraska. The Lexington, (NE) school board voted to fire Mrs. Peterson and revoke her state teaching license (Spagat, 2007).

The U.S. is not the only country to experience this problem. In 2002 Amy Gehring, a 26-year-old Canadian supply teacher working in the U.K., was acquitted on charges of sexually assaulting three male students, ages 14-15. At the time of the jury's decision, they were unaware that Gehring had been investigated previously by police and social services for having sex with a young boy and kissing another at her first teaching assignment. Mrs. Gehring stated, "I confess to liking younger men. They are fitter and better looking, and good looks are important to me" (Amiel, 2002:20). One must question Mrs. Gehring's definition of "younger men" given that her victims were 14- to 15-year-old boys, not "younger men."

Cases such as these illustrate two significant problems in female teacher male student sexual abuse. The first problem is victim blaming, which has been discussed previously. The second problem is referred to as "passing the trash" which will be discussed further below.

In many of the cases listed above, the victims have been held responsible for provoking, encouraging, or contributing to their victimization. Amy Gehring said, "I lost count of the number of boys who scrawled their phone numbers on scraps of paper and threw them into my handbag." The reporter interjects that such behavior on the part of the boys "makes a mockery of the notion that any of them were victims" (Amiel, 2002:20). Vili Fualaau impregnated Mary Kay Letourneau twice before he was of legal age. The second pregnancy was after her conviction for sexually abusing him. Some find it hard to see him as a "victim" when he seems to be acting under his own free will. Victor Gomez forced his way into his abuser's apartment with a shotgun, after she plead guilty to abusing him, in order to be with her. Kelsey Peterson's victim continued having contact with her after she told him to stop, wrote her love letters, and fled with her to Mexico. Are these the actions of victims or, as male sexual scripts posit, natural reactions for males who are ready, willing, and able to have sex with a willing female? Are we not perpetuating the "Mrs. Robinson myth" that every young boy's fantasy is to be initiated into sex by an older woman (Valios, 2002)? Paul Roffey, a

Director of Adolescent Services, stated, "I'm not sure what the difficulty is in seeing what women do as child abuse. Boys may believe they are giving consent, but in the cold light of day, when the woman is not there controlling them...There is a dangerous presumption that a boy would not find it a negative experience" (Valios, 2002:19).

"Passing the trash" is a phrase used to describe situations where school employees are allowed a number of options, other than official sanctions, when allegations of sexual misconduct arise. Rather than investigate and deal with the problem, administrators allow the accused to leave quietly or handle the situation internally to avoid negative publicity and public scrutiny (Lilienthal & Mowrey, 2006). Because there is no investigation and no record of the misconduct, the offender is free to apply for jobs elsewhere and often continue their abusive behaviors. Ironically, many of these offenders are also the most beloved and respected people at the school. Shakeshaft (2004) reports it is not unlikely to see "Teacher of the Year" awards on the walls of the offender's classroom. Coaches who offend can have winning records in their sport and thus parents and students, who are unaware of the misconduct, hate to see them go. This beloved status can add to the power offenders have over students and the reluctance of victims to report their victimization to authorities.

Educator Sexual Misconduct: A Synthesis of Existing Literature, (Shakeshaft, 2004), is the most comprehensive collection of research about this topic to date. In her report, Shakeshaft reviews volumes of literature related to sexual misconduct and educators and offers suggestions as to ways to correct the problem. Of particular interest in this chapter is her findings related to female sexual offenders and students.

When official data, such as investigations into misconduct allegations, were used to calculate the rates of female and male offenders, males accounted for 96 percent of the offenders and females only 4 percent. Keep in mind, such statistic might reflect administrative responses to allegations and thus be biased by decisions to investigate allegations or not (i.e., passing the trash). In stark contrast to the use of official reports, when students were asked about sexual misconduct at school they reported 57 percent of the offenders were male and 43 percent were female. Similarly, when victim-reporting rates were examined, official sources showed greater percentages of female students reporting sexual abuse than male students. However, when students were asked about victimization female and male students reported similar rates. The conclusion is that males experience similar rates of abuse as females but are even more reluctant to report their victimization or perhaps to define what happened to them as abuse, especially when the offender is female.

Outraged by the differential treatment of male students victimized by female teachers, Stennis (2006) wrote, "Equal Protection Dilemma: Why Male Adolescents Students Need Federal Protection from Adult Female Teachers Who Prey on Them." In his article, Stennis asserts the current treatment of male victims violates the victim's Constitutional right to equal protection. Responses to this problem on the part of the criminal justice system are woefully inadequate. Laws are not written using gender-neutral language and thus do not acknowledge males as victims of sexual abuse, law enforcement does not treat male victims of sexual abuse with respect, and courts offer lenient sentences and plea bargains to female offenders. Stennis also points out that many state courts require male victims of sexual abuse to financially support any children resulting from the abuse, once the male reaches the age of majority. "In essence, family courts view a male victim's parental obligation separate from the abusive act that created the child" (2006:402).

Conclusion

Female sex offenders, like their male counterparts, contribute to a cycle of sexual victimization. Researchers have shown that victims of sexual abuse are more likely to victimize others in the future (Lewis & Stanley, 2000; Denov, 2001; Chandy, Blume & Resnick, 1997). Female sex offenders are likely to have been the victim of sexual abuse at some time in their life. Denov (2003) found 72 percent of the female sex offenders in her study had been victims of sexual abuse. In a study of men who are sexually aggressive towards women, 80 percent had been sexually abused by a female during childhood (Denov, 2001). Statistics such as these confirm the notion that without stopping sexual victimization we will not be able to stop the cycle of abuse.

Also imperative to ending sexual victimization is understanding the impact gender roles and sexual scripts have on society. Both hinder our understanding of human behavior in general. False assumptions about which behaviors are "natural" for females and males stifle our ability to see people as diverse individuals. Enforcing gender roles and sexual scripts in the case of female sex offenders, adds to the problem of underreporting and prevents victims from seeking help from law enforcement, social services, and therapists. Finally, blaming the victim of sexual abuse for their victimization is illogical and unjust. Female sex offenders might account for only a small percentage of sex offenders but any amount is too much.

References

Amiel, B. (2002). "Amy Gehring's Legacy." *Maclean's*, 115:20.

Spagat, E. (2007). "U.S. Case Illustrates Patterns in Teacher Sex Abuse Cases." *Associated Press*, (November 11).

Byers, E. (1996). "How Well Does the Traditional Sexual Script Explain Sexual Coercion?" *Journal of Psychology and Human Sexuality*, 8, 6-26.

Canadian Center for Justice Statistics (2001). *Adult Criminal Court Data Tables 1999/00*. Ottawa, ON: Canada.

Chandy, J.M., RW. Blum & M.D. Resnick (1997). "Sexually Abused Male Adolescents: How Vulnerable Are They?" *Journal of Child Sexual Abuse*, 6:1-16.

Davies, M., P. Pollard & J. Archer (2006). "Effects of Perpetrator Gender and Victim Sexuality of Blame Toward Male Victims of Sexual Assault." *The Journal of Social Psychology*, 146:275-291.

Denov, M. (2003). "The Myth of Innocence: Sexual Scripts and the Recognition of Child Sexual Abuse by Female Perpetrators." *The Journal of Sex Research*, 40: 303-314.

Denov, M. (2001). "A Culture of Denial: Exploring Professional Perspectives on Female Sex Offending." *Canadian Journal of Criminology*, 43, 303-329.

Elliott, M. (1993). *The Female Sexual Abuse of Children*. London, England: The Guilford Press.

Federal Bureau of Investigation (2006). *Crime in the United States: Uniform Crime Report*. Washington, DC: U.S. Department of Justice.

Federal Bureau of Investigation (2002). *Crime in the United States: Uniform Crime Report*. Washington, DC: U.S. Department of Justice.

Garland, T. (2005). "An Overview of Sexual Assault and Sexual Assault Myths." In F. Reddington & B. Wright Kreisel (eds.) *Sexual Assault: The Victims, the Perpetrators, and the Criminal Justice System*, pp. 5-27. Durham, NC: Carolina Academic Press.

Hetherton, J. & L. Beardsall (1998). "Decisions and Attitudes Concerning Child Sexual Abuse: Does the Gender of the Perpetrator Make a Difference to Child Protection Professionals?" *Child Abuse and Neglect*, 22:1265-1253.

Home Office (2001). *Statistics on Women and the Criminal Justice System*. London, England: Her Majesty's Stationery Office.

Irvine, M. & R. Tanner (2007). "Sexual Misconduct Plagues U.S. Schools." *Associated Press*, (October 20).

Lewis, C.F. & C.R. Stanley (2000). "Women Accused of Sexual Offenses." *Behavioral Science and the Law*, 18:73-81.

Lilienthal, S. & J. Mowrey (2006). "Stop 'Passing the Trash': Addressing the Circulation of Repeat Sex Offenders in Coaching." *Journal of Physical Education, Recreation & Dance*, 77:3-5 & 54.

Mendel, M.P. (1995). *The Male Survivor: The Impact of Sexual Abuse*. London, England: Sage Publications.

Nathan, P. & T. Ward (2002). "Female Sex Offenders: Clinical and Demographic Features." *The Journal of Sexual Aggression*, 8:5-21.

Nelson, E. (1994). "Females Who Sexually Abuse Children: A Discussion of Gender Stereotypes and Symbolic Assailants." *Qualitative Sociology*, 17:63-87.

O'Hagan, K. (1989). *Working with Child Sexual Abuse*. Milton Keynes, U.K.: Open University Press.

Redmond, D.E. Jr., T.R. Kosten & M.F. Reiser (1983). "Spontaneous Ejaculation Associated with Anxiety: Psychophysiological Considerations." *American Journal of Psychiatry*, 140:1163-1166.

Richey-Suttles, S. & R. Remer (1997). "Psychologists' Attitudes Toward Adult Male Survivors of Sexual Abuse." *Journal of Child Sexual Abuse*, 6:43-61.

Rothenberg, P. (1998). *Race, Class, and Gender in the United States: An Integrated Study*. New York, NY: St. Martin's Press.

Shakeshaft, C. (2004). *Educator Sexual Misconduct: A Synthesis of Existing Literature*. Washington, DC: U.S. Department of Education.

Smith, R.E., C.J. Pine & M.E. Hawley (1988). "Social Cognitions about Adult Male Victims of Female Sexual Assault." *Journal of Sex Research*, 25:101-112.

Snyder, H. (2000). *Sexual Assault of Young Children as Reported to Law Enforcement: Victim, Incident and Offender Characteristics*. Washington, DC: U.S. Department of Justice, Bureau of Justice Statistics.

Stennis, J. (2006). "Equal Protection Dilemma: Why Male Adolescent Students Need Federal Protection from Adult Female Teachers Who Prey on Them." *Journal of Law and Education*, 35:395-403.

Struckman-Johnson, C. & D. Struckman-Johnson (1994). "Men Pressured and Forced into Sexual Experience." *Archives of Sexual Behavior*, 23:93-114.

Valios, N. (2002). "Teacher Sex Allegations Expose Flaws in Regulation of Supply Agencies." *Community Care*, 1409:18-19.

Vandiver, D.M. (2006). "Female Sex Offenders: A Comparison of Solo Offenders and Co-Offenders." *Violence and Victims*, 21:339-354.

Vandiver, D.M. & G. Kercher (2004). "Offender and Victim Characteristics of Registered Female Sexual Offenders in Texas: A proposed Typology of Female Sexual Offenders." *Sexual Abuse: A Journal of Research and Treatment*, 16:121-137.

Vandiver, D.M. & J.T. Walker (2002). "Female Sex Offenders: An Overview and Analysis of 40 Cases." *Criminal Justice Review*, 27:284-300.

Walker, J., J. Archer & M. Davies (2005). "Effects of Rape on Men: A Descriptive Analysis." *Archives of Sexual Behavior*, 34:69-80.

Homicide Survivors

A Summary of the Research

MARTIE P. THOMPSON

On November 10, 1992, I saw my son at school, and at 3:30 I was leaving. We hugged. He said, "Mama, I love you." I said I love you too and I'll see you tonight. I was going to my second job. . . . Later that evening, I called my grandmother's house where he was, and we talked. He was cooking French fries. About 9:00, security came and told me someone wanted to see me upstairs. It was my uncle, and the feeling I got—I knew something was wrong. He said, "Gwen, you've got to come home." The first thing I asked was "where's Mike?" He said "Mike is at home . . . we need you at home." I could see tears in his eyes. My grandmother had just had heart bypass surgery so I thought maybe she was sick. So I got in his truck and he said "Gwen, Mike's dead." It was like I didn't hear what he said. It was like I was in shock. It was like I could hear him calling me way off. I tried to get out of the truck—if I could have just run—run all the way to where I had to go, I would have felt better. He started shaking me and said, "Gwen, Mike is dead." I could hear myself screaming, just screaming. And I thought "Wow—my world is going to come to an end." He couldn't drive fast enough. He was running red lights. When we got to my grandmother's house, I saw all these people I knew. It was like they were waiting to see what I would do. And it was like all I wanted was to see and to hear was Mike. So I went upstairs and I didn't see Mike. And people were like "Honey, it's going to be okay." And I was thinking, "What's going to be okay, what's wrong with these folks?" So I said "where is Mike?" And they said, "he's really dead." And I said "not Mike." So I ran out of the house and I went on the hill where they said he was killed. And I said "Mike!" I was just calling him. Whenever I called my son, he would always answer. I don't care how far we were, if he was a long way from me, when I started calling him, he would come running—"here I come, Mama." So that's what I was looking for. And so the paramedics came and they say I was in shock. . . .I told them I wanted to see him.

So we went to the morgue and some guy rolled him out. And he was just laying there. I mean, he was just there, and the guy said I couldn't touch him. I felt that if I could touch him I could bring breath back into his body. He had on his jacket, his lunch card. . . . I just saw and hugged this child at 3:00 today, just talked to him at 7:00 this evening. And I just could not believe it.

—From author's interview with a homicide survivor

There is a vast amount of research literature on crime victims, in terms of both its prevalence and its consequences. Little attention, however, has been given to the consequences of violence on secondary or indirect victims, such as family members of homicide victims. In this chapter, I first provide a discussion of the prevalence of homicide and estimates of the number of people who have lost a family member to homicide (i.e., homicide survivors). Second, I discuss the effects of loss of a family member to homicide, including psychological, behavioral, and cognitive consequences. Third, I focus on factors that affect family members' recovery, such as social support and coping resources. Fourth, I focus on family members' interactions with the criminal justice system and how these interactions can impact the recovery process. Last, I present information on mental health services for homicide survivors.

PREVALENCE

In 2002, homicide was the 14th leading cause of death in the United States, resulting in an estimated 17,368 fatalities (CDC, 2003). Violent death rates are about twice as high in low- to mid-income level countries (32.1 per 100,000) than in high-income level countries (14.4 per 100,000) such as the United States (Krug, Dahlberg, Mercy, Zwi, & Lozano, 2002). However, the homicide rate in the United States is twice as high as the rates found in other high-income countries (Mercy, Dahlberg, & Krug, 2003).

Homicide rates vary significantly by different demographic groups. Homicide was the forth leading cause of death for children ages 1 to 14, and the second leading cause of death for 15- to 24-year-olds. Homicide is more common among males (13th leading cause of death) than females (not in top 20 leading causes of death). The most pronounced demographic differences in homicide rates are between Blacks and Whites. Whereas homicide was the 20th leading cause of death for Whites, it was the 6th cause of death for Blacks in 2002. Among black males ages 15 to 34, homicide was the leading cause of death (CDC, 2003).

These data underscore the prevalence of homicide in the United States and reflect the vast number of people who are the family members of these victims. It is difficult to estimate the number of family members or "survivors" of these homicide victims. Using a national probability sample, researchers estimate that 5 million U.S. adults have lost an immediate family member to criminal or vehicular homicide, and 16 million have lost an immediate family member, other relative, or close friend to homicide (Amick-McMullan, Kilpatrick, & Resnick, 1991).

RESEARCH ON REACTIONS TO LOSS OF A FAMILY MEMBER TO HOMICIDE

The death of a family member is almost always a stressful event. The loss of a family member to homicide is even more traumatic for a variety of reasons. First, it is almost always sudden. Second, it is a violent event, and the bereaved family members know that their loved ones suffered when they died. Third, there are often feelings of guilt associated with loss of a family member to homicide, as bereaved family members may feel they could have done something to prevent the death. Fourth, because of the nature of the death, the criminal justice system becomes involved. Family members may be questioned about the deceased and about various circumstances of the victim's life, such as their acquaintances and their lifestyle patterns. Fifth, there is stigma associated with murder, as many people may blame the victim's lifestyle for the murder.

Every study that has been conducted with homicide survivors indicates that they experience many types of posttrauma symptoms that manifest themselves psychologically, behaviorally, and cognitively (Amick-McMullan et al., 1991; Bard, Arnone, & Nemiroff, 1980; Thompson, Norris, & Ruback, 1998). The opening story at the beginning of this chapter provides a look into how a survivor of homicide is impacted from the tragedy of loss to murder. The psychological, behavioral, and cognitive reactions to loss of a family member to homicide are discussed next.

Psychological Consequences

High levels of psychological distress, including post-traumatic stress disorder (PTSD), depression, and anxiety have been found among family members of homicide victims. For example, in a nationally representative sample of U.S. adults, 19% of those who lost an immediate family member to homicide had PTSD at some time during their lives, and 5% had current PTSD (Amick-McMullan et al., 1991). To place homicide survivors' distress in context, it is worth comparing their distress levels to those of victims of direct crime (e.g., rape victims) as well as family members who have lost a loved one to death other than homicide. One study indicated that homicide survivors had significantly higher PTSD symptoms than did rape victims or individuals who lost a significant other to a nonhomicide death (Amick-McMullan, Kilpatrick, & Veronen, 1989). In a second study, 150 family members of homicide victims were identified through the medical examiner's office. The number of

years elapsing between interviewing respondents and the death of their loved ones ranged from 1½ to 5 years ($M = 3$). These homicide survivors were compared to a group of 108 demographically similar individuals who had experienced another type of traumatic event (e.g., robbery, physical assault, sexual assault) within the past 5 years (Thompson, Norris, et al., 1998). Homicide survivors reported significantly higher PTSD symptoms than the other trauma group. A third study found that parents whose children had been murdered reported higher levels of PTSD than parents whose children had died accidentally (Applebaum & Burns, 1991). It is interesting to note that both homicide and accidental deaths are sudden, so the differences in PTSD were due to aspects of the homicide other than its suddenness.

More studies are needed that focus on the trajectory of survivors' distress over time. A prospective study by Murphy, Braun, Cain, Johnson, and Beaton (1999) provides important information on homicide survivors because it was longitudinal and sampled parents whose children died by different modes. A sample of 173 parents of children who died by homicide, suicide, or accidental death was identified from official death records in six counties in the northeastern United States. The sample was assessed at one-, two-, and five-year follow-up periods. At four months postdeath, twice as many parents who had lost a child to homicide met diagnostic criteria for PTSD compared to parents who lost a child to suicide or accidental death (Murphy, Braun, et al., 1999). Mothers (41%) were more likely than fathers (14%) to report PTSD symptoms. Reexperiencing symptoms were the most common symptoms reported by mothers (87%) and fathers (67%). PTSD symptoms declined by the two-year follow-up period for women only; 21% of mothers and 14% of fathers still met diagnostic criteria for PTSD two years later (Murphy, Braun, et al., 1999). At the five-year follow-up period, mothers (28%)

continued to show higher levels of PTSD than did fathers (13%), but mode of death did not predict PTSD status anymore (Murphy, Johnson, Chong, & Beaton, 2003; Murphy, Johnson, & Lohan, 2002). These data suggest that it may take several years to cope with the homicide of a loved one.

Homicide survivors also evidence other types of psychological distress in addition to PTSD. In the study described earlier that compared the distress levels of 150 family members of homicide victims with other trauma victims, homicide survivors reported significantly more distress than adults from the general population (Thompson, Norris, et al., 1998). Twenty-six percent of the homicide survivors scored in the clinically significant range on depression, anxiety, hostility, or somatization, compared to only 3% of the no trauma group (see Table 7.1). Of note, hostility was the only symptom on which homicide survivors differed significantly from violent crime victims.

Data from Murphy's prospective study with parents who lost children to homicide, suicide, or accidental death also indicate elevated rates of distress at four months postdeath across various types of symptoms. Compared to a general population sample of adult women mothers who lost children were significantly more likely to score in the clinical range for depression (3.5 times more likely), anxiety (3.8 times more likely), somatization (2.1 times more likely), and hostility (2.5 times more likely). Similarly, bereaved males were more likely than a normative sample of men to score in the clinical range for depression (4.3 times more likely), anxiety (3.0 times more likely), somatization (1.8 times more likely), and hostility (2.5 times more likely). Although these symptoms significantly declined by two years postdeath, they were still significantly higher than those found in the normative samples (Murphy, Gupta, et al., 1999). It should be pointed out, however, that this sample

Table 7.1   Sample Means and Standard Deviations on Distress Measures of Homicide Victims Compared to Published Norms (Thompson, Norris, et al., 1998)

	Homicide Survivors (N = 150)	Nonpatient Adults (N = 341)	Psychiatric Outpatients (N = 576)	Violent Crime Victims (N = 175)
Depression				
M	.91[ab]	.28	1.80	.91
SD	.76	.46	1.08	.88
Anxiety				
M	.87[ab]	.35	1.70	.93
SD	.80	.45	1.00	.81
Somatization				
M	.78[a]	.29	.83	.62
SD	.82	.40	.79	.73
Hostility				
M	.50[abc]	.35	1.16	.85
SD	.53	.42	.93	.73

NOTE: BSI norms for nonpatient and outpatient adults were taken from Derogatis and Spencer (1982); those for violent crime victims were taken from Norris and Kaniasty (1994).

a. Homicide sample significantly different from nonpatient adults ($p < .05$).

b. Homicide sample significantly different from psychiatric outpatients ($p < .05$).

c. Homicide sample significantly different from recent violent crime victims ($p < .05$).

included parents who lost their children to suicide and accidental death in addition to homicide. Given the finding reported earlier that loss of a child to homicide was related to a greater likelihood of PTSD than loss of a child to other types of death, these data may actually underestimate the increased psychological distress experienced by homicide survivors.

Behavioral Consequences

How a family member reacts to losing a loved one to homicide is not limited to psychological difficulties. Research indicates that family members of homicide victims also can experience negative behavioral consequences, such as suicidal behaviors, avoidant behavior, and alcohol and drug use. Murphy compared parents who lost a child to homicide, suicide, and accidental death on the likelihood of suicidal ideation. Whereas 19% of the parents whose children had been murdered expressed suicidal ideation, 7% of parents whose children died by suicide and 14% of parents whose children died accidentally reported suicidal ideation. Not surprisingly, parents who reported suicidal ideation were more likely than their nonsuicidal counterparts to score higher on other indicators of psychological distress, such as depression and PTSD, and report lower acceptance of their children's deaths (Murphy, Tapper, Johnson, & Lohan, 2003).

Another negative behavioral consequence to loss of a family member to homicide is the avoidance of things that serve as reminders of the homicide or the deceased (Burgess, 1975). For example, one respondent in a study conducted with 200 parents who had lost a child to murder was quoted as saying, "I stay at home all the time now. I'm scared to death to go for a walk in my own neighborhood" (Rinear, 1988). In another study, a woman who had lost a brother to an unsolved homicide said that she was afraid to let people walk behind her (Burgess, 1975). In the Murphy, Gupta, et al. (1999) study, psychological distress significantly declined over time for 8 of the 10 distress indicators assessed (e.g., depression, anxiety). However, social alienation and interpersonal sensitivity did not improve over time, suggesting that survivors might be avoiding social contacts and situations, particularly those that remind them of the homicide, and thus becoming isolated and detached.

Although no study could be located that assessed if homicide survivors had elevated rates of substance use, research indicates that bereaved individuals in general are at increased risk for elevated consumption of alcohol (Clayton, 1990; Umberson & Chen, 1994). In a large cohort study that followed 1.5 million 35- to 84-year-old adults for five years, those who experienced the death of a spouse were at increased risk of dying from alcohol-related causes (Martikainen & Valkonen, 1996). Thus it is likely that homicide survivors may also be at risk for substance use related problems.

Cognitive Consequences

Research with crime victims indicates that one of the more insidious and common consequences of being violently victimized is the undermining of certain cognitive schemas or assumptions that people hold about themselves, the world, and their relationship to it (Frieze, Hymer, & Greenberg, 1987; McCann, Sakheim, & Abrahamson, 1988; Norris & Kaniasty, 1991). Researchers have focused on different schemas and have referred to them by different names. These schemas include assumptions about the world as safe, meaningful, and predictable. Research suggests that the shattering of these assumptions contributes to the psychological distress associated with victimization (Norris & Kaniasty, 1991; Taylor, 1983).

The importance of cognitive schemas also applies to coping with the loss of a family member to homicide. Homicide survivors evidence negative consequences in several cognitive domains following the murder, including feelings of fear and vulnerability, lack of perceived control, and loss of meaning. Because homicide is typically the result of intentional maliciousness on the part of one person toward another, family members of the victim are likely to experience feelings of fear and vulnerability. In some cases, survivors may literally fear for their lives if a suspect has not been apprehended. For example, in a study with 200 parents who had lost a child to homicide, a quarter of the parents reported fears about their safety and the safety of their surviving children and other family members (Rinear, 1988). One respondent interviewed was quoted as saying, "I am much more concerned about the safety and life of my remaining daughter. Before, I never thought anything like this could happen to us. . . . We're still scared that what happened once might happen again."

Losing someone to homicide also can undermine one's faith in the world as meaningful and predictable. Murder is an event that few would expect to happen to them and can shatter one's sense of control over one's life and the world. The story at the beginning of this chapter illustrates how a survivor's sense of the world as predictable and understandable can be shattered upon learning of the loss of a family member to homicide. In general, homicide survivors who are able to restore their perceptions of the world as meaningful and predictable are able to combat their sense of helplessness and cope better than those who cannot restore this perception. Interestingly, in a study with parents whose children died in a fatal bus crash, the search for factual information about the crash was unrelated to psychological symptomatology in the first three years following the death, but was related to poorer psychological adjustment after that. Those parents who continued to feel the need for information showed poorer adjustment than parents who felt adequately informed (Winje, 1998). Although this sample was comprised of parents who lost their children

to a nonhomicide death, it indicates that the need to find meaning in the event is a critical aspect of posttrauma recovery.

The importance of finding meaning also was supported in the prospective study by Murphy, Johnson, et al. (2003). Murphy asked parents at each data collection point (4, 12, 24, and 60 months after the child's death), "How have you searched for meaning in your child's death as well as your own life?" Parents who reported responses that indicated finding a new appreciation of what really matters were considered successful in finding meaning. Parents who were able to find some meaning in their child's death reported significantly less psychological distress, higher marital satisfaction, and better physical health than parents who did not find meaning. One year after the deaths of their children, only 12% of the parents found any meaning in their child's death, but by five years postdeath, 57% had found meaning.

One way survivors may attempt to restore their sense of the world as predictable and controllable is to find someone or something to blame for the murder of their loved ones. In that way, the event can be explained and the world can still be perceived as fair. Targets of blame for the murder may include the perpetrator, the criminal justice system, society at-large, and sometimes even the victim or the survivors (Burgess, 1975; Rinear, 1988). In a study with parents of murdered children, parents reported a high amount of self-blame for the murder (Rinear, 1988). For example, one parent was cited as saying, "I helped him to buy the Corvette that attracted the murderers to him." Another parent was quoted as saying, "I should have insisted that he wear a bullet-proof vest since there was danger in one of the neighborhoods where he delivered papers." Although these statements may not sound rational, they exemplify the self-blame that survivors often experience.

FACTORS THAT AFFECT
FAMILY MEMBERS' RECOVERY

Although loss of a family member to homicide invariably has negative consequences on survivors' well-being, the pattern of recovery is not the same for everyone. Other factors may moderate or mediate the effects of the homicide on survivor's recovery. Factors that have been studied in relation to homicide survivors are discussed in the following sections.

Relationship to Victim. One factor that has been shown to be associated with survivors' psychological reactions to the homicide is their relationship to the victim—in terms of both type of relationship as well as quality of relationship. For example, in the study with 150 adult family members of homicide victims described earlier, mothers who lost a child to homicide scored significantly higher on psychological distress variables than did other types of relatives (Thompson, Norris, et al., 1998). This finding was replicated in Murphy's prospective study with parents whose children died by homicide, suicide, or accident; mothers had higher PTSD levels than fathers at both one year and five years after their child's death (Murphy, Johnson, et al., 2003). Research also indicates that family members who lived with the victim and reported being very close to the victim had the highest rates of posttraumatic stress symptoms and depression and lower self-reported esteem (Thompson, Norris, et al., 1998).

Social Support. Research indicates that crime victims who report high levels of social support cope better than crime victims without adequate support (Ruback & Thompson, 2001). Unfortunately, although social support is beneficial to survivor's recovery, it is often hard to obtain. Many people do not know how to respond effectively. This could be due to several reasons (Wortman, Battle, & Lemkau, 1997). Others may feel that survivors have more control over their symptoms and should be coping with their loss in a timely manner. Their abilities to provide support also may be impeded by their own feelings of vulnerability that the homicide incites. In order to offset their own fears that this could happen to their loved one too, they may attribute the homicide to a nonrandom cause, such as the victim's living a dangerous lifestyle, rather than a random cause, such as the victim's being in the wrong place at the wrong time. The need to believe in a just world can make it difficult for others to provide adequate emotional support to survivors.

Secondary Stressors. Another factor that can affect recovery is the precipitation of secondary stressors. Homicide can set into motion a series of other life events and stressors, and these stressors can exacerbate survivors' distress. These events that occur after the homicide have been referred to as secondary stressors. In a study comparing children who lost a parent to homicide, children who lost a parent to natural death, and a nonbereaved control group, secondary stressors were integral to understanding the psychological consequences of parental death (Thompson, Kaslow, Price, Williams, & Kingree, 1998). Bereaved children experienced more bereavement-related stressors (people at school acted uncomfortable around child after parent's death; child's relatives told him/her to act differently than he/she did before parent's death) and general stressors (e.g., family moved to new house) than did the children who had not lost a parent to death. The more stressors experienced, the greater the children's psychological distress. The increase in secondary stressors accounted for bereaved youth's higher distress scores, especially among those who had lost a parent to homicide. In other words, high levels of psychological distress levels among homicide survivors were partly due to the changes in their lives that were set in motion by their parents' deaths.

Coping Style. Another factor that can affect recovery is coping style. As with all traumatic events, people use different coping styles, and these coping activities are associated with how well a victim or survivor adjusts to trauma. Among bereaved parents, including parents who lost a child to homicide, repressive and affective styles of coping have been found to be related to PTSD, but in divergent ways. Repressive coping (e.g., denial, substance use) was related to higher levels of PTSD, whereas effective coping (e.g., seeking social support, acceptance) was related to lower levels of PTSD. However, coping styles were only important in predicting PTSD in the first year after the death, but not five years later (Murphy, Johnson, et al., 2003).

Resources. Homicide does not strike randomly. Certain subgroups of the population are more likely to be killed than other subgroups. People with fewer economic resources are at greater risk for being murdered than people of higher socioeconomic status (Cohen, Farley, & Mason, 2003; Hsieh & Pugh, 1993). Because homicide victims are more likely to have few economic resources, their surviving family members also are likely to have few economic resources. This lack of resources is likely to compound the effects of loss of a family member to homicide. According to the conservation of resources theory (Hobfoll, 1988), a trauma, such as homicide, can cause a rapid loss of resources, including loss of objects (e.g., housing), conditions (e.g., job, marriage), personal resources (e.g., self-esteem), and energies (e.g., time, knowledge). People who lack resources before a traumatic event are more susceptible to post-trauma psychological problems than people who have a reservoir of resources before the trauma. The concept of loss spiral has been used to describe how initial loss can provoke future loss, particularly when pretrauma resources are limited (Hobfoll & Lilly, 1993). Although there are no data on whether homicide survivors with few economic resources are at greater risk for maladjustment than survivors with more resources, the conservation of resources theory would suggest that this is the case.

INVOLVEMENT WITH THE CRIMINAL JUSTICE SYSTEM

Homicide is a crime that most always is investigated by law enforcement agencies. Consequently, homicide survivors must interact with criminal justice system personnel and navigate the criminal justice system while coping with their bereavement. Unfortunately, this involvement with the justice system can exacerbate many of the negative consequences precipitated by the homicide (Thompson, Norris, & Ruback, 1996). In the words of a man whose mother was one of the 168 people killed in the Oklahoma City bombing, "The last year or so, we have been able to kind of put it out of our minds because of all of the other things going on. But with the trial starting up again, it kind of brings it all back. . . . It reopens the scab" (Atlanta Journal/Constitution, 1997). In the words of another homicide survivor, "You never bury a loved one who's been murdered, because the justice system keeps digging them up" (Schlosser, 1997).

Many times, homicide survivors have their views of the criminal justice system challenged and violated. Before the murder of their loved one, many survivors likely held fairly benevolent or neutral views of the criminal justice system and perceived its function as one in which justice was meted out. However, when these expectations are violated, the survivors can feel vulnerable, helpless, and angry. According to one homicide survivor who wrote a book about her own and other survivors' experiences, "Murder is a crime against the state, not the survivor. . . . Homicide survivors have to contend with light sentences, the crime never being solved, or the murder presented to the grand jury and not prosecuted, as well as the release of the perpetrator" (Bucholz, 2002, p. 115).

The quality of contacts after a homicide is critical for successful coping. When family members are treated sensitively by justice system personnel, they can start to trust in society again. However, if they have unsatisfactory experiences with the justice process, they are likely to have pessimistic and cynical attitudes regarding justice (Frieze et al., 1987; Greenberg, Ruback, & Westcott, 1983). For example, in the Oklahoma City bombing case against Terry Nichols, family members and relatives of bombing victims were disappointed and angry that the jury did not convict Nichols of first-degree murder charges and did not sentence him to the death penalty. They were also distraught over comments made by the jury forewoman, who announced to reporters that the case against Nichols was circumstantial. Family members likely felt that the justice process did not do "justice" for their loved ones who were killed, thereby exacerbating their distress over their loved ones' murders.

It is important that the justice system provides homicide survivors with information about the murder in order to help attenuate their high levels of distress. If family members are not informed about the investigation and prosecution of the homicide (e.g., if the offenders have been caught, plans for the cases, and when court cases will be heard), they will experience what is referred to as the "second injury to victims" (Symonds, 1980). When a police officer does not take the time to explain to family members what happened to their loved one, family members are likely to feel ignored and unimportant. When a defense attorney paints a portrait of their loved one as having brought about the crime, family members are likely to be hurt and angered. When a plea bargain takes place without their knowledge, family members are likely to feel devalued. One woman whose son was murdered was so distraught over the lack of information and action provided by the police that she started looking for the killers herself.

"I was down there every weekend . . . doing my own investigation. . . . Every time I went down there, I hoped that someone would shoot me. I wasn't fearful. My only child, all I had in my life, was gone" (McDonald, 1995).

In one study, 80% of homicide survivors reported feeling that the justice system should provide them with legal assistance and information on the status of the case, but only 33% reported that they had received this service (Amick-McMullan et al., 1989). Over 80% also believed that the system should provide an advocate, yet only 27% reported that they were adequately served in this area. Eighty percent also believed that the courts should provide personal protection for family members, while only 10% reported receiving this service. In this study, those who reported the most psychological distress were the least satisfied with the criminal justice system. The feelings of dissatisfaction and frustration with the criminal justice process are illustrated by the words of a woman who lost her husband to murder: "I would love to be able to put this in the past and go on, but the laws of our justice system don't allow me to do that. Regardless of how many years go by, I have to relive this every time he (the murderer) is up for parole" (Ogelsby, 1997).

INTERVENTIONS WITH HOMICIDE SURVIVORS

Even though homicide survivors have a high need for mental health services, little research has been conducted on their use of mental health services. Estimates of the percentage of violent crime victims in general who seek professional mental health services indicate that only about 23% sought professional mental health services within the first few months of the incident, and only 22% of those who received services thought the services were "very helpful" (Norris, Kaniasty, & Scheer, 1990). In another study with victims with some involvement with the criminal justice system, rates of service use varied by type of crime: 50% of sexual assault victims, 22% of physical assault victims, and 16% of homicide survivors had used mental health services (Freedy, Resnick, Kilpatrick, Dansky, & Tidwell, 1994).

A recent review of mental health service utilization among people who experienced traumatic events, including violent crime, identified several factors that were important in predicting mental health service use after a traumatic event (Gavrilovic, Schutzwohl, Fazel, & Priebe, 2005). The authors applied a behavioral model of health service use to mental health service use and examined how predisposing, enabling, and need factors were related to service use. Predisposing factors include characteristics of the individual, most typically demographic factors such as age, sex, and race. Enabling factors include characteristics that allow for an individual to seek mental health services, such as transportation, employment, insurance, and knowledge of the availability of services. Need factors include the individual's degree of psychological distress. Using data from 24 published studies, the researchers found that predisposing factors inconsistently predicted use of mental health services. For example, some studies found that younger age, unemployment, and being married predicted treatment seeking, whereas other studies found that older age, employment, and being separated or divorced predicted treatment seeking. Enabling factors that significantly predicted treatment seeking were insurance benefits and compensation. The effects of income were inconsistent. Several need factors were associated with treatment seeking. Most notably among these were psychological symptoms, with higher levels of distress predictive of a higher likelihood of seeking services. Other factors associated with treatment seeking among trauma victims were the occurrence of other stressful life events,

previous use of services, and social support. Other researchers also have found that higher depressive symptoms and more severe crimes are associated with an increased likelihood of seeking mental health services. Among a subset of violent crime victims, predictors of mental health service utilization included urban residence, high social support, internal locus of control, and prior crime experience (Norris et al., 1990).

Although little research has focused on the use of professional mental health services among homicide survivors, several articles have been published on other types of support services for homicide survivors. Salloum and Vincent (1999) presented information on community-based support groups they conducted with adolescent homicide survivors. The general goals of their intervention were to educate adolescent homicide survivors about the nature of trauma and grief, facilitate the expression of trauma-related thoughts and feeling, and reduce PTSD symptoms. They provided recommendations for implementing the intervention, as well as a synopsis of the content of their group sessions. In terms of facilitating successful implementation, they recommend the following: (1) offering support groups in community-based settings, such as schools; (2) educating the administration and teachers about traumatic loss from homicide and explaining the purpose of the group; (3) securing consistent and private space for the group; (4) consulting with administrators when scheduling the groups to ensure that they coincide with the school schedule (e.g., do not fall on holidays); (5) screening to ensure that the group includes only adolescents who have lost a family member to homicide; (6) keeping the group to an optimum size (a maximum of 8 to 10); (7) obtaining written informed consent from youth's guardian for them to participate; and (8) matching the facilitator's ethnicity to the ethnicity of the group.

The content of their intervention sessions is briefly provided below.

Session 1   Explain purpose of group, explain time frame of group, discuss importance of confidentiality, introductions

Session 2   Administer measure of PTSD symptoms, educate about normal reactions, discuss what happened and relationship to the person that died. Worksheets (e.g., a favorite memory) can be used to facilitate discussions

Session 3   Discuss group goals, discuss grieving process

Session 4   Recognize types of losses, find creative ways to cope

Session 5   Identify traumatic reactions (e.g., avoidance of people or places that remind them of homicide), discuss ways to reduce negative reactions, discuss safety issues, teach relaxation techniques

Session 6   Discuss ways to cope during special occasions (e.g., holidays)

Session 7   Discuss feelings of revenge and teach anger management techniques

Session 8   Discuss support, spirituality

Session 9   Review progress toward goals, readminister PTSD symptoms measure; discuss future goals

Session 10   Recognize progress, distribute certificates

Salloum, Avery, and McClain (2001) have evaluated the intervention and reported favorable results. Forty-five African American youth ages 11 to 19 participated in the 10-week intervention. The community-based intervention was conducted at four different public schools in New Orleans. After participating in the group, adolescents experienced significant decreases in PTSD symptoms (assessed at Sessions 2 and 9), particularly in the areas of reexperiencing and avoidance symptoms of PTSD. More than half (58%) of the youth had PTSD symptom scores in the clinical range at the beginning of the intervention. At postintervention, 22% had PTSD scores in the clinical range. However, because there was no control group of bereaved children who did not receive the intervention, it is not possible to know if the decreases in PTSD were due to the intervention or to the passage of time.

In another study specifically with homicide survivors, Rynearson (1995) contacted family members of homicide victims in the Seattle area within three months of the murder. Among the families they were able to contact (75%), 22% agreed to participate in a survey on trauma. Families were then offered supportive intervention services. Because only a portion of families accepted the intervention services, it was possible to compare family members who accepted services (62%) to those who did not seek services (38%). Comparisons revealed that homicide survivors who desired treatment were younger, less religious, less likely to be married, more likely to have had prior therapy, and more likely to have a childhood history of physical and sexual abuse. Results also showed that homicide survivors who desired intervention services reported higher levels of grief, posttraumatic stress, and dissociation symptoms than their counterparts who did not want services.

Another study on service use patterns of homicide survivors in Tennessee used case records from the homicide response program of the county government Victims Assistance Center to gather data on the relationship of the victim to the survivor and the degree of service utilization for counseling, court advocacy, and case management during the four months following the homicide. Survivors were more likely to utilize all three forms of services during the initial eight weeks after the homicide than in the following eight weeks. Further, intrafamilial homicide survivors utilized services more frequently than extrafamilial homicide survivors during the initial eight weeks (Horne, 2003).

SUMMARY AND SUGGESTIONS FOR FUTURE RESEARCH

Because homicide is a leading cause of death in the United States, many people have experienced this tragic loss. One national study indicated that approximately 5 million U.S. adults have lost an immediate family member to criminal or vehicular homicide, and another 11 million have lost another relative or close friend to homicide (Amick-McMullan et al., 1991). Losing a family member to homicide can have negative affective, behavioral, and cognitive consequences. These reactions can include PTSD, depression, suicidal behavior, substance use, and schema shifts regarding fear, control, and meaning. As with a direct experience with crime, losing a family member to murder can negatively affect the indirect victim in multiple ways. However, people who lose a family member to homicide do not all react the same way. Other factors, such as survivors' relationships to the victims, the quality of their social support, and their coping strategies, impact their psychological, behavioral, and cognitive reactions.

The criminal justice system and mental health services also influence reactions of survivors. Because death by homicide, unlike death by natural causes, necessitates the justice system's involvement, it is important to understand how this involvement affects survivors' reactions. Unfortunately, the justice system can exacerbate many of the negative consequences precipitated by the homicide. Survivors' views of the criminal justice system are often violated, and survivors can feel helpless and angry. The quality of contacts after a homicide is critical for successful coping. Regarding mental health services, one study

estimated that 16% of homicide survivors sought mental health services after the crime (Freedy et al., 1994).

Among homicide survivors, predictors of seeking services include being related to the perpetrator, less elapsed time since the homicide (Horne, 2003), being younger and unmarried, being less religious, having a childhood history of abuse, and having higher levels of grief, posttraumatic stress, and dissociation symptoms (Rynearson, 1995). One community-based intervention specifically for homicide survivors indicated that the intervention was effective in reducing PTSD (Salloum et al., 2001).

There are many methodological difficulties inherent in studying family members of homicide victims. One of these difficulties is the inability to use optimal research designs such as randomization to experimental or control group. Obviously, it is not possible to randomly assign people to experience loss of a family member to homicide. However, future research should incorporate nonrandomized control groups into study designs. This would allow for comparing homicide survivors to demographically similar people who have not experienced loss to homicide, thereby enabling researchers to disentangle the psychological consequences due to the homicide from the effects due to other confounding factors, such as limited economic resources. Research on interventions with homicide survivors should try to randomly assign participants into control and intervention groups. Without a control group, it is not possible to determine if improvements in mental health functioning are due to the passage of time or to the intervention. Another suggestion for future research is to utilize longitudinal designs. The studies by Murphy and colleagues on parents who lost a child to death number among the few studies to examine distress levels longitudinally (Murphy, Braun, et al., 1999; Murphy, Gupta, et al., 1999). This work has shed light on the trajectories of parent's distress levels over time. A third suggestion for future research is to examine moderators when studying post-loss consequences. For example, future research should investigate the role of economic resources in coping with loss to homicide. Are survivors with few resources at greater risk for maladjustment compared to their wealthier counterparts? Not all survivors experience a loss to homicide in the same way. It is important for researchers to identify factors that help to buffer the negative consequences of loss to homicide. In this way, clinicians can be alerted as to what factors may predispose some survivors to have poorer outcomes and some survivors to be resilient. Interventions then can be designed that bolster those factors that buffer against the negative effects of loss of a family member to homicide.

REFERENCES

Amick-McMullan, A., Kilpatrick, D., & Resnick, H. (1991). Homicide as a risk factor for PTSD among surviving family members. *Behavior Modification, 15,* 545–559.

Amick-McMullan, A., Kilpatrick, D., & Veronen, L. (1989). Family survivors of homicide victims: A behavioral analysis. *Behavior Therapist, 12,* 75–79.

Applebaum, D. R., & Burns, G. L. (1991). Unexpected childhood death: Posttraumatic stress disorder in surviving siblings and parents. *Journal of Clinical Child Psychology, 20,* 114–120.

Bard, M., Arnone, H., & Nemiroff, D. (1980). Contextual influences on the post-traumatic stress adaptation of homicide survivor-victims. In C. Figley (Ed.), *Trauma and its Wake: Vol. 2. Traumatic stress theory, research, and intervention* (pp. 292–304). New York: Brunner/ Mazel.

Bucholz, J. (2002). *Homicide survivors: Misunderstood grievers.* Amityville, NY: Baywood.

Burgess, A. (1975). Family reactions to homicide. *American Journal of Orthopsychiatry, 45,* 391–398.

Centers for Disease Control and Prevention. (2003). Web-Based Injury Statistics Query and Reporting System (WISQARS). National Center for Injury Prevention and Control, Centers for Disease Control and Prevention (producer). Retrieved February 5, 2006, from www.cdc.gov/ncipc/wisqars

Clayton, P. J. (1990). Bereavement and depression. *Journal of Clinical Psychiatry, 51*(Suppl.), 34–40.

Cohen, D. A., Farley, T. A., & Mason, K. (2003). Why is poverty unhealthy: Social and physical mediators. *Social Science and Medicine, 57,* 1631–1641.

Derogatis, L., & Spencer, P. (1982). *The Brief Symptom Inventory (BSI): Administration, scoring, and procedures manual-1.* Baltimore, MD: Author.

Freedy, J. R., Resnick, H. S., Kilpatrick, D. G., Dansky, B. S., & Tidwell, R. P. (1994). The psychological adjustment of recent crime victims in the criminal justice system. *Journal of Interpersonal Violence, 9,* 450–468.

Frieze, I., Hymer, S., & Greenberg, M. (1987). Describing the crime victim: Psychological reactions to victimization. *Professional Psychology: Research and Practice, 18,* 299–315.

Gavrilovic, J. J., Schutzwohl, M., Fazel, M., & Priebe, S. (2005). Who seeks treatment after a traumatic event and who does not? A review of findings on mental health service utilization. *Journal of Traumatic Stress, 18,* 595–605.

Greenberg, M., Ruback, R. B., & Westcott, D. (1983). Seeking help from the police: The victim's perspective. In A. Nadler, J. Fisher, & B. DePaulo (Eds.), *New directions in helping: Vol. 3. Applied perspectives on help-seeking, and -receiving* (pp. 71–103). New York: Academic Press.

Hobfoll, S. (1988). *The ecology of stress.* New York: Hemisphere.

Hobfoll, S., & Lilly, R. (1993). Resource conservation as a strategy for community psychology. *Journal of Community Psychology, 21,* 128–148.

Horne, C. (2003). Families of homicide victims: Service utilization patterns of extra- and intrafamilial homicide survivors. *Journal of Family Violence, 18,* 75–82.

Hsieh, C., & Pugh, M. D. (1993). Poverty, income inequality, and violent crime: A meta-analysis of recent aggregate data. *Criminal Justice Review, 18*, 182–202.

Krug, E., Dahlberg, L. L., Mercy, J. A., Zwi, A. R., & Lozano, R. (2002). *World report on violence and health.* Geneva, Switzerland: World Health Organization.

Martikainen, P., & Valkonen, T. (1996). Mortality after the death of a spouse: Rates and causes of death in a large Finnish cohort. *American Journal of Public Health, 86*, 1087–1093.

McCann, L., Sakheim, D., & Abrahamson, D. (1988). Trauma and victimization: A model of psychological adaptation. *Counseling Psychologist, 16*, 531–594.

McDonald, R. R. (1995, March 20). Son's slaying haunts mom. *Atlanta Journal & Constitution*, p. B2.

Mercy, J. A., Dahlberg, L. L., & Krug, E. (2003). Violence and health: The United States in a global perspective. *American Journal of Public Health, 92*, 256–261.

Murphy, S. A., Braun, T., Cain, K., Johnson, L. C., & Beaton, R. D. (1999). PTSD among bereaved parents following the violent deaths of their 12–28-year old children: A longitudinal prospective analysis. *Journal of Traumatic Stress, 12*, 273–291.

Murphy, S. A., Gupta, A. D., Cain, K. C., Johnson, L. C., Lohan, J., Wu, L., et al. (1999). Changes in parents' mental distress after the violent death of an adolescent or young adult child: A longitudinal prospective analysis. *Death Studies, 23*, 129–159.

Murphy, S. A., Johnson, L. C., Chong, I., & Beaton, R. D. (2003). The prevalence of PTSD following the violent death of a child and predictors of change 5 years later. *Journal of Traumatic Stress, 16*, 17–25.

Murphy, S. A., Johnson, L. C., & Lohan, J. (2002). The aftermath of the violent death of a child: An integration of the assessments of parents' mental distress and PTSD during the first 5 years of bereavement. *Journal of Loss and Trauma, 7*, 203–222.

Murphy, S. A., Tapper, V. J., Johnson, L. C., & Lohan, J. (2003). Suicide ideation among parents bereaved by the violent deaths of their children. *Issues in Mental Health Nursing, 24*, 5–25.

Norris, F. H., & Kaniasty, K. (1991). The psychological experience of crime: A test of the mediating role of beliefs in explaining the distress of victims. *Journal of Social and Clinical Psychology, 10*, 239–261.

Norris, F., & Kaniasty, K. (1994). Psychological distress following criminal victimization in the general population: Cross-sectional, longitudinal, and prospective analyses. *Journal of Consulting and Clinical Psychology, 62*, 111–123.

Norris, F. H., Kaniasty, K., & Scheer, D. (1990). Use of mental health services among victim of crime: Frequency, correlates, and subsequent recovery. *Journal of Consulting and Clinical Psychology, 58*, 538–547.

Ogelsby, C. (1997, April 18). Widow protests parole of mall killer. *Atlanta Journal & Constitution*, p. F8.

Rinear, E. (1988). Psychosocial aspects of parental response patterns to the death of a child by homicide. *Journal of Traumatic Stress, 1*, 305–322.

Ruback, R. B., & Thompson, M. P. (2001). *Social and psychological consequences of violent victimization.* Newbury Park, CA: Sage.

Rynearson, E. K. (1995). Bereavement after homicide: A comparison of treatment seekers and refusers. *British Journal of Psychiatry, 166*, 507–510.

Salloum, A., Avery, L., & McClain, R. P. (2001). Group psychotherapy for adolescent survivors of homicide victims: A pilot study. *Journal of the American Academy of Child and Adolescent Psychiatry, 40*, 1261–1267.

Salloum, A., & Vincent, N. J. (1999). Community-based groups for inner-city adolescent survivors of homicide victims. *Journal of Child and Adolescent Group Therapy, 9*, 27–45.

Schlosser, E. (1997, September). A grief like no other. *Atlantic Monthly*, pp. 37–76.

Symonds, M. (1980). The "second injury" to victims. In L. Kivens (Ed.), *Evaluation and change: Services for survivors* (pp. 36–38). Minneapolis, MN: Medical Research Foundation.

Taylor, S. (1983). Adjustment to threatening events: A theory of cognitive adaptation. *American Psychologist, 38*, 1161–1173.

Thompson, M. P., Kaslow, N. J., Price, A., Williams, K., & Kingree, J. B. (1998). The role of secondary stressors in the parental death—Child distress relation. *Journal of Abnormal Child Psychology, 26*, 357–366.

Thompson, M. P., Norris, F., & Ruback, B. (1996). System influences on posthomicide beliefs and distress. *American Journal of Community Psychology, 24*, 787–812.

Thompson, M. P., Norris. F., & Ruback, B. (1998). Comparative distress levels of inner-city family members of homicide victims. *Journal of Traumatic Stress, 11*, 223–242.

Umberson, D., & Chen, M. D. (1994). Effects of a parent's death on adult children: Relationship salience and reaction to loss. *American Sociological Review, 59*, 152–168.

Winje, D. (1998). Cognitive coping: The psychological significance of knowing what happened in the traumatic event. *Journal of Traumatic Stress, 11*, 627–643.

Wortman, C. B., Battle, E. S., & Lemkau, J. P. (1997). Coming to terms with the sudden, traumatic death of a spouse or child. In A. Lurigio, W. Skogan, & R. Davis (Eds.), *Victims of crime* (2nd ed., pp. 108–133). Newbury Park, CA: Sage.

THE COSTS OF VICTIMIZATION

by William G. Doerner and Steven P. Lab

INTRODUCTION

This chapter takes a look at some of the costs associated with becoming a crime victim. As we all know, victims suffer at the hands of their criminals. Some people may be injured physically. Others may lose property during the attack. All will be gripped to some extent with fear and mental anguish. This aspect of their victimization experience will affect their quality of life and probably will not subside for quite a while.

Victims who turn to the criminal justice system for comfort and solace quickly learn that they run the risk of being exploited. The system, through its impersonal and detached mechanisms for sorting through cases, aggravates the victim's condition. For example, inconsiderate habits may force some victims to wait in hallways for a hearing to start, only to learn later that it has been canceled. No one bothered to telephone them. Other victims are bewildered by what is transpiring around them. No one has taken the time to explain what is happening in the case or why. Instead, these victims find system officials quickly shepherding them through the courthouse doors without so much as a simple "thank you." This chapter visits some of the problems that victims and witnesses encounter during their treks through the system.

Being victimized results in a number of both direct and indirect costs for the victim, his or her family, the community, and the criminal justice system. Victimization surveys provide insight into the costs associated with the crime. Beyond direct costs from the criminal event, victims and witnesses face additional losses when dealing with the authorities.

THE FIRST INSULT: CRIMINAL VICTIMIZATION

Early victim studies concentrated on documenting the calamity and woes that accompany the victimization experience. The Milwaukee Victim/Witness Project, for example, was undertaken to assess the difficulties stemming from the criminal episode (Knudten et al., 1976, 1977; Knudten & Knudten, 1981). In addition to sustaining physical injury and property loss or damage, a sizable proportion of victims reported losing time from work and having their normal routines disrupted. They also endured emotional anguish and interpersonal complications with family members and friends. Despite their perception that these problems were serious, most victims forged ahead alone. Even though many social service agencies were in operation, victims remained largely unaware of service availability. As a result, relatively few victims received help coping with their crime-induced problems (Doerner et al., 1976). Table 3.1 illustrates the range of costs associated with crime for the victim and a host of other people.

TABLE 3.1 List of Costs Associated with Crime

Costs of Crime	Party Who Directly Bears Cost
Direct Property Losses	
Losses not reimbursed by insurance	Victim
Losses reimbursed by insurance	Society
Administrative cost of insurance reimbursement	Society
Recovery by police	Society
Medical and Mental Health Care	
Costs not reimbursed by insurance	Victim/Family/Society
Costs reimbursed by insurance	Society
Administrative overheads of insurance coverage	Society
Victim Services	
Expenses charged to victim	Victim
Expenses paid by agency	Society
Temporary labor and training of replacements	Society
Lost Workdays	
Lost wages for unpaid workday	Victim
Lost productivity	Society/Employer
Lost School Days	
Forgone wages due to lack of education	Victim
Forgone non-pecuniary benefit of education	Victim
Forgone social benefits due to lack of education	Society
Lost Housework	Victim
Pain and Suffering/Quality of Life	Victim
Loss of Affection/Enjoyment	Family
Death	
Lost quality of life	Victim
Loss of affection/enjoyment	Family
Funeral and burial expenses	Family
Psychological injury/treatment	Family
Legal Costs Associated with Tort Claims	Victim or Family
"Second-Generation Costs"	
Future victims of crime committed by earlier victims	Future Victims
Future social costs associated with above	Society/Victims

Source: Miller et al. (1996: 11).

Economic Losses

The direct economic loss due to crime can be large. It is possible to gain some insight into the loss from individual crimes through both official and self-report data. Table 3.2 provides a monetary breakdown for crimes that involve property loss. Based on the 2014 UCR, property crimes and robberies resulted in more than $14 billion in total loses (Federal Bureau of Investigation, 2015a). Using the average loss figures for the different offenses in the 2008 NCVS adjusted for inflation as a base, property crimes in the NCVS result in more than $16.6 billion in losses.

Burglary losses account for $3.9 billion according to the UCR and $5.1 billion in victimization data. In the UCR, this works out to an average loss of $2,251. It is important to note that this corresponds to burglary of any structure, including businesses. The NCVS average loss of $1,693 reflects only burglary of households. The impact of theft is equally great. Based on UCR figures, the average loss in larceny/thefts was $941 (Federal Bureau of Investigation, 2015a). When extrapolated to the U.S. population, approximately $5.5 billion was lost due to larceny in 2014. The NCVS also offers sobering statistics on theft loss. In 2014, there were almost 12 million household theft victimizations with an average loss (adjusted for inflation) of $576. While the individual losses are not great ($576), the total loss of $6.8 billion is substantial. There can be little doubt that theft has a major economic impact on both the individual and society.

While the actual number of motor vehicle thefts is not as high as other property crimes, the financial impact of the crime is large. The average loss due to

TABLE 3.2 Monetary Losses Due to Property-Related Victimizations			
Offense	N	Total $ Loss	Avg. $ Loss[a]
UCR			
Robbery	325,802	$400 million	$1,227
Burglary	1,729,806	$3.9 billion	$2,251
Larceny Theft	5,858,496	$5.5 billion	$941
Motor Vehicle Theft	689,527	$4.5 billion	$6,537
NCVS			
Robbery	664,210	$1.1 billion	$1,630
Household Burglary	2,993,480	$5.1 billion	$1,693
Household Theft	11,760,620	$6.8 billion	$576
Motor Vehicle Theft	534,370	$3.6 billion	$6,685

Note: [a] NCVS loss figures based on 2008 NCVS average loss adjusted for inflation.

Source: Constructed by the authors, from the Federal Bureau of Investigation (2015a) and Bureau of Justice Statistics (2016a).

motor vehicle theft was more than $6,500 in 2014. Nationally, the total loss was more than $4.5 billion (Federal Bureau of Investigation, 2015a). Approximately three-quarters of the theft and loss was of automobiles. Victimization data present an equally troubling set of figures, with an average loss of $6,685 and a gross national loss of approximately $3.6 billion (Bureau of Justice Statistics, 2016a).

Arson offenses added more than $629 million in property losses in 2014. The average fire resulted in damages of $16,055 (Federal Bureau of Investigation, 2015a). This ranges from a low of $2,189 for "other" forms of property to a high of $167,545 for "industrial/manufacturing" fires.

It is also possible to look at monetary impacts from some personal crimes. When considering robbery, the UCR reports a total loss of $400 million in 2014 (Federal Bureau of Investigation, 2015a). This is an average of $1,227 per offense. Robberies of banks incurred an average loss of $3,816 per event. Based on NCVS data, robbery victims incurred $1.1 billion in losses in 2014. This corresponds to an average loss of $1,630. Unfortunately, the UCR and NCVS do not offer any information on economic loss due to homicide, and the UCR offers nothing for assault. The NCVS does include data on losses due to assaults. In 2014, based on an average loss of $260, more than $1.1 billion was lost as a result of assaults.

Included in these losses from personal crimes area losses related to medical costs; unfortunately, the figures from the UCR and NCVS underreport these costs. The Centers for Disease Control and Prevention (CDC) offers more in-depth cost figures due to both medical costs and work losses from homicides, sexual assaults, and other assaults (see Table 3.3). The average medical cost of a homicide is almost $11,000, resulting in $178 million in losses in 2010. Medical costs due to hospitalizations for sexual assaults and other assaults equal $20,000 and $29,000, respectively. Total medical costs from death, hospitalization, and emergency department visits in 2010 are almost $8.5 billion. Costs from lost time at work greatly increase the financial drain due to crime. Total costs for homicide are $25 billion, those for hospitalization due to assaults are $20 billion, and emergency department visits for assaults add another $10 billion.

There are other property offenses besides those that appear in the UCR Part I offense categories and the yearly NCVS data. Among these are offenses like identity theft, fraud, and cybercrime. Identity theft impacts victims in multiple ways. Most directly is the cost of the crimes, both to the individuals and to society. The 2014 NCVS: Identity Theft Supplement reports that the average loss to victims is $1,343 (Harrell, 2015). The Nilson Report (2015) put credit card/debit card/prepaid card losses in 2014 at almost $7.9 billion in the U.S.A. and over $16.3 billion worldwide.

TABLE 3.3 Costs Related to Homicide, Sexual Assault, and Other Assaults

	Homicide	Hospitalization		Emergency Department	
		Sexual Assault	Assault	Sexual Assault	Assault
N	16,259	5,247	135,563	62,645	1,531,219
Medical Costs					
Avg.	$10,944	$19,998	$29,201	$3,365	$2,646
Total	$178 million	$105 million	$4 billion	$211 million	$4 billion
Work Loss					
Avg.	$1.5 million	$66,293	$120,081	$4,905	$3,863
Total	$25 billion	$348 million	$16 billion	$307 million	$5.9 billion
Combined Costs					
Avg.	$1.5 million	$86,291	$149,281	$8,270	$6,509
Total	$25 billion	$453 million	$20 billion	$518 million	$10 billion

Source: Compiled by the authors, from Centers for Disease Control and Prevention (2010).

Estimating the financial impact of mass-marketing fraud is extremely difficult. A survey in the U.K. puts the loss at more than $6.8 billion a year (U.K. Office of Fair Trading, 2006). The Internet Crime Complaint Center (ICCC), a component of the FBI and the National White Collar Crime Center, serves as a repository for citizen complaints of fraud. Data for 2015 show almost 290,000 complaints, of which 127,145 victims report losses totaling more than $1 billion (ICCC, 2015). This works out to an average loss of $8,421 per victim.

The economic impact of cybercrime upon society is not inconsequential. What information is available on cybercrime losses typically reflects its impact upon businesses. Lloyd's, the British insurer, claims that, worldwide, businesses lose $400 billion a year due to cybercrime (Gandel, 2015). The Ponemon Institute (2015), surveying 252 companies in seven countries on cybercrime, reports that U.S. businesses experience an average loss of $15.4 million. The loss varies by the size of the organizations. While these losses are tied to the organizations, it is important to note that they are tied to higher costs of the products/services provided to the general public.

These monetary estimates would escalate considerably if complete information were available on every single crime incident. At the same time, one should realize that these figures refer only to a handful of crimes. Other statutory violations (e.g., tax evasion, white-collar crime, corporate crime, and the like) need to be factored in to arrive at a more comprehensive assessment.

Non-Economic Costs

Crime victims suffer from a variety of ills beyond the direct monetary losses from victimization. First, many victims may not have insurance to cover any losses, or their insurance company will not reimburse them for the type of loss they incurred. Certainly, falling victim to a mass-marketing inheritance scam is not something covered by insurance policies. In many cases, the loss is borne solely by the victim. For victims without property insurance, even a burglary, arson, or motor vehicle theft leaves the individual with out-of-pocket losses for which there is no recompense.

Second, there are many different physical and emotional consequences that may follow victimization. The Office for Victims of Crime (OVC) (1998a) has pointed out that victims often experience shame, guilt, and self-blame for the event. Langton and Truman (2014) note that 57 percent of violent crime victims experience socio-emotional problems as a result of the event. More than two-thirds of serious violent crime victims (75 percent of rape/sexual assault victims; 74 percent of robbery victims; 62 percent of assault victims) and approximately half of simple assault victims report experiencing problems. Table 3.4 shows the types of socio-emotional symptoms experienced by victims of violent crimes. These include worry, anger, feelings of vulnerability, distrust, trouble sleeping, fatigue, headaches, and other problems. Many victims opt not to tell anyone about the events out of a sense of guilt or shame (Office for Victims of Crime, 1998a). They may isolate themselves from others who they perceive may ridicule them for their lack of foresight or judgment that "allowed" them to be victimized. Indeed, some observers may condemn the victim as "getting what he deserved" (Office for Victims of Crime, 1998a). The emotional costs can be more debilitating than the financial losses resulting from the crime.

A third consequence of many types of crime is a lost sense of security in both the home and society. In the case of home burglary, victims lose the belief that they can be safe in their homes from the crime and turmoil that occur "out there." Whether the crime occurred when the resident was home or not, there is an increased sense of insecurity and anxiety that can permeate every facet of daily living. Where do you go to feel safe if you cannot do so in your home? Anxiety and a loss of trust also emerge as a result of any type of fraud. Victims may lose all sense of trust in banks/financial institutions, charities, the use of credit cards, or anything they equate with their victimization.

Many victims are injured and require medical attention. Table 3.5 presents data from the 2014 NCVS. Almost half of all rape victims, one-third of robbery and aggravated assault victims, and one-fifth of simple assault victims report being injured. More than 20 percent of robbery victims require medical treatment, while the same is true for approximately 15 percent of aggravated assault

TABLE 3.4 Physical and Emotional Symptoms Suffered by Violent Crime Victims, 2009–2012

Symptom	Types of crime		
	Total Violence	Serious Violence	Simple Assault
Emotional	91%	96%	87%
Worried or anxious	72	78	67
Angry	70	76	67
Unsafe	65	73	60
Violated	61	69	56
Vulnerable	60	64	58
Distrustful	56	66	50
Sad or depressed	53	58	50
Other	12	13	12
Physical	61%	67%	57%
Trouble sleeping	47	51	44
Fatigue	34	36	33
Upset stomach	31	32	30
Muscle tension	31	34	28
Headaches	30	37	25
Problems with eating/drinking	27	33	23
High blood pressure	15	16	15
Other	9	12	7

Source: Langton and Truman (2014).

TABLE 3.5 Victim Injury and Medical Care, 2014

	Injured	Medical Treatment
Robbery	34.4%	20.7%
Aggravated Assault	30.6	15.3
Simple Assault	20.6	8.6
Rape	45.7	16.1

Source: Bureau of Justice Statistics (2016a).

and rape victims and less than 10 percent of simple assault victims. The medical treatment is tied to substantial financial costs, as seen earlier in Table 3.3.

Adding to these measures of crime impact is the time lost by the victims. Victims often lose time from work or school (not to mention just relaxation time) as a result of the victimization (see Table 3.6). They spend time at the doctor, recuperating from an injury, talking to the police or prosecutor, coming to court, replacing lost or damaged goods, or doing other things related to the crime. Over 75 percent of robbery and over two-thirds of assault, household burglary, and motor vehicle theft victims report losing at least one day of time due to the victimization (Bureau of Justice Statistics, 2010b). More than 60 percent of household theft victims report losing at least one day of work due to the victimization. It should also be noted that it is very difficult, if not impossible, to gauge the impact upon lost productivity from the labor force even after the victim returns to the work site. One outcome of the lost time from work is the accompanying financial loss (see Table 3.3).

Beyond lost time from work, victims experience considerable lost time trying to resolve the problems. Eighteen percent of households report that problems are ongoing, with another 17.2 percent reporting that it took more than one month to resolve the problems (Baum, 2007). A survey by the Federal Trade Commission on fraud victimization reports that victims are harassed by collectors, are rejected for credit cards and loans, have accounts frozen, experience insurance problems, and may be subjected to criminal investigation or civil lawsuits (Synovate, 2007). Businesses reported almost 324,000 hours of downtime due to some form of cybercrime, with two-thirds of that time due to a cyber attack (Rantala, 2008).

There can be little doubt that victimization comes with high costs for both the victim and society. Not included in any of these figures are the intangible harms of increased fear and anxiety brought on by the events. These other problems are much harder to quantify in any way but may be the most problematic for many victims.

TABLE 3.6 Lost Time Due to Victimization, NCVS				
Offense	Lost Work Time	Loss < 1 Day	Loss 1–10 Days	Loss > 10 Days
Robbery	12.4%	13.8%	66.5%	11.7%
Assault	7.0%	24.3%	43.7%	25.8%
Household Burglary	9.7%	29.3%	60.1%	4.8%
Motor Vehicle Theft	15.7%	27.8%	65.7%	1.7%
Household Theft	5.7%	36.1%	58.3%	2.9%

Source: Constructed by the authors, from the Bureau of Justice Statistics (2010b).

Victims of an alleged swindler wait in line to enter the courtroom for the arraignment of the suspect. Among the many things causing time lost by victims is time attending court, sometimes only to find that another court date has been scheduled.

CREDIT: AP Photo/*The Canadian Press*, Graham Hughes

Beyond such obvious costs as injury, medical expenses, lost days from work, and economic loss, victimization generates a broader public impact. Many citizens, whether or not they have been victimized, report being afraid of crime, and the fear may manifest itself in various ways depending on the person involved and the basis for his or her anxiety. Some individuals fear walking on the streets in their neighborhood, while others fear physical attack within their own home. As a result, there may be a shift in physical functioning, such as high blood pressure and rapid heartbeat. Alternatively, the individual may similarly alter his or her behavior in certain places or avoid various activities. To a great extent, the source of the fear for the individual will determine the response to the fear.

Surveys report that more than 40 percent of the public are fearful of crime (Gallup, 1992; Skogan & Maxfield, 1981; Toseland, 1982). Survey results find that one-third of the public report that there are areas near their homes where they would be afraid to walk alone at night (Gallup, 2009; Maguire, 2010). In 2016, the Gallup Poll found that 53 percent of U.S. adults worry "a great deal" and another 26 percent worry "a fair amount" about crime and violence (Davis, 2016). This is the highest level of worry since 2001. Jones and Saad (2014) report that 18 percent of respondents to the 2014 Gallup Poll worry frequently or occasionally about being murdered, 45 percent worry about having their credit card information stolen by computer hackers, and 62 percent worry about having their computer or smart phone hacked. Obviously, fear of crime has become an added burden affecting both those who are victimized and the general public (see Table 3.7).

Societal/System Costs

While the above information paints a serious picture of the impact of crime, the actual impact extends beyond the direct financial loss due to the crime or the time lost by victims as reflected in the UCR or the NCVS. Indeed, crime exacts a wide range of additional costs from the individual and society. Among these are the criminal justice system costs of investigating, arresting, prosecuting, adjudicating, and incarcerating/punishing the offender. Besides the direct crime losses suffered by the victims, there are the medical costs related to injuries and lost income, as well as *intangible costs*, which include pain and suffering,

TABLE 3.7	Percent Worried Frequently or Occasionally About Being a Victim of Select Crimes	
Having the credit card information you have used at stores stolen by computer hackers		69%
Having your computer or smart phone hacked and the information stolen by unauthorized persons		62
Your home being burglarized when you are not there		45
Having your car stolen or broken into		42
Having a school-aged child physically harmed attending school		31
Being the victim of terrorism		28
Getting mugged		31
Your home being burglarized when you are there		30
Being a victim of a hate crime		18
Being sexually assaulted		18
Being attacked while driving your car		20
Getting murdered		18
Being assaulted/killed by a co-worker/employee where you work		7

Source: Compiled by authors, from Jones & Saad (2014).

psychological impacts, and reduced quality of life. Yet another consideration is the costs associated with the offender's choice to pursue crime rather than socially acceptable forms of production (McCollister et al., 2010).

Miller and colleagues (1996) combed through a variety of data sources, including the NCVS, to gain a fuller picture of the costs and consequences of criminal victimization. They began by compiling a lengthy list of costs extracted by the victimization experience. As Table 3.8 shows, the annual loss due to just these ten crime classifications reached $450 billion during the 1987 to 1990 period. These costs include not only medical costs and property loss but also losses due to time, mental health care, and criminal justice system costs. These monetary estimates would escalate considerably if complete information were available on every single crime incident. At the same time, one should realize that these figures refer to only a handful of street crimes. Other statutory violations, such as fraud, mass-marketing fraud, identity theft, white-collar crime, and corporate crime, need to be factored in to arrive at a more comprehensive assessment.

 **WEB ACTIVITY**

The entire report by Miller et al. (1996) may be found on this textbook's companion website at **www.routledge.com/cw/doerner.**

Aos and colleagues (2001) computed the economic costs related to the criminal justice system's processing of individual crimes for the State of Washington.

TABLE 3.8 Annual Losses Due to Crime During 1987–1990, in Millions, Expressed in 1993 Dollars[a]

Type of Crime	Medical	Other Tangible[b]	Quality of Life	Total
Fatal Crime	$700	$32,700	$60,000	$93,000
Child Abuse	$3,600	$3,700	$48,000	$56,000
Rape and Sexual Assault	$4,000	$3,500	$119,000	$127,000
Other Assault or Attempt	$5,000	$10,000	$77,000	$93,000
Robbery or Attempt	$600	$2,500	$8,000	$11,000
Drunk Driving	$3,400	$10,000	$27,000	$41,000
Arson	$160	$2,500	$2,400	$5,000
Larceny or Attempt	$150	$9,000	$0	$9,000
Burglary or Attempt	$30	$7,000	$1,800	$9,000
Motor Vehicle Theft or Attempt	$9	$6,300	$500	$7,000
Total	$18,000	$87,000	$345,000	$450,000

Notes:

[a] Totals may appear not to add up due to rounding.

[b] "Other Tangible" includes Property Damage and Loss, Mental Health Care, Police and Fire Services, Victim Services, and Productivity.

Source: Miller et al. (1996: 17).

Their computations are based solely on the costs related to the various criminal justice system agencies involved in handling the offender and the offense as it moves through the system. Included are the costs to the police, courts, and correctional systems. Based on cost figures from the mid-1990s, the estimated cost of a homicide is $355,086; the cost of an aggravated assault is $56,790; and the cost of a robbery is $92,705 (Aos et al., 2001). While these figures are for only one state, it is reasonable to assume that other states would expend similar high-dollar costs in processing these offenses.

WEB ACTIVITY

Details and discussion on calculating the economic costs of crime to society may be investigated at **http://www.wsipp.wa.gov/pub.asp?docid=03-01-1202.**

McCollister and colleagues (2010) provide a detailed discussion of the data and computations on the costs of crime to society. The authors draw data from the UCR, National Incident-Based Reporting System (NIBRS), the NCVS, the Federal Emergency Management Agency, the U.S. Fire Administration (for arsons), the Bureau of Justice Assistance (for jail and prison data, criminal justice system employment data, and expenditures), and the Bureau of Labor Statistics (for income and earnings). They also rely on data and input from other analyses, including the work of Miller et al. (1996) and Aos

TABLE 3.9 Tangible and Intangible Costs of Crime

Offenses	Victim Costs	Criminal Justice System Costs	Crime Career Costs	Total Tangible Costs	Pain and Suffering Costs
Murder	$737,517	$392,352	$148,555	$1,278,424	$8,442,000
Rape/Sex Assault	5,556	26,479	9,212	41,247	198,212
Aggravated Assault	8,700	8,641	2,126	19,537	13,435
Robbery	3,299	13,827	4,272	21,398	4,976
Motor Vehicle Theft	6,114	3,867	533	10,534	262
Arson	11,452	4,392	584	16,428	5,133
Household Burglary	1,362	4,127	681	6,170	321
Larceny/Theft	480	2,879	163	3,523	10
Stolen Property	n/a	6,842	1,132	7,974	0
Vandalism	n/a	4,160	701	4,860	0
Forgery/Counterfeiting	n/a	4,605	660	5,265	0
Embezzlement	n/a	4,820	660	5,480	0
Fraud	n/a	4,372	660	5,032	0

Source: Constructed by the authors, from McCollister et al. (2010).

(2003). Table 3.9 presents the tangible and intangible costs for 13 crime types in 2008 dollars. The total costs range from a high of almost $9 million for each murder to a low of $3,523 for each larceny/theft. While these per crime figures are themselves staggering, multiplying the costs of homicides by the number of homicides in 2010 reveals a total cost of more than $132 billion just for this one offense category. Carrying out this same computation for all 13 crime categories reveals a total cost of more than $295 trillion in 2010!

The economic impact of crime upon the individual and society is huge. Simply looking at the immediate loss due to the victimization itself is short-sighted. To these losses, you need to add the costs of the criminal justice system, other costs to the victim and his or her family, pain and suffering, and lost productivity by the offender. While the actual level of crime has fallen in recent years, the staggering economic costs to the individual victims and to society cannot be ignored.

Summary

The data and figures on the impact of crime suggest that many victims, as well as the general public, become the "walking wounded." They endure their problems and tribulations in silence, often without help from external sources. On top of the crime-related losses come more difficulties when a victim's case finds its way into the criminal justice system. As the following section explains, these costs can be substantial.

THE SECOND INSULT: SYSTEM PARTICIPATION

A victim's problems have only just begun if the case is processed through the criminal justice system. The costs listed in Table 3.9 include a number of costs associated with the victim's decision to report the victimization to the authorities. A number of these costs accrue to the victims themselves. Others are borne by the criminal justice system and society at large.

The system extracts further costs as soon as people enter the halls of justice. In fact, the plight of victims and witnesses has led at least one prosecutor to chastise the system for victimizing its own patrons. Ash (1972: 390) describes typical system encounters in the following terms:

> [T]he witness will several times be ordered to appear at some designated place, usually a courtroom. . . . . Several times he will be made to wait tedious, unconscionable long intervals of time in dingy courthouse corridors or in other grim surroundings. Several times he will suffer the discomfort of being ignored by busy officials and the bewilderment and painful anxiety of not knowing what is going on around him or what is going to happen to him. On most of these occasions he will never be asked to testify or to give anyone any information, often because of a last-minute adjournment granted in a huddled conference at the judge's bench. He will miss many hours from work (or school) and consequently will lose many hours of wages. In most jurisdictions he will receive at best only token payment in the form of ridiculously low witness fees for his time and trouble.

Besides addressing the direct impact of a criminal event upon victims, the Milwaukee Victim/Witness Project identified problems that the criminal justice system provoked for victims and witnesses (Doerner et al., 1976; Knudten et al., 1976; Knudten & Knudten, 1981). Interviewers learned that common problems for system participants included time loss, a corresponding reduction in income, time wasted waiting needlessly inside the courthouse, and problems getting to and from the courthouse. In addition, court appearances for subpoenaed witnesses translated into lost wages—a significant concern for many people. Waiting conditions were another critical problem. At the time of the study, all victims and witnesses reported to a large waiting room at the courthouse. Bailiffs would retrieve witnesses when it was time for their testimony. In one particular case, a sexual assault victim took a seat before the trial began. A number of other people shuffled in and out waiting for their cases to start. A few minutes later, much to her chagrin, the victim realized her suspected assailant was sitting next to her. Intimidation tactics can be very discomforting (Healey, 1995). In many cases, numerous delays and postponements may result in cases taking in excess of one year to resolve (Cassell, 1997). Needless to say, situations such as the one described here do nothing to alleviate the stress and anxiety associated with system participation.

Probably the best way to characterize the reactions of victims and witnesses would be to say that their courthouse experiences leave them bewildered and frustrated. Although victims have gone there to discharge a civic duty, they learn the hard way that the system takes undue advantage of their goodwill. They spend time away from work, lose money, and are not treated courteously (Norton, 1983: 146–147). As one research team explained:

> [T]here is a serious gap between . . . . . problems faced by crime victims and the help available to them. Unless this gap is bridged, victims may come to realize they stand a good chance of incurring even greater financial losses if they cooperate with the criminal justice system. The anticipated financial loss due to entrance into the system may be sufficient to deter such citizen involvement. It is ironic that the system which is designed to protect the constitutional rights of the offender fails even to recognize the victim's position and then turns around and wonders why its citizenry is apathetic.
>
> (Doerner et al., 1976: 489)

Rather than claim apathy on the part of victims, it is more realistic to view the lack of participation in the criminal justice system as a rational choice. That is, victims make a *cost–benefit analysis* and see exacerbated costs accruing from system participation. Accordingly, the American criminal justice system is facing a critical loss of citizen trust and support.

Results from the 2011 National Crime Victimization Survey indicate that more than 40 percent of serious violent victimization episodes, 60 percent of property victimizations, and half of all simple assaults go unreported to the police (Langton et al., 2012). When interviewers ask these victims why they did not call the police, several consistent refrains emerge (see Table 3.10). Most commonly, victims report that the police would not or could not help. Others claim that the victim handled it another way, it was not important enough to report, or they feared reprisal (Langton et al., 2012). Consequently, victims turn to other officials or individuals besides the police (Bureau of Justice Statistics, 2010a). Other reasons typically revolve around apparent frustrations

WEB ACTIVITY

The issue of non-reporting is a persistent problem. You can read more about this issue at **www.bjs.gov/ content/pub/pdf/vnrp0610.pdf.**

TABLE 3.10 Percent of Victimizations Not Reported to the Police by Reason for Not Reporting, 2006–2010

	Total Crime	Serious Violence	Simple Assault	Personal Larceny	Burglary	MVT	Theft
Dealt with in another way/personal matter	20%	25%	38%	17%	12%	16%	16%
Not important enough to victim to report	27	13	21	24	27	26	31
Police would not or could not help	31	21	14	43	40	30	35
Fear of reprisal or getting offender into trouble	5	19	11	2	4	7	3
Other reason or not one most important reason	17	21	17	14	17	21	16

Source: Compiled by the authors, from Langton et al. (2012).

that nothing can be done to solve the situation. In short, many victims see no benefits to be gained from initiating contact with system representatives.

These sentiments are not confined to the police. Many people harbor genuine doubts that the courts will punish an offender sufficiently once he or she is apprehended and prosecuted (Maguire & Pastore, 1996; Schneider et al., 1976). They realize that there is no "truth in sentencing" for convicted felons. Homicide offenders, for example, usually net a 16-year state prison term from the courts. However, they typically spend only half of this time behind bars. Judges solemnly pronounce ten-year terms for rapists, but they are often out in fewer than seven years. Robbers can expect to fulfill four-and-a-half years out of an eight-year sentence. Aggravated assault convicts often serve approximately three years, although their sentences officially extend for eight years (Maguire & Pastore, 2006). What this boils down to is that the system is not making good on its promises.

Given this climate, it is not surprising that Gallup reports that only 23 percent of its survey respondents expressed quite a lot or a great deal of confidence in the criminal justice system (Gallup, 2016). Citizen reluctance to become involved in the criminal justice system is reaching epidemic heights. A substantial number of victims and witnesses who have gone through the criminal justice process confide that they would not return if they could avoid doing so in the future (Cannavale & Falcon, 1976; Finn & Lee, 1987; Knudten et al., 1976; Norton, 1983). System personnel complain that citizens are growing increasingly apathetic. However, such a self-serving portrayal is difficult to accept. An alternative description is that victims have grown disenchanted and are rebelling against further abuse. Because of past mistreatment, they are making a very deliberate and rational decision to bypass the criminal justice system.

SECTION V

Responding to Crime Victimization

VICTIMS' ADVOCACY PROGRAMS

by Michelle Perin

With community-based policing strategies increasing, law enforcement agencies struggle to incorporate social justice within their overloaded criminal justice role. One common way is incorporation of victims' advocacy programs.

A teenager had enough sexual abuse at the hands of her biological father. After reporting the incident to the Phoenix, AZ Police, detectives initiated a confrontation call with the abuser. He admitted his crime. At the end of the call, the detectives, concerned about the way the abuser was acting, attempted to contact him. The abuser had killed himself. Now the officers faced telling the victim her father was dead, dealing with her guilt and grief and the notification of the family members, who were unaware of the accusation or the outcome. The detectives called out their victims' advocate team.

About the call, Kerry Ramella, Phoenix Community Assistance Program (CAP) manager, said, "The fact the officers took the step to help the family with what they would encounter was great. Together as partners, we took care of all their needs." Changes in police roles, including mandatory victims' rights responsibilities, makes the collaboration between officers and advocates essential.

"The victims' rights laws require us as a state to move forward," said Mark Roberts, commander, Arizona State University Polytechnic Campus Patrol Bureau. "The officers understand in this day and age there is quite a bit of social work involved in what they do." Many federal mandates, especially ones associated with grant funding, require agencies to establish victims' rights policies. Establishing a victims' advocacy program or partnering with a nonprofit agency are two ways agencies comply with mandates.

Accomplishments

Many departments are moving away from the reactive, professional model of policing and toward preventative strategies. Advocacy programs assist with this task. "A lot of time when people are traumatized, they might not be comfortable with the uniformed presence there," said Brian McLean, the Houghton, MI sheriff. "They get their needs attended to."

Chris Parks, MC, victim services coordinator for the Phoenix, AZ Police Victims' Service Unit (VSU) added, "Criminal justice is sometimes referred to as a second victimization, and we want to reduce that by giving information and understanding to victims. The general public most of the time does not understand how the police department operates, how investigations are done, what is needed to prove probable cause, or what is needed to get a conviction when a case goes to court. Often they have unrealistic expectations of the police department, so we try to explain what the role of the police department is."

Victims' advocacy programs offer a host of services, including 24/7 crisis intervention; emergency needs assessments, including shelter placement; information and referral; crisis counseling; food and transportation; case management; liaison with law enforcement, and other criminal justice professionals and legal assistance.

"Victim advocacy, in my opinion, is actually a mixture of social work, criminal justice and mental health but should not be evaluated under any of the three," Parks said. "It is founded in four core measures: healing, safety, justice and restitution and is its own discipline with its own standards and

ethics." Many victims' advocacy programs began because first responders felt helpless to do more for victims.

Ramella explained how CAP started. "Fire trucks were going on scene and taking care of putting out the fire at the house, and their job was done. The fire was out, and they were getting ready to leave, and a family was just sitting on the curb not knowing what to do. The firefighters didn't know what to do." This was in 1995. Currently, CAP, which works out of the fire department facility, assists numerous agencies, including Phoenix Police, the AZ Department of Public Safety (DPS), and other surrounding law enforcement agencies.

Advocates can be called out to provide crisis intervention, including emotional support and resource referral. After the initial crisis, advocates continue to follow up with the victims, facilitating their contact with detectives and continuing to provide infor-

mation about the case and avenues of healing. Moving through the criminal justice system, the advocate attends court hearings, explains processes and assists with paperwork.

An advocate works with a victim through to the sentencing phase and often will follow up for many months after just to check and see how the victims are doing and if they need anything. This type of relationship improves the community's view of the police department.

"It is designed to lessen the trauma they have already received by being victimized and to train law enforcement, prosecutors, nurses and advocates to respond to people who have been victimized so they aren't retraumatized," said Terry Sayatovich, victim service coordinator at Dial Help Inc. in Houghton, MI. "We have set standards and protocols across the whole team so that if a victim contacts anyone, [he gets] the same response. The benefit is in its consistency."

Different Agencies, Different Agendas

A standard victims' advocacy program is hard to come by. Many large municipal agencies have in-house programs, while smaller, rural departments share nonprofit agencies. Although both types of agencies provide similar services and utilize common victims' rights approaches, each has advantages and disadvantages.

"The advantage (of a nonprofit) is that their advocacy for the victim has the potential of being less inhibited by the governmental or law enforcement influences, resulting in a greater range of possibilities," Parks said. Another aspect of nonprofit advocacy is that they do not often require the victim to report the crime. Although this might seem at odds with the mission of holding criminals accountable, assisting victims to heal in any way possible is the goal. Advocates hope that by teaching skills, they can assist in preventing further victimization.

Also, even if a victim does report a crime and desires accountability, the case might not be strong enough to

prosecute. "She might feel let down by the police department and me too as her advocate here at the police department," Lessa Johnson, victims' service coordinator, Anderson (IN) Police Department, said. "So, she may prefer to continue her communication with a private organization."

In-house victims' advocacy programs offer a host of benefits. "One of the benefits to being an in-house program is the daily contact with sworn personnel and the opportunity to build trust and professional respect," Parks said. Johnson agreed, "I prefer to work here in the police department because I have face-to-face contact with officers and detectives. I also have access to our computer system, so I can read every report ever made." Having the advocates in-house allows the officers to get to know them, which builds trust.

Benefits

Regardless of whether an advocacy program is in house or a nonprofit, the benefits for both officers and victims are enormous. "Law enforcement can provide immediate protection and safety and possibly the arrest of a suspect," Roberts said. "The advocate knows how to work with the victim, how to notify friends and family, get them necessary paperwork and provide resources such as shelter services."

One important benefit to officers is that the advocate allows them to focus on the investigation. An advocate concentrates on the needs of the victim. This allows the officer to perform the law enforcement role, knowing the victim is not being left to fend for himself. Advocates can also calm victims, providing a better witness for detectives. "We are a resource for them," Ramella said. "Typically, we arrive on scene, they brief us, and we tell them what we can do, or they tell us what they are in most need of."

Advocates also can reduce on-scene time. "We can take over the call, and they can go back in service," Ramella said. A third benefit is that the advocate is a liaison for the officers. "They have a person they can contact 24 hours a day in regards to the case," Sayatovich said. Johnson agreed, "We are time efficient. We have time to listen to people talk. Sometimes they want to tell their life story. We can provide some insight to the detective about what the bigger picture is. Officers want to do more than take statements, gather evidence and make cases. They want to help people and follow up, but they don't have time."

Along with benefiting law enforcement officers, victims' advocates make a profound difference to victims. "We can provide an advocate typically within 60 minutes of an officer arriving on a call, depending on the time of day and location," Roberts said. "For the victim, it means a quicker response." A victim's comfort level can be increased by the presence of an advocate.

Victims benefit in a variety of ways from the myriad tasks advocates perform. Each victim is unique, and advocates assess their needs and provide appropriate services. Advocates assist at the hospital during sexual assault exams. They can sit with family members and explain what is going on and what usually occurs next. Advocates accompany victims to speak with detectives and for court dates. Advocate not only provide a stable face in the often transitory justice system, but they also provide an ear 24 hours a day. Many victims state they felt left out of their case. An advocate can help ease this frustration.

Roles

An issue surrounding victims' advocacy is educating advocates and officers about their roles. "Each side perceives the other in their own way," said Matthew Ecker, Maricopa County, AZ Sheriff's deputy. He believes the advocates see the police as disinterested and the police see the advocates as agenda driven. "Each side needs to understand the other's objective," he said. "Police want to punish the bad guy. The advocate wants to help the victim."

Although officers also want to help the victim, the advocate slips into this role when an officer's primary focus must be on the facts. "We want to come along side [officers, prosecutors, and judges] and have an important part in helping them reach their goal of protecting victims, of holding perpetrators accountable," Johnson said.

An advocate's role is seen as more of a social helper. This frees officers to concentrate on the crime itself. "The advocates need to have a good understanding of the investigative process, crime-scene preservation and where the officers are coming from and what they need to do," Ramella said. When each part of the team understands the other's role, they can work together to benefit each other, the victim and the case.

In a time when budgets are tight, funding another program can be a challenge. "We are funded by general city funding and grants, including Victims of Crime Act (VOCA) and Arizona Criminal Justice Commission (ACJC) grants," Ramella said. "My hope is that it becomes a standard so people don't have to rely on grant funding. I hope it becomes more institutionalized." Johnson said their program is also funded in part by grants and the rest from the city budget. As research continues to support victims' advocacy programs and community policing expands, more departments will be able to get funding written into their budgets.

Management

Law enforcement management plays an important role in maintaining a victims' advocacy program. "First line staff, both officers / detectives and advocates work very well together. Probably because by working together, each of their jobs is easier. Trust and respect will always be critical though," Parks said. "When issues occur, it is more often management that may forget to respect the importance of each others' roles and understand and accept the differences."

Johnson said, "It sure has meant a lot through the years to have good support from the chief and assistant chief. Not only financial support, but respect. I know that they will do their best to assist us to do the best job we can." Like most collaborations, communication is key.

"Two lieutenants do our policy writing," Johnson said. "They get suggestions from me and officers. If new laws occur, we keep in contact with other agencies and keep up to date. As we get new officers, we have to communicate with them and let them know what our role is, what services we provide, how we can help the officer." Sayatovich said their program coordinator is always in contact with the agencies asking, "What can we do to make your job easier and service victims better?"

To facilitate communication, training should be collaborative. "I'm real proud of our folks," Roberts said. "We have received training with our counseling and consultation staff. Typically at one of our annual trainings, we'll have a counselor come in and explain how they are going to work with us, what their job is and what it isn't and establish their relationship."

Phoenix's program includes a huge training program, the Regional Crisis Intervention Training Academy. Ramella said this program is used to train personnel from various departments. "They come and we all train together," she said. Ride-alongs are another popular method of training that spurs the relationship building essential to officer / advocate trust. "We have ridden out in patrol cars," Johnson said. "I would get to know the officers, and they would get to know me. We would talk about advocacy and what I do. Then they understood that we worked better as a team, especially during a crisis situation."

Relationship building helps foster communication and trust and inspires a team spirit. "We can be the softer, gentler part when we team up," Sayatovich said. "It helps the victim to see us as a team." Ramella agreed, "We have a great relationship with the law enforcement officers. We do briefings with them. They treat us as a part of them."

She said, "I continue to see how the criminal justice system can be improved. We never get to the point where we can pat ourselves on the back and say we have accomplished what we wanted to do. We make steps in that direction, but there is always more to do." As police departments recognize the need to assist victims in more ways, victims' advocates can join the team. "It just makes sense," Roberts said.

Michelle Perin worked as a telecommunications operator with Phoenix, AZ police for eight years and currently writes full time from Michigan's Upper Peninsula. She has been published in Chief of Police, Police Times, The UP Mag, Beyond the Badge, and she has a monthly column on Officer.com. She can be reached at thewritinghand@highstream.net.

Demeanor also plays a part in making or breaking the team spirit. "We have a good rapport with the officers," Johnson said. "When I came in 1990, I was accepted by many, but a few were rather skeptical of me. A few were cool in the beginning. My approach and my personality were key in gaining their trust and their confidence. I couldn't come in here and start pounding on my desk and telling them how to do their jobs. That wouldn't go over well with anyone and especially a police officer."

Victims' advocacy programs are proving to be an asset to many communities and their police departments across the country. Community policing philosophy encourages the use of resources to address underlying social issues—not only law enforcement issues. Police departments want to address this new philosophy but find they are overwhelmed by the criminal justice needs of policing. Victims' advocates can assist.

"When it first started [the biggest challenge] was distrust, but now that we have been working together for a while, there isn't much of a challenge," Roberts said. "We have grown to know what each other does and the response to a call. In the beginning, we weren't sure how to share information with each other. We don't have that handicap anymore." Johnson said victims' advocacy assists in "more successful cases, more follow-through, better statements and higher convictions."

The Development of Crime Victims' Rights in the United States

by Robert C. Davis, James M. Anderson, and Julie Whitman

Legal rights for crime victims have been developed and expanded in the past three decades. These rights have transformed the relationship between the crime victim and the criminal-justice system, as victims gained the rights to be informed, present, and heard during the criminal- and juvenile-justice processes. This change has been driven largely by crime victims and survivors, with the support of advocacy organizations, leaders within the criminal-justice field, and policymakers.

The adoption of victims' rights accelerated in the early 1980s following the release of the final report of President Ronald Reagan's Task Force on Victims of Crime (1982). That task force had been assembled to investigate the treatment of victims by the criminal-justice system. Its 1982 final report defined an agenda for bringing a balance between the rights of defendants and victims. It called for increased participation by victims throughout criminal-justice proceedings and restitution in all cases in which victims suffer financial loss.

At the same time the task force was undertaking its work, Congress was developing legislation to provide protections for victims at the federal level. The 1982 Victim and Witness Protection Act (Pub. L. 97-291) authorized victim restitution and the use of victims' impact statements at sentencing in federal cases. It also required the attorney general to issue guidelines for the development of further policies regarding victims and witnesses of crimes. Soon after, the 1984 Victims of Crime Act (VOCA) (Pub. L. 98-473) implemented more of the task force's recommendations on victim compensation and assistance. This second act by Congress redistributed monies levied from federal offenders to states, funding local aid to victims ("Constitutionalizing Crime Victim Rights," 1997; Smith and Hillenbrand, 1999, pp. 247–249).

In 1990, Congress passed the Victims' Rights and Restitution Act (Pub. L. 101-647), giving crime victims in federal cases the right to notification of court proceedings and the right to attend them, the right to notice of changes in a defendant's detention status, the right to consult with prosecutors, and the right to protection against offender aggression.

In 1994, the Violent Crime Control and Law Enforcement Act (Pub. L. 103-322) gave victims in federal cases the right to speak at sentencing hearings, made restitution mandatory in sexual-assault cases, and expanded funding for local victim services. Rights for federal crime victims were further strengthened as part of the Antiterrorism and Effective Death Penalty Act of 1996 (Pub. L. 104-132), and the Victim Rights Clarification Act of 1997 (Pub. L. 105-6).

Then in 2004, Congress passed the Crime Victims' Rights Act (CVRA) as part of the Justice for All Act of 2004 (Pub. L. 108-405). The CVRA generally strengthened the rights of federal crime victims and transferred them from Title 42, the Public Health and Welfare Code, to Title 18, the Crimes and Criminal Procedure code, elevating their profile within the federal justice system. The rights protected under the CVRA include the right to be reasonably protected from the accused; the right to be informed of criminal proceedings and the custody status of the defendant; the right to be present in the courtroom; the right to be heard at proceedings involving release, plea agreement, sentencing, or parole; the right to confer with the prosecutor; the right to restitution from the defendant; the right to proceedings free from unreasonable delay; and the right to be treated with fairness, dignity, and respect.

Victims' rights at the state level also progressed dramatically during this same time period. By the early 1980s, four states had broad laws providing a range of rights to victims, eight required a victims' impact statement at sentencing, six had open parole hearings, and eight mandated restitution for victims (DOJ, 1986). The first state victims' rights legislation was largely advisory; many such laws were called "guidelines" for the treatment of victims, rather than conferring "rights."

As at the federal level, the release of the final report of the President's Task Force on Victims of Crime in 1982 spurred the states to strengthen and expand victims' rights. By the early 1990s, every state provided violent-crime victims the right to victim compensation and provided victims of serious crime with a set of legal rights, including the rights to be informed, present, and heard during the criminal-justice process and to receive restitution from the offender.[1] Many also gave victims rights to protection from the defendant, speedy trial, privacy, and other rights to fair treatment by the criminal- and juvenile-justice systems.

Along with statutory rights for victims, 32 states amended their constitutions to provide additional protection for the rights of victims. While amending a state's constitution is a cumbersome process, typically requiring multiple levels of approval by a state legislature as well as ratification by the voters, victims' advocates pursued these amendments for the additional authority they give to victims' rights. Rights protected by the constitution cannot be diminished by anything in a state's statutes, court rules, or administrative code provisions. A constitutional amendment also provides a level of permanency to the victims' rights, since they can be changed only by another cumbersome, multiyear amendment process. And constitutional rights offer a level of implied enforceability.

State victims' rights amendments generally take one of two forms. The first is a short and broad statement of rights. Colorado's amendment takes this approach:

> Any person who is a victim of a criminal act, or such person's designee, legal guardian, or surviving immediate family members if such person is deceased, shall have the right to be heard when relevant, informed, and present at all critical stages of the criminal justice process. All terminology, including the term "critical

---

[1] Every state provides rights to victims of violent felonies. Most states extend rights to victims of any felony as well as any violent misdemeanor. A few states provide rights to a victim of any crime.

stages", shall be defined by the general assembly. (Colo. Const. art. II, §16a)

In contrast, Arizona's amendment provides a list of 12 rights, as well as a definition of *victim* and other language to guide implementation (Ariz. Const. art. II, §2.1).

Most of the state amendments mandate notification of victims concerning events in court and the parole or release of offenders, and permit victims to participate in their cases through oral or written input at sentencing. Fewer state constitutions extend other rights, such as the right to a speedy trial and the right to participate in parole proceedings or proceedings involving pretrial release.

States also began to amend their court rules of criminal procedure and evidence to incorporate the rights of victims. While victims' rights across the states are not uniform in scope or application, most victims of serious crime are entitled to basic rights under the law.

Enforceability of Crime Victims' Rights

Despite this remarkable progress in the passage of crime victims' rights, advocates have been dismayed to see that, too often, victims' rights were violated with impunity. An NIJ-funded survey of crime victims in 1998 found that, even within states with strong victims' rights legislation, many victims were not notified about key hearings and proceedings, many were not given the opportunity to be heard, and few received restitution (Kilpatrick, Beatty, and Howley, 1998). Although victims in these states generally fared better than those in states with weak victims' rights legislation, as many as one-third of victims in strong-protection states were not afforded the opportunity to exercise certain rights.

Few states—even those that have adopted constitutional amendments—provide recourse to victims when their rights are not honored. With the exception of Arizona, all states ban any civil action for damages caused by a violation of rights. State victims' rights laws also typically provide that a violation of rights will not constitute grounds for a new trial or to overturn a sentence or other disposition. Several states restrict enforceability even further, providing that the victims' bill of rights creates no cause of action against the state. In those states, the term *cause of action* is not specifically limited to actions for damages, so the language could be interpreted in some courts to bar any action to enforce the rights of victims.[2] Two states, New York and North Dakota, have legislative language providing that a violation of their victims' bills of rights gives rise to no cause of action for money damages or injunctive relief (N.Y. Exec. Law §649[2008]; N.D. Cent. Code §12.1-34-05[2008]).[3]

Only four states—Arizona, Florida, Indiana, and Texas—provide victims express legal standing through their constitution or statutes to assert their rights (Ariz. Rev. Stat. §13-4437 [2008]; Fla. Stat. §960.001[7][2008]; Ind. Code §35-40-2-1[2008]; Tex. Const. art. I, §30 [2008]). Another two—Maryland and Utah—provide a clear right for victims to seek an appeal where their rights are denied (Md. Code Ann. Crim. Proc. §11-103 [2008]; Md. Rules 8-111 and 8-204[2008]; Utah Code Ann. §77-38-11[2008]), and several others expressly allow a limited legal remedy, such as authorizing the prosecutor or a state victims' advocate to assert a victim's rights, or allowing the victim or others to seek a writ of mandamus ordering an official or agency to comply with the victims' rights law (e.g., Ala. Code §15-23-83[2008], authorizing attorney general or district attorney to assert victims' rights; Conn. Gen. Stat. §46a-13c [2008], authorizing the state victims' advocate to file a limited special appearance for the purpose of advocating for a victim's rights; N.C. Gen. Stat. §15A-840[2008],

---

[2] This is not necessarily the case, however. Florida's victims' bill of rights both provides that "Nothing in this section or in the guidelines adopted pursuant to this section shall be construed as creating a cause of action against the state or any of its agencies or political subdivisions" and gives crime victims standing to assert their rights. See Fla. Stat. §960.001(5) and (7). Thus, it would seem that the intent of "cause of action" here is restricted to monetary damages, although it is not specifically stated.

[3] In both of these states, however, this prohibition is limited to the general listing of rights, in both states called the Fair Treatment Standards, and does not appear to apply to other, discrete rights of victims that appear elsewhere in the code, such as the right to be heard at specific proceedings or the right to restitution.

authorizing a victim to seek a writ of mandamus enforcing the victim's rights).

At least nine states have created or designated an entity to receive and investigate reports of violations of victims' rights. These may take the form of a state ombudsman, a committee or board, a state victims' advocate or victims' rights office, or another designated office or individual.

The issue of enforceability of victims' rights came to the federal level in 2004, when Congress passed the CVRA as part of the Justice for All Act of 2004. Along with listing the rights of victims, the CVRA gave victims legal standing to enforce their rights in court and called for the creation of a mechanism to receive and investigate reports of victims' rights violations. The larger Justice for All Act also promoted the enforceability of victims' rights at the state level by authorizing funding for legal clinics to represent the rights of victims in criminal proceedings. The statute specified that funding would be provided to the OVC for the NCVLI to provide grants and assistance to lawyers to help victims of crime in court.

Victim Participation in the Criminal Justice System

EDNA EREZ

JULIAN ROBERTS

According to the adversarial model of justice, a criminal trial entails a conflict between two theoretically equal adversaries, the state and the defendant, played out before an impartial adjudicator—the judge. The victim of the crime serves as the principal witness for the prosecution, and having served this function, has no further role to play. The victim is essentially a passive participant; she or he appears when called to testify and responds to examination in chief and cross-examination, if necessary. However, over the past 30 years, much has changed in the theory, policy, and practice of adversarial criminal justice. The role of the crime victim has been transformed from passive witness to active participant. While still lacking full "standing" as a party to the proceedings, victims nevertheless are consulted, informed, and participate more than ever before. To traditionalists, this evolution represents an unwelcome threat to core values central to the adversarial model. Victims' rights advocates hold a different perspective, viewing the new powers of the victim as evidence of progress toward an as yet unattained goal of full participation in the criminal process.

Until the 1970s crime victims were invisible to the general public and had little profile within the criminal justice system. The names of high-profile offenders were well recognized: Charles Manson, Peter Sutcliffe, Ted Bundy. Their victims, however, remained unknown. Public and media attention continues to focus on offenders and still overlooks their victims. However, this is no longer true for the criminal justice system. The governments of most Western nations have legislated many victim rights and created a wide range of services for the victims of crime. Victims have the right to receive information about the status of the case in which they are involved, and they also have the right to apply for financial and psychological assistance. More importantly, in many jurisdictions victims also enjoy participatory rights throughout the criminal process (Hall, 1991). Although most rights and benefits for victims have been generally accepted, the right to actively participate in the judicial process has proved controversial and continues to be the subject of heated debate.

Victim participatory rights apply throughout the criminal justice process, beginning with the arrest of a suspect and ending with the prisoner's release from prison. They pertain to hearings on bail or pretrial release of the offender, through plea agreements or sentencing, to posttrial relief or release hearings, including probation and commutation or pardon hearings. Victim participation is buttressed by laws that mandate victim notification, protection, and financial compensation in the event that they incur expenses in the course of participating. For instance, notification applies to the victim or victim's family, who should receive advance notice of proceedings where the victim has the right to attend and/or make a statement, as well as when hearings have been canceled and rescheduled. The right to protection from intimidation and harassment by the offender or the offender's family or associates may be extended to the victim's family members. The participation of victims whose victimization renders them particularly vulnerable to intimidation, such as domestic violence, is facilitated by rights that ensure police escorts to and from court, secure waiting areas separate from those of the accused and his/her family during court proceedings, and witness stands that are shielded from the direct view of the offender. This protection is particularly significant if the victim is a child, in which case many courts now allow videotaped testimony to be used to protect the child from the trauma of the courtroom and further exposure

to the accused. Other special circumstances allow for the closing of the courtroom to those who are not parties to the case and for the residence relocation of victims.

Victims' rights have also assumed a constitutional dimension in the United States. The Victims' Right Amendment is a proposed constitutional amendment that would enumerate various participatory rights for crime victims. These include notification of guaranteed admission to and the right to speak during the course of legal proceedings, including pretrial release, plea bargains, sentencing, and parole. The amendment also requires courts to consider victims' interests to ensure that trials occur without "unreasonable delays" and to consider the victim's safety when prisoners are considered for conditional release from prison. To be enacted, the proposed amendment requires a two-thirds vote in U.S. Congress (both the House and the Senate) as well as ratification by two thirds of all the states. To date, despite campaigns for its passage, including presidential endorsement in the last round, the proposed Victims' Rights Amendment has failed to gain the necessary number of states in support. The major argument against its passage has been that victim participation can be accomplished by enforcing existing laws found in state constitutional amendments or statutes.

This chapter surveys victim participatory rights and explores the continuing debate surrounding victims' claim to have a voice in criminal proceedings involving "their" offender. Exploring the issues and research on all stages of the system is beyond the scope of the chapter. Instead, after exploring some general issues and describing important participatory rights, we focus on the sentencing process. It is at sentencing that victims express greatest interest in participating and where victim input has generated the most opposition. We begin by describing the background from which victim participation emerged. Second, we summarize some important participatory reforms that have been adopted. Third, we consider some arguments for and against victim participation in sentencing. We pay particular attention to the victim impact statement (VIS). The VIS is in many respects the paradigm example of victim input, having been implemented in almost all common law jurisdictions. We then review future directions for victim participation in the judicial system, including attempts to inject restorative justice elements into an adversarial system that is fundamentally retributive in nature.

CRIME VICTIMS AND THE JUSTICE SYSTEM

The role of victims in a criminal prosecution has changed drastically over the centuries in common law countries—from an eye-for-an-eye system in which victims were expected to deal with their offenders directly, through a system in which the monarch assumed the duty of imposing punishment, to the present system in which the state prosecutes a defendant on behalf of the surrogate victim who is relegated to a role of (at best) lead witness (Zeigenhagen, 1977). For most victims, even their role as witness never materializes. As a result of attrition in the criminal process, most cases do not result in arrest, much less prosecution. Many crimes remain unreported to the police, and of those that are, a charge is laid in only a portion of incidents. Some charges are subsequently stayed or withdrawn by the prosecutor acting in the public interest or because there is no reasonable prospect of a conviction. In a large percentage of cases—estimates range as high as 90%—the offender enters a guilty plea, often following negotiations with the prosecutor. This obviates the need for a trial and the victim therefore has no opportunity to testify.[1] If the offender pleads guilty to a much less serious offense than the crime with which he was charged, victims may feel let down by the criminal process. The victim's principal role is as a backup—a

threat waiting in the wings if plea bargaining breaks down.

Unlike continental legal systems (see Joutsen, 1994), the adversarial system accords victims no formal standing in the prosecution of their offenders, and until fairly recently, the crime victim provided no input into the treatment of "their" offender. Even today, in most states crime victims have no legal rights for input into the system that are guaranteed by remedies for nonenforcement, only courtesies to be extended or withheld at the discretion of the police or prosecutor. The result is a curious blend of independence and dependence, with the result that victims have little influence over whether or how the state chooses to proceed against their offenders. At the same time, the state is highly dependent on the cooperation of victims, without which a criminal prosecution is unlikely to succeed.

In the early 1970s victims began to exert more influence over decisions taken in the criminal justice system. This was largely due to an unexpected alliance of feminist scholars and advocates (advocating to improve the treatment of victims of rape and intimate partner violence) and law-and-order groups (lobbying to "get tough" on crime). As a result of their combined efforts, criminal justice procedures were adapted to make the justice system more sensitive to victims' needs and concerns. Efforts initially focused on responses to the economic and psychological problems that victims experienced as a result of the crime, leading to the creation of programs that addressed the psychological consequences of the crime (Erez, 1989). For instance, rape shield laws were enacted to limit the scope of defense efforts to introduce a victim's past sexual history in evidence at trial. In a similar way, domestic violence laws were enacted that are distinct from other laws against assault. Police departments began to offer specialized training regarding the investigation of crimes of sexual aggression and the needs of rape and domestic violence victims. These reforms were motivated both by a newfound compassion for victims and by a realization that the criminal justice system would benefit by treating victims with more sensitivity.

Victimization surveys at the time revealed that a large proportion of crimes were not reported to the police (Bureau of Justice Statistics, 1983), because, among other reasons, victimized citizens were apprehensive about how they would be treated by the justice system and whether they would be believed (Kidd & Chayet, 1984; Kilpatrick & Otto, 1987). Studies also showed that victims and witnesses were "uncooperative" with respect to prosecutorial efforts to bring offenders to justice because they were intimidated by the criminal justice system or were uninformed as to what was expected of them (Cannavele, 1975). Accordingly, victim-witness assistance units were established to respond to victims' desire for better treatment and information, as well as to address the state's need for cooperative witnesses. Today, such units form part of most Western criminal justice systems and provide a variety of services to crime victims from first contact with the police to the sentencing of the offender. Victims began to be notified when hearings were scheduled so that they would not be kept waiting in court unnecessarily. In many courthouses, separate waiting rooms were established for defense and state witnesses. In the past, victims and accused persons often came into close contact at the courthouse.

CLAIMS FOR PARTICIPATORY RIGHTS

Although these changes were welcome, crime victims demanded more than sympathy and support; they wanted to have a *voice* in the criminal justice system. A number of studies have found that while some victims prefer to stay out of the criminal justice system, many others wish to participate (e.g., Kelly, 1984; Shapland, Villmoare, & Duff, 1985). Moreover,

the need to accord victims participatory rights has been recognized by many national committees established to study victims in the criminal justice process, of which the following are examples:

- United States: the President's Task Force on Victims of Crime (1982)
- Canada: the report of the Standing Committee on Justice and Human Rights (1998)
- New Zealand: the Victim's Task Force (1987)
- England and Wales: Justice Committee on the role of the victim in criminal justice (1998)

The international community has also recognized the need to integrate victims into the criminal justice process. In 1985, the United Nations Seventh Congress on the Prevention of Crime and Treatment of the Offender adopted a declaration that required that victims be allowed to present their views and concerns at appropriate stages of the criminal justice process. As advocates pressed for victims' rights to participate in proceedings, their demands were met with considerable resistance. Victim participation threatened to disturb established routines at the courthouse, undermine the predictability of case outcomes and slow the processing of cases. Studies showed that prosecutors, defense attorneys, and judges operated as a "work group," sharing the mutual goal of disposing of cases as fast as time and justice would permit (Eisenstein & Jacob, 1977). It was feared that allowing victims to have some input would impair the efficiency of the work group and exacerbate the pressure of cases on the court's already overloaded docket.

EMERGENCE OF VICTIM PARTICIPATORY REFORMS

United States

In the midst of this debate, a new generation of participatory reforms emerged. Many of these reforms were prompted by the recommendation of the President's Task Force on Victims of Crime (1982) that the Sixth Amendment be amended to guarantee victims a right to be present and to be heard at all critical stages of a judicial proceeding. Most states in the United States adopted laws that address victims' right to be present in proceedings by excluding victims from sequestration requirements or otherwise accommodating their wish to participate. The 1991 Omnibus Crime Bill (Pub. L. No. 101–647) stated that victims have a right to "be present at all public court proceedings related to the offense." Title V, the Victims' Rights and Restitution Act of 1990, provides that victims in federal courts have rights to restitution; to be present "at all public court proceedings related to the offense" (unless the court determines that the victim's testimony would be affected by the testimony of other witnesses at trial); to confer with the U.S. attorney; and to be informed of the arrest, conviction, sentencing, imprisonment, parole, release, or death of the offender.

Many states in the United States have enacted victims' bills of rights, which vary in their scope from mandating that criminal justice officials show respect toward victims, to establishing a victim's right to be present and heard, to allowing victims to sit at the prosecutor's table during trial. In several states, victims' rights legislation is by specific statute, but a substantial number of states have adopted constitutional amendments to give victims' rights greater permanence and visibility. The majority of the states also allow for victim participation in sentencing and parole hearings. States also provide for victim participation in plea bargaining. For example, crime victims in Arizona have the right to be consulted with respect to any potential plea agreement. Furthermore, prosecutors are required to demonstrate that they have complied with victims' rights legislation (U.S. Department of Justice, 2002; see Verdun-Jones & Tijerino, 2004, for discussion).

However, the extent to which victims are allowed to participate in plea discussions varies widely, with no state providing victims with a veto over plea agreements.

Reforms addressing circumstances in which victims are afraid or reluctant to provide testimony or input into proceedings (such as domestic violence cases) were also adopted. These laws or statutory amendments require police to make arrests, regardless of whether the victim signs the complaint. Similarly, prosecutors are allowed to proceed with a case, even if the victim refuses to cooperate (known as a "no-drop" policy). Mandatory arrest laws and no-drop prosecutorial policies recognize that victims of domestic violence are especially vulnerable to retaliation for pressing charges and therefore remove this decision from victims. These mandatory charging and prosecuting policies create a potential conflict with the principal goal of victims' advocates: to give victims a say in decisions that affect their lives. Accordingly, some battered women's advocates and feminist scholars have criticized the mandatory element of these policies, arguing that they further disempower the crime victim.

Other Jurisdictions

Other jurisdictions have also adopted victims' rights legislation of various kinds, although not to the degree found in the United States. In Canada, victims have a statutory right to submit a victim impact statement at sentencing and to deliver the statement orally if they so desire (Roberts, 2003). Victims may also submit impact statements to parole board hearings. In Manitoba, according to the Victims' Rights Act, crime victims have the right to be consulted with respect to decisions taken at all stages of the criminal process, including whether the state appeals a conviction or a sentence. Some jurisdictions such as England and Wales have adopted "Victims' Charters," which are largely aspirational in nature, creating expectations that the system will conform to certain standards without actually conferring legal rights upon crime victims. Finally, the importance of victim participatory rights is apparent from Article 68 of the Rome Statute of the International Criminal Court. This provision recognizes the security interests and participatory rights of victims and witnesses.

Victim Impact Statements

Of all the participatory reforms, victim input into sentencing decisions, or victim impact statements (VIS), have attracted the most opposition. The remaining sections of this chapter focus on victims' right to submit a VIS—as the term is referred to in the United States and Canada—or victim personal statement (VPS), its counterpart in England and Wales.[2] We focus on VIS, as this reform represents a good example of a participatory mechanism, which on the evidence can be of considerable benefit to the victim and the court to which it is submitted. The VIS is a statement in which the victim describes the impact of the crime on his or her life, including physical, social, psychological, and financial harms. The VIS may be delivered at the sentencing hearing in writing, orally, or visually (in countries or jurisdictions that allow victim allocution or presentations through a video). VIS forms differ in content and form, ranging from simple checklists in some jurisdictions to lengthy descriptive statements in others (McLeod, 1988). Some permit considerable latitude in terms of the information that may be included; other forms restrict the victim to a much greater degree. In most jurisdictions, courts are directed to take the statement into account. For example, in Canada, a provision in the Criminal Code makes it mandatory for a court to consider the victim impact statement at sentencing.

THE DEBATE SURROUNDING VICTIM PARTICIPATION AT SENTENCING

Arguments for Victim Input

Advocates of victims' rights to participate in the criminal justice process have advanced a variety of arguments, some moral, some penological, and others practical in nature. Victim participation recognizes victims' wishes to be treated as a party to the proceeding and with dignity (Henderson, 1985). It reminds judges, juries, and prosecutors that behind the "state" stands an individual with an interest in how the case is resolved (Kelly, 1987). Some argue that sentencing outcomes will be more proportionate if victims provide accurate information about the impact of the crime (Erez, 1990) and that the criminal justice process will be more democratic and better reflect the community's response to crime (Rubel, 1986). Victim participation may also lead to increased victim satisfaction with the judicial process (Australian Law Reform Commission, 1988), and cooperation with the criminal justice system may thereby enhance the system's efficiency (McLeod, 1986). It may well also increase perceptions of the fairness of proceedings. Thus, when the court hears from offenders' family and friends, fairness dictates that the people who actually were injured should be allowed to speak (Sumner, 1987).

Victim participation may also promote psychological healing by helping victims to recover from the emotional trauma associated with their victimization and court experiences (Erez, 1990; Ranish & Shichor, 1985). In contrast, a criminal justice system that provides no opportunity for victims to participate may exacerbate the feelings of helplessness that often arise as a result of the crime (Kilpatrick & Otto, 1987, p. 19). Victim participation may also promote the rehabilitation of the offender, who upon hearing the victim's statement must confront the reality of the harm that he or she inflicted on the victim (Talbert, 1988). Later in the chapter we examine the validity of these claims.

Arguments Against Victim Input

The objections to victim participation at sentencing range from assumptions that vengeful justice will result to predictions that the system will grind to a halt as a result of the additional time needed to process cases if victims provide input (Erez, 1990, 1994). Some argue that allowing victims to participate will expose the court to precisely the public pressure from which it should properly be insulated (Rubel, 1986), or will result in substituting the victim's "subjective" approach for the allegedly "objective" one practiced by the court (Victorian Sentencing Committee, 1988). The legal profession, in particular, has found the prospect of allowing material that may be highly emotional in the courtroom unacceptable. Critics argue that a victim's input into sentencing is "irrelevant to any legitimate sentencing factor, lacks probative value in a system of public prosecution, and is likely to be highly prejudicial" (Hellerstein, 1989, p. 429).

Permission to deliver a VIS in person—exercising victim allocution right—has been regarded as particularly objectionable, as an oral version in a very serious crime may be very moving for the judge or jury, and this may increase sentence severity or promote sentencing disparity.[3] Critics argued that similar cases might end·up being disposed of differently depending on whether a VIS is available and how persuasive the victim is (Grabosky, 1987, p. 147).[4] Legal professionals and scholars also argued that victim input violates the fundamental principles of the adversarial legal system, which, as previously noted, do not recognize the victim as a party to proceedings (Ashworth, 1993, 2002). Including victims would transform the trial between the state and the defendant into a tripartite court proceeding (state—victim—offender). Such practices, it was argued, belong only in so-called continental legal systems with adhesive prosecution or *partie civil* procedures, or to restorative justice schemes.[5]

Prosecutors sometimes object to victim input in sentencing because they fear that their control over cases will be undermined, with the consequence that court outcomes will become more unpredictable (Davis, Kunreuther, & Connick, 1984), and the system will be overburdened (Australian Law Reform Commission, 1988). Others argue that victim input is redundant or adds very little information that is not already available to the court, given that the criminal law already takes into account the harm done to the victim through its charging decisions and submissions from the prosecution at sentencing (Hellerstein, 1989; Paciocco, 1999). Moreover, as the law typically punishes offenders for harm that was foreseeable, critics argue that only effects on the "typical" victim should be considered (Victorian Sentencing Committee, 1988) and that the offender should not be held accountable for unforeseen consequences—for example, the effects of the crime on victims who turned out to be particularly vulnerable in ways unforeseen by the perpetrator (Ashworth, 1993).

It has also been argued that VIS may create unrealistic expectations in victims that are not or cannot be met (Fattah, 1986). For example, if a judge imposes a sentence that is at odds with the victim's wishes as expressed in a VIS, the victim may become resentful (Henderson, 1985). Although victims are not obliged to, they may feel compelled to submit a statement, and the process may be traumatic for victims who do not want offenders to know the extent of the harm they inflicted (Australian Law Reform Commission, 1988). Victims who do submit impact statements may feel as if they are responsible for the sentencing outcome and some may prefer not to assume this responsibility (Reeves & Mulley, 2000). In addition, it has been suggested that filling out a VIS raises the prospect in the victim's mind that his or her "submission" on sentencing will carry the same weight as any representations by the prosecution or defense counsel. When the court ignores a victim's sentence recommendation, the victim may feel that submitting a statement was in vain.

Other objections to victim input are based on ideological grounds. Opponents allege that any gain for victims constitutes a loss for defendants. They argue that victims have been exploited by a conservative "law-and-order" ideology, whose real goal is to get tough on offenders, not to help victims (Henderson, 1985), suggesting that the reform is just a euphemistic label to camouflage efforts to make sentencing harsher. The true intention behind the victim rights rhetoric, it has been suggested, is to mobilize hostility toward offenders or to demonstrate the leniency of the sentencing system. Critics depicted victims as merely "pawns" used in these politics of law and order. Because victims were portrayed as vindictive and motivated by a desire to maximize sentence severity, some scholars have attributed recent increases in punitiveness to the movement to grant victims participatory rights. A recurrent theme emerging in objections to victim input involves concern for defendants' rights.[6] The argument is advanced that victim input reflects a desire to strengthen the prosecution and therefore undermine the interests of defendants.[7]

The Context of the Debate and the Ensuing Research

Because the campaign to allow victim input into sentencing encountered such strong opposition from the legal profession, the justification for the reform was refashioned from its original purpose—advocating victim voice as a measure of healing (the expressive aim of VIS; see Roberts & Erez, 2004)—to emphasizing its potential to help judges impose sentences commensurate with the (intended) harm (the instrumental aim).[8] The time was ripe to connect and jointly address victim input and the quantum of sentences: In criminology, there was disenchantment with the idea of rehabilitation as the basis for punishment, and calls to replace it with "just deserts" philosophy were growing. According to just deserts principles, the punishment should be based on the offender's level of culpability and the extent of harm inflicted on the victim. Victim input, it was suggested, could be useful in this regard by providing full details on the extent of injury. In victimology, ample evidence accumulated on "secondary victimization" of crime victims—their wounds, frustration, and alienation from a justice system in which they had no voice, except as witnesses at trial. The framing of the VIS as a tool to help the court in meting out "justice" led to sometimes contradictory justifications for victim voice in sentencing, resulting in what has been described as "incoherence." It also redirected the discussion to questions such as whether the VIS fulfills its intended purpose, whether it meets the needs of the court, or what are its impacts on sentencing. More recent critics, however, claim that the goal of improving victim welfare, or the therapeutic benefits of having a voice—the original purpose of the VIS reform—is merely rhetoric, if not an illusion (Sanders et al., 2001).

RESEARCH FINDINGS ON THE EFFECTS OF VICTIM INPUT INTO SENTENCING

Research provides answers to some of the issues raised in the debate about victim input into sentencing. It suggests that (a) victim participation does not clog the criminal justice system by protracting the time taken to arrive at an adjudication, (b) victim participation does not necessarily result in harsher punishment of offenders, (c) victim participation has the potential to increase victim satisfaction with the judicial system, and (d) the implementation of victim input laws is still problematic, and many victims do not benefit from these reforms. First, however, we briefly discuss the levels of participation and the reasons that victims offer for wishing to provide impact evidence into sentencing.

Levels of Participation

In practice, many victim-related reforms never reach victims. Victims either are unaware of their rights to participate or elect not to exercise them (Erez & Tontodonato, 1990; Hillenbrand & Smith, 1989; Villmoare & Neto, 1987). Studies also reflect considerable confusion about the nature and purpose of VIS. Victims often do not know what VIS are or claim that they did not fill out such statements when, in fact, they did (Erez & Tontodonato, 1992; Erez, Roeger, & Morgan, 1994). This may be because victims are questioned by a seemingly endless array of people and may become confused about the purpose of particular interviews. Some jurisdictions have overcome this problem by having victims prepare their own VIS rather than merely provide the information to the investigating officer (the counterpart of probation or victim assistance officers in other countries).

One observation applicable to victim impact schemes in all common law jurisdictions is that only a minority of all victims participate by submitting a VIS. Based on research in England and Wales, Sanders et al. (2001) report a submission rate of 30%, while judges in surveys conducted in Canada reported seeing a VIS on average in 11% of cases proceeding for sentencing (Roberts & Edgar, 2006). The likelihood of an impact statement being submitted will depend greatly on the nature and seriousness of the crime as well as many other variables. Analysis of court files and surveys of criminal justice professionals such as prosecutors and judges confirm that most sentencing hearings take place without the benefit of an impact statement from the victim. There are a number of explanations for this state of affairs.

First, not all victims wish to submit a statement, or indeed to have any contact with the justice system. Some victims may be quite satisfied that the prosecutor will accurately describe the harm inflicted on the victim. Second, the justice system may fail in its duty to inform victims of their right to submit a statement. Third, issues such as plea bargaining may play a role. If the prosecution and defense agree to place a joint sentencing submission before the court, sentencing may take place before the system has had a chance to inform the victim. If this is the case, unless an impact statement was submitted early in the proceedings and filed for later use at the time of sentencing, the opportunity to provide input is lost. It is also clear that part of the low rate of participation arises from the fact that many victims of property crimes see little benefit or no need to submit an impact statement. This explains the fact that the submission rate is much lower for property crimes than crimes of violence.

The nature of the implementation of VIS schemes may also affect the participation rate. To the extent that victims learn of their right to submit a VIS only if the police or court officials tell them, victims' involvement depends on official support for such reforms. Criminal justice officials sometimes believe that VIS are redundant and contain no new information (Paciocco, 1999). Prosecutors may be reluctant to have the judge know the full impact of the crime for fear that it would jeopardize a negotiated plea (Corns, 1988) and may be skeptical about the extent to which judges consider victims' views (Davis & Smith, 1994; Erez et al., 1994). In addition, there may be practical problems in obtaining a VIS or an ideological resistance to giving victims a voice in criminal justice decisions, despite legislative authority to do so (e.g., Hellerstein, 1989; Victorian Sentencing Committee, 1988).

Reasons for Submitting a Victim Statement at Sentencing

Findings with respect to this issue vary across jurisdictions. Hoyle, Cape, Morgan, & Sanders (1998) found that the majority of the victims in their study in England and Wales explained that they had submitted a VIS for expressive reasons (i.e., to communicate a message of impact to the court). Slightly more than half cited an instrumental reason, namely the desire to influence the outcome of the sentencing hearing. In the survey of crime victims in South Australia, Erez et al. (1994) report that the main reason that victims cited for providing information for a VIS was to ensure that justice was done (cited by more than two thirds of the respondents). The most recent Canadian research found that victims were twice as likely to cite "want court to understand effect of crime" than "thought statement would affect sentence" as a reason for submitting a VIS (Prairie Research Associates, 2004). The other reasons cited included communicating the impact of the crime to the offender, and in order to discharge a civic duty. Clearly, there are many reasons why victims submit an impact statement. Indirect evidence also suggests that victims may be interested in participating for the purpose of "justice," even though it means reliving the experience of victimization. A study in Australia found that victims of serious crimes, in particular, were interested in receiving information concerning the case at all stages of the process (Gardner, 1990).

It is also apparent that the extent to which victims understand the purpose and function of a VIS varies considerably, and this level of understanding may affect submission rates. Some VIS forms may contribute to confusion among victims. For example, one Canadian VIS guide states, "The Victim Impact Statement *may* be used during the sentencing hearing," and "the judge will decide whether or not to consider the victim impact statement when determining the sentence" (see Roberts, 2003). In fact, there is a statutory obligation on judges to consider the VIS at sentencing in that country. Not surprisingly, research has found that some participants were unclear as to whether judges are required to actually read the statements that they had prepared (Meredith & Paquette, 2001). In addition to holding misperceptions about the purpose of a VIS, many victims are simply confused about the nature of their input (e.g., Erez & Tontodonato, 1990). The fact that some victims want to influence sentencing is not unexpected; indeed it is a natural reaction, reflecting widespread public confusion over the role of the victim in the sentencing process and the nature of a criminal proceeding under the adversarial system. But victims may well accept the role currently assigned to them if it is explained thoroughly, with sensitivity, and by the relevant authorities.

The Effect of Victim Input on Criminal Justice Administration

Researchers have evaluated the effects of victim input in many ways, through the analysis of criminal justice statistics as well as surveys of criminal justice professionals such as prosecutors and judges. Research in jurisdictions that allow victim participation indicates that including victims in the criminal justice process does not cause delays or additional expense (Davis & Smith, 1994; Erez et al., 1994; Roberts & Edgar, 2006) and that very few court officials believe that victim input creates or exacerbates problems or slows down the proceedings (Hillenbrand & Smith, 1989). Court officials (prosecutors, defense attorneys, as well as judges) even in very busy jurisdictions generally view victim input positively (e.g., Henley, Davis, & Smith, 1994; Roberts & Edgar, 2006).

Perceptions of the Judiciary

The views of judges are particularly relevant to the debate, as they are best placed to know whether victim impact statements contain probative or extraneous information. Surveys of the judiciary demonstrate that most judges see a benefit to receiving crime impact information directly from the victim by means of a victim impact statement. Although much of the information in VIS should already be reflected in evidence adduced at trial or prosecutorial submissions at sentencing, at times VIS may provide additional information useful to the judge when determining a sentence. According to surveys in Canada and Australia, most judges acknowledge that VIS contain information that is relevant to the purposes of sentencing (D'Avignon, 2001; Erez & Rogers, 1999; Roberts & Edgar, 2006). Studies of judges in the United States and Australia suggest that judges find VIS helpful for learning how victims are affected by crime (Davis & Smith, 1994). Judges in one study also indicated that without VIS they would have a less accurate idea of the true impact of the crime on the victim (Davis & Smith, 1994).

In most jurisdictions victims are discouraged from making specific sentencing recommendations in their VIS. Yet judges report that they do encounter sentence recommendations in VIS (Roberts & Edgar, 2006). The presence of sentence recommendations suggests that the form used, or the information conveyed to victims who submit a statement, may be at fault. If victims are encouraged to tell the court anything they wish, the victim may lose sight of the expressive, communicative function of the idea and see the statement in instrumental terms: to influence the court with respect to the sentence imposed. The justice system therefore needs to specify clearly the format, content, and exact use of a VIS. However, although judges report that they do sometimes read such recommendations, they appear to have little difficulty in setting the victim's views in this regard aside. Professional judges are trained to ignore testimony that has prejudicial but not probative value.[9]

In short, the most critical constituency at this stage of the criminal process—sentencing judges—perceive considerable utility in VIS. This is particularly true for crimes of violence, crimes in which property was stolen or damaged, or offenses in which the impact on the victim was disproportionate or unusual. Furthermore, judges in Australia reported that VIS not only educated them about the effects of crimes on victims but sometimes benefited the defendant—for example, when the information disclosed that the injury was not as severe as one might expect from the charge of conviction (Erez & Rogers, 1999).[10]

The VIS also creates an opportunity for the court to acknowledge the victim as the aggrieved party and to communicate state recognition of the harm sustained by the victim. If the victim is in court, the sentencing judge also has the opportunity to speak directly to the victim, validating his or her harm. Victims who hear their own words quoted in judges' sentencing remarks appreciate the validation and report being more satisfied with the justice system (Erez, 1990). As for the criticism that some victims use the opportunity to criticize or attack the defendant, judges who witness abuse of the right to communicate have the authority to intervene and stop the abusive communication, whether it is from the victim or from the defendant (Roberts & Erez, 2004). Judges are commonly aware of their power to acknowledge victims as the injured person, and that quoting the VIS in sentencing remarks enhances victims' sense of being recognized as victims. Judges appreciate the therapeutic value such recognition has, and many make use of it in court (Erez & Rogers, 1999; Roberts & Edgar, 2006).

Validity of VIS

Although defense lawyers occasionally express concern that victim statements are inaccurate, research indicates that, in fact, victim statements seldom include inflammatory or prejudicial material (Erez et al., 1994; Henley et al., 1994; Roberts & Edgar, 2006). On the rare occasions when this occurs, the prosecution can edit the statement to prevent the inflammatory phrases from coming to the attention of the court. Another erroneous criticism of the VIS is that victims often exaggerate the level of harm that they sustained. This appears to happen only rarely, and when it does, judges and prosecutors report that these exaggerations involve financial matters, not emotional or mental suffering (Erez & Rogers, 1999).

There is conflicting research as to whether impact statements improve the quality of justice by influencing restitution awards (Erez et al., 1994; Hillenbrand & Smith, 1989). Research has found that most judges and prosecutors believe it does. These findings are consistent with research in England suggesting that compensation is more likely to be ordered if it was mentioned in court proceedings (Shapland et al., 1985). Because prosecutors may be unaware of victims' preferences, or for various reasons may fail to convey them to the court, allowing victims to express their wishes directly by means of a VIS may be the only way to guarantee that the sentencing authority learns of their requests. Research in Australia, however, did not find any increase in the rate of restitution or compensation orders following the introduction of VIS because, unless offenders have means to pay, judges are precluded from imposing restitution or compensation orders (Erez et al., 1994).

The Impact of Victim
Input on Sentencing Practices

As noted, critics of VIS have claimed that the presence of these statements will tip the scales against the defendant, resulting in harsher sentencing patterns. Research largely refutes assumptions that victim participation results in harsher sentences for defendants. Studies suggest that sentences are determined predominantly on the basis of legal considerations such as the seriousness of the offense and the offender's criminal record (Davis & Smith, 1994; Erez & Tontodonato, 1990; Erez & Roeger, 1995). Victim participation either has no effect on sentence severity or cuts both ways in the sense that it sometimes results in a more lenient disposition. As a practical matter, VIS will have limited relevance in the U.S. federal system or in jurisdictions that employ a determinate sentencing scheme (Hellerstein, 1989). Judges and prosecutors in one study (Erez & Rogers, 1999) reported that VIS result in harsher sentences in some cases (e.g., when the intended harm was particularly serious or the crime was especially heinous) and in less severe sentences in other cases (e.g., when no harm occurred or when the harm was much less than would be expected). This may in part explain why aggregate studies (e.g., Erez & Tontodonato, 1990) do not find any effect of victims' participation on sentencing trends (Erez & Roeger, 1995).

With regard to victims' views on sentencing, a study of impact statements submitted in sexual assault cases found that the court was most likely to recognize the desires of the victim when they were consistent with the court's own view of the appropriate sentence. This study refutes the stereotype that all victims thirst for vengeance. It revealed that the court was *more* punitive than victims and was likely to ignore victims' desire for probation sentences over imprisonment (Walsh, 1986; see also Sherman & Strang, 2003). Moreover, once a prison sentence was imposed, the victim's opinion regarding sentencing did not significantly affect the length of term (Erez & Tontodonato, 1990). Other studies reaffirm that victim participation does not result in more severe sentences. One study that used an experimental design to examine the effect of VIS on sentences found that the use of VIS did not result in harsher sentences for offenders or increase the likelihood of incarceration as opposed to probation. Instead, the researchers concluded that the seriousness of the charge, rather than the harm described in the VIS, most affected the sentence imposed (Davis & Smith, 1994).

In contrast to victims' rights to file a written statement, one study of victims' right to speak, or allocate, in court found that it was victims' presence rather than their oral delivery that had an effect on the length of sentence. Typically, victims who attend court during sentencing tend to be involved in many phases of the trial process, thus providing a constant (and in our view, salutary) reminder to the judge that an individual and not the state is the principal injured party (Erez & Tontodonato, 1990). When a case proceeds to sentencing, the decision has already been made, so allocution is unlikely to affect the outcome. In this sense, the right to allocution is more symbolic than effective. By the time the victim comes to court, a well-prepared judge has already received the probation report, and there is little room for modification of the court's intended decision. An emotional appeal to the court by the victim cannot carry more weight than facts and sentencing precedent (Villmoare & Neto, 1987, p. 37). In contrast, because the written VIS is submitted *prior to* sentencing, it has a greater chance to influence sentencing, if at all (Erez & Tontodonato, 1990).

The Effect of VIS on Victims' Welfare and Satisfaction With the Justice System

Findings on the effect[11] of providing input into sentencing are inconsistent with respect to the issue of victim welfare and satisfaction and suggest, at best, modest effects. The lack of evidence on satisfaction, however, may simply reflect a problematic implementation of the law. One study found that filing VIS usually results in increased satisfaction with the outcome (Erez & Tontodonato, 1992), while a study of rape victims found that victim participation generally increases victims' satisfaction (Kelly, 1984). Another study that randomly assigned victims' cases to various treatments found that VIS had no effect on victims' feelings of involvement or satisfaction with the criminal justice process or its outcome (Davis & Smith, 1994). There was no effect of VIS on satisfaction levels. Similarly, studies of the VIS program in Canada and in Australia (Erez et al., 1994) revealed that victims who submit an impact statement are not necessarily more satisfied with the outcome or with the criminal justice system. The Australian study found that lack of evidence may be related to the problematic implementation of the law; many victims did not realize that the purpose of the interview they had was to gather input that would be provided to the judge. In some cases, filing VIS heightens victims' expectations that they will influence the outcome. When that does not happen, victims may be less satisfied than those who do not submit a statement (Erez et al., 1994). In contrast, a comparative study of victims in the continental criminal justice systems (which allow victims a party status and significant input into the proceedings) suggests that victims who participated as subsidiary prosecutors or acted as private prosecutors were more satisfied than victims who did not participate (Erez & Bienkowska, 1993). These differences suggest that in jurisdictions in which victims have more input into proceedings, levels of satisfaction are higher.

Research on victims' involvement in parole proceedings indicates that participation at this stage may enhance the image of the criminal justice system in the eyes of the crime victim. One study found that many victims who testified in parole hearings were dissatisfied with the criminal justice system's handling of their cases to that point because they had been excluded from earlier proceedings. These victims especially appreciated the opportunity to be heard by parole authorities (Parsonage, Bernat, & Helfgott, 1992).[12]

The effect of victim participation on victims' distress levels has not been systematically studied. Those few studies conducted were limited to rape victims, and their results are inconclusive (Lurigio & Resick, 1990). The only study that has examined the effect of VIS on victims' distress levels (Tontodonato & Erez, 1994) suggests that although distress is not directly influenced by filing a VIS, opportunities for such participation nonetheless may be important because they may affect whether a request for restitution is awarded (Erez & Tontodonato, 1990). Restitution, in turn, influences victims' perception of equity and their satisfaction with justice (Erez & Tontodonato, 1992; see also Boers & Sessar, 1991).

Research has identified three major factors that increase victims' overall satisfaction with the justice system and reduce their trauma. They include (a) procedural justice concerns such as whether the victim had the opportunity to be heard, and whether he or she was treated with respect and informed of key developments in their cases (see Wemmers, 1996); (b) the final decision of the court (e.g., whether the victims received financial compensation); and (c) whether there was an admission of guilt or request for forgiveness from the perpetrator (see Orth, 2002, 2003; Wemmers, 1996). These variables were found to be more predictive of victim satisfaction than the severity of punishment imposed. This research suggests that victims' interests or concerns relative to proceedings are not simply to generate a severe sentence but pertain to the court addressing a broad range of issues that are within its purview, issues that a well-implemented VIS program can facilitate. Finally, research with victims of violent crime in several countries has revealed that victims appreciate judicial recognition of the harm they sustained (Erez,

1999; Roberts & Edgar, 2006). Judicial acknowledgment may be expressed in a direct statement if the victim is present in court at sentencing, or it may be articulated in the reasons for sentence. Judges appear aware of the importance of this validation of the harm: a survey of the judiciary found that most reported acknowledging victim harm directly by addressing the victim in court or indirectly by citing victim impact in their reasons for sentencing (Roberts & Edgar, 2006).

RESTORATIVE JUSTICE, THERAPEUTIC JURISPRUDENCE, AND THE VIS

Victims have benefited greatly from the rise—worldwide—of interest in restorative justice (see Dignan, 2005, for discussion). This perspective offers an alternative to the conventional retributive model of criminal justice, and one that assigns a very prominent role to the victim. Victim rights and restorative justice are not interchangeable;[13] indeed, some scholars such as Zedner (2002) have questioned "whether, and how far, restorative justice is about serving the interests of victims" (p. 447). In our view, victims' rights and restorative justice are best viewed as related initiatives with overlapping interests. The importance of victim voice in proceedings on the one hand, and victims' role in the reentry of offenders[14] on the other, has been increasingly recognized in justice practices. This change is due in part to victim advocates' efforts on behalf of victims, and in part to research findings that challenge prevailing beliefs and myths about victims' interests, motives, and consequences of input into sentencing.

It is impossible to characterize all victims as vengeful, forgiving, or expressive. Some victims will be outraged by what they perceive as a lenient sentence. Others may seek a noncustodial sentence accompanied by compensation, whereas the court favors imprisoning the offender. And some victims will want nothing to do with the justice system, preferring to deal with the victimization experience in their own way and time. However, it is clear that many crime victims, particularly of serious offenses,[15] are eager to describe their victimization experiences. They want a voice to communicate a sense of the harm they sustained more than they wish to influence the sentence (Erez, 1999). In this context, the VIS can serve as a restorative justice element in adversarial proceedings, facilitating supervised communication between victims and offenders.

The idea that VIS can be recognized as injecting a restorative element into adversarial proceedings has precedence and support. The National Institute of Justice (NIJ) Web site lists the VIS as an example of restorative justice practices. It refers to it as "one of the most effective means to communicate the 'voice of the victim' throughout the criminal and juvenile justice systems," listing it together with restorative justice remedies or procedures such as restitution, sentencing circles, community service, family group conferencing, victim-offender mediation, victim impact panels, and victim impact classes. The therapeutic value of the VIS is similarly evident in official documents that state,

> It is significant for victims' healing that the judge acknowledge at the time of sentencing that victims have been injured, solicit specific information from victims on the crime's impact on their lives, and explain the terms of the offender's sentence. (U.S. Department of Justice, 1998, p. 108)

The inclusion of the VIS among restorative justice practices underscores its significance for improving victims' well-being. Beyond its symbolic value, the VIS is situated at the apex of the criminal justice process, when key courtroom participants determine the disposition of the case. As such, victim voice can trigger helpful reactions, and it can evoke appropriate emotions that serve therapeutic

ends. The emerging field of therapeutic jurisprudence,[16] which focuses on the law's impact on the emotional life and psychological well-being of the people its proceedings or remedies affect, has considered the VIS as an important reform that can promote the welfare of those engaged in it (see Wiebe, 1996; Herman, 2003).

The restricted opportunity for victim-offender exchanges in adversarial proceedings further highlights the importance of allowing and encouraging victims to deliver their statements in person. The victim is ideally placed to sensitize the offender to the consequences of the crime. Presentation of the VIS by the victim is preferable to having prosecutors convey impact information, as the offender would be able to relate to what a victim conveys more than to impact details presented by a legal professional who has the role of prosecuting the case. As most victims and offenders are laypersons rather than criminal justice professionals, and are often unfamiliar with its legal jargon, a direct appeal by the victim to the offender may be a more effective route to encourage offenders to accept responsibility.

Not all victims who are present in court during sentencing will wish to exercise the right to speak. Fear of public speaking, fear of the defendant, or just not feeling the need to express oneself may be some of the reasons for which victims would be reluctant to speak in open court. A sizeable proportion of victims nevertheless would wish to make use of this right and communicate with the defendant (see, e.g., Villmoare & Neto, 1987). Allowing victim-defendant communication at sentencing may serve as a step toward making the adversarial process more restorative in nature, thereby increasing defendants' awareness of the consequences of the crime on the victim. Research in various countries has shown that victims have an interest in communicating with the offender. A VIS delivered by the victim is more likely to induce a defendant to apologize and accept responsibility.

Victims may also feel empowered by their ability to confer or withhold forgiveness, and victims' aggressive feelings are likely to be attenuated following genuine requests for forgiveness (see Petrucci, 2002). When victims and offenders know each other, victims sometimes prefer (or request, in jurisdictions that permit victim statements at sentencing) a lenient sentence. Also in crimes involving strangers, where victims are more likely to express punitive sentiments, providing an occasion for victim-defendant exchanges benefits both: it increases victims' familiarity with the offender and the offender's circumstances, and it enhances offenders' understanding of the consequences of their acts. Victims may become more understanding if they hear the offender's story, particularly if it is preceded or accompanied by the expression of remorse, which a moving VIS may elicit (see Roberts & Erez, 2004, for discussion).

The VIS may well have therapeutic potential for defendants as well as their victims—for instance, by providing offenders with a concrete and unmediated picture of the harm their actions have caused, and an opportunity for apology following the VIS presentation. The option to formally submit a VIS should be considered as an occasion for communication between the victim and his or her violator and should become a vital legislated right. Victims who feel the need to express their harm should be afforded the option to submit a VIS, even in circumstances that may render the VIS "irrelevant" for sentencing purposes, such as a negotiated plea or a mandatory sentence.[17]

CONCLUSION

Victim participatory rights are now recognized as an important component of criminal justice proceedings. Reports from practitioners indicate that few administrative problems,

serious defense challenges, longer trials, or harsher sentences result from victim participation. Similarly, there is no evidence that incarceration levels in countries that allow victim input have increased due to victims' participation in proceedings. However, because victim participation in sentencing decisions challenges traditions and established patterns within the criminal courts, these rights often amount to lip service or encounter resistance in their implementation. Legislative reforms typically lack remedies for noncompliance. Victims' participation at times depends on the luck of the draw, or whether a victim encounters criminal justice personnel who support victims' rights (see Douglas, Laster, & Inglis, 1994; Kury, Kaiser, & Teske, 1994). Although legislatures were probably motivated to adopt victims' reforms as a way of ensuring victim cooperation, ultimately the decision of whether to allow or require victim participation largely rests on subjective moral judgments (Erez, 1994). Clearly, victims' participation is viewed skeptically by many in the legal community (e.g., Hall, 1991; Hellerstein, 1989) and the social science community (e.g., Davis & Smith, 1994; Sanders et al., 2001) because of fears that if only some victims avail themselves of these rights, the treatment of defendants in the criminal justice system will become more disparate.

There is a need for further research on the effect of victims' reforms. Even if such research confirmed that victims' rights pose no great danger to the system or to its defendants and resulted in recommendations to put "teeth" in such statutes (presumably by creating cases of actions against those who fail to notify victims of their rights, or to implement their rights in practice), such recommendations would probably never be adopted. Creating rights with remedies in the event that rights are violated would rupture the fragile alliance of victims' advocates, legislators, and prosecutors. As a result, victims are likely to remain where they are, hoping to work with sympathetic criminal justice personnel who will inform them of their rights and help ensure that these rights are respected.

Research has demonstrated that the right to participate in proceedings, including the right to be heard at various points in the criminal justice process, is important to many crime victims. Most victims are interested in participating in the justice process, and they want an opportunity to tell, in their own words, the way that the crime has affected them. Court procedures rarely provide victims with an occasion to construct a coherent and meaningful narrative (Herman, 2003). The VIS represents a means to provide victims with a voice at sentencing and allows them to express the impact of the crime on their lives. In adversarial legal systems, the VIS is the only tool by which victims can articulate their suffering, identify their concerns, and communicate the way their lives have been affected by the crime.

As legal cultures are transformed, and victims are increasingly perceived as a legitimate party in proceedings (see Cassell 1999; Pizzi, 1999), forms of victim input such as the VIS can become a routine practice of injecting restorative justice elements into adversarial justice systems. Ultimately, it is the underlying value system and ideology, not data, that will determine whether victims are meaningfully integrated into proceedings. The road to incorporating a victim voice in adversarial proceedings has not been smooth (see U.S. Department of Justice, 1998). Attempts to integrate victims outside the adversarial justice system through restorative justice schemes have worked for some victims but they have not served those who wish to remain within the protective structure of adversarial systems.

Perceptions of victims as "barbarians at the gates"[18] or arguments about alleged violation of "defendants' rights" should no longer be used in unsympathetic, if not hostile,

adversarial legal cultures to deny victims the right to be heard and to participate.[19] A careful reading of research findings requires the position that victims do not belong in adversarial proceedings be reassessed, as should the notion that restorative justice practices and adversarial principles cannot coexist when it comes to integrating victim voice in sentencing (see Erez, 2004).

REFERENCES

Ashworth, A. (1993, July). Victim impact statements and sentencing. *Criminal Law Review,* 498–509.

Ashworth, A. (2000). Victims' rights, defendants' rights and criminal procedure. In A. Crawford & J. Goodey (Eds.), *Integrating a victim perspective in criminal justice: International debates* (pp. 185–204). Aldershot: Dartmouth.

Ashworth, A. (2002). Restorative rights and restorative justice. *British Journal of Criminology, 42,* 578–595.

Australian Law Reform Commission. (1988). *Sentencing.* Report No. 94. Canberra: Attorney General's Publication Service.

Boers, K., & Sessar, K. (1991). Do people really want punishment? On the relationship between acceptance of restitution, needs for punishment and fear of crime. In K. Sessar & H.-J. Kerner (Eds.), *Developments in crime and crime control research: German studies on victims, offenders and the public.* New York: Springer-Verlag.

Braithwaite, J. (2002). Restorative justice and therapeutic jurisprudence. *Criminal Law Bulletin, 38,* 244–262.

Bureau of Justice Statistics. (1983). *Reports to the nation on crime and justice.* Washington, DC: Institute for Law and Social Research.

Cannavele, F. (1975). *Witness cooperation.* New York: Lexington.

Cassell, P. G. (1999). Barbarians at the gates? A reply to the critics of the Victims' Rights Amendment. *Utah Law Review, 2,* 479–544.

Cole, M. (2003). *Perceptions of the use of victim impact statements in Canada: A survey of Crown Counsel in Ontario.* Unpublished master's thesis, University of Ottawa, Ottawa.

Corns, C. (1988). Offender and victims. In D. Biles (Ed.), *Current Australian trends in corrections* (pp. 204–216). Sydney: Federation Press.

D'Avignon, J. (2001). *Victim impact statements: A judicial perspective.* Winnipeg: University of Manitoba.

Davis, R., Kunreuther, F., & Connick, E. (1984). Expanding the victim role in the criminal court dispositional process: The results of an experiment. *Journal of Criminal Law and Criminology, 75,* 491–505.

Davis, R., & Smith, B. (1994). Victim impact statements and victim satisfaction: An unfulfilled promise? *Journal of Criminal Justice, 22,* 1–12.

Department of Justice Canada. (1990). *Victim impact statements in Canada, 7: Summary of the findings.* Ottawa: Department of Justice Canada, Research and Development Directorate.

Dignan, J. (2005). *Understanding victims and restorative justice.* Maidenhead: Open University Press.

Douglas, R., Laster, K., & Inglis, N. (1994). Victim of efficiency: Criminal justice reform in Australia. *International Review of Victimology, 3,* 95–110.

Edwards, I. (2001). Victim participation in sentencing: The problems of incoherence. *Howard Journal of Criminal Justice, 40,* 30–54.

Eisenstein, J., & Jacob, H. (1977). *Felonious justice: An organizational analysis of criminal courts.* Lanham, MD: University Press of America.

Erez, E. (1989). The impact of victimology on criminal justice policy. *Criminal Justice Policy Review, 3,* 236–256.

Erez, E. (1990). Victim participation in sentencing: Rhetoric and reality. *Journal of Criminal Justice, 18,* 19–31.

Erez, E. (1994). Victim participation in sentencing: And the debate goes on . . . *International Review of Victimology, 3,* 17–32.

Erez, E. (1999, July). Who is afraid of the big bad victim: Victim impact statements as victim empowerment and enhancement of justice. *Criminal Law Review,* 545–556.

Erez, E. (2004). Victim voice, impact statements and sentencing: Integrating restorative justice and therapeutic jurisprudence principles in adversarial proceedings. *Criminal Law Bulletin, 40,* 483–500.

Erez, E., & Bienkowska, E. (1993). Victim participation in proceedings and satisfaction with justice in the Continental systems: The case of Poland. *Journal of Criminal Justice, 21,* 47–60.

Erez, E., & Roeger, L. (1995). Crime impact vs. victim impact: Evaluation of victim impact statements in South Australia. *Criminology Australia, 6,* 3–8.

Erez, E., Roeger, L., & Morgan, F. (1994). Office of Crime Statistics, South Australian Attorney General's Department, *Victim impact statements in South Australia: An evaluation.* Adelaide: Office of Crime Statistics, South Australian Attorney General's Department.

Erez, E., & Rogers, L. (1999). Victim impact statements and sentencing outcomes and processes. *British Journal of Criminology, 39,* 216–239.

Erez, E., & Tontodonato, P. (1990). The effect of victim participation in sentencing on sentence outcome. *Criminology, 28,* 451–474.

Erez, E., & Tontodonato, P. (1992). Victim participation in sentencing and satisfaction with justice. *Justice Quarterly, 9,* 393–415.

Fattah, E. (1986). *From crime policy to victim policy.* New York: Macmillan.

Gardner, J. (1990). *Victims and criminal justice.* Adelaide: Office of Crime Statistics, Department of the Attorney General.

Grabosky, P. (1987). Victims in the criminal justice system. In G. Zdenkowski, C. Ronalds, & M. Richardson (Eds.), *The criminal injustice system* (Vol. 2, pp. 143–157). Sydney: Pluto Press.

Hagan, J. (1982). Victims before the law: A study of victims' involvement in the criminal justice process. *Journal of Criminal Law and Criminology, 73,* 317–329.

Hall, D. (1991). Victim voices in criminal court: The need for restraint. *American Criminal Law Review, 28,* 233–266.

Hellerstein, D. (1989). Victim impact statement: Reform or reprisal? *American Criminal Law Review, 27,* 391–430.

Henderson, L. (1985). The wrongs of victims' rights. *Stanford Law Review, 27,* 391–430.

Henley, M., Davis, R., & Smith, B. (1994). The reactions of prosecutors and judges to victim impact statements. *International Review of Victimology, 3,* 83–93.

Herman, J. (2003). The mental health of crime victims: Impact of legal intervention. *Journal of Traumatic Stress, 16,* 159–166.

Herman, S., & Wasserman, C. (2001). A role for victims in offender re-entry. *Crime and Delinquency, 47,* 428–445.

Hillenbrand, S., & Smith, B. (1989). *Victim rights legislation: An assessment of its impact on criminal justice practitioners and victims.* Washington, DC: American Bar Association.

Hoyle, C., Cape, C., Morgan, R., & Sanders, A. (1998). *Evaluation of the "one stop shop" and victim statement pilot projects.* London: Home Office Research Development and Statistics Directorate.

Joutsen, M. (1994). Victim participation in proceedings and sentencing in Europe. *International Review of Victimology, 3,* 57–67.

Justice Committee on the Role of the Victim in Criminal Justice. (1998). *Victims in criminal justice: Report of the Justice Committee on the Role of the Victim in Criminal Justice.* London: Justice.

Kelly, D. (1984). Victims' perceptions of criminal justice. *Pepperdine Law Review, 11,* 15–22.

Kelly, D. (1987). Victims. *Wayne Law Review, 34,* 69–86.

Kidd, R., & Chayet, E. (1984). Why victims fail to report: The psychology of criminal victimization. *Journal of Social Issues, 40,* 34–50.

Kilpatrick, D., & Otto, R. (1987). Constitutionally guaranteed participation in criminal justice proceedings for victims: Potential effects of psychological functioning. *Wayne Law Review, 34,* 7–28.

Kury, H., Kaiser, M., & Teske, R. (1994). The position of the victim in criminal procedure: Results of a German study. *International Review of Victimology, 3,* 69–81.

Lurigio, A., & Resick, P. (1990). Healing the psychological wounds of criminal victimization: Predicting postcrime distress and recovery. In A. Lurigio, W. Skogan, & R. Davis (Eds.), *Victims of crime: Problems, policies and programs* (pp. 50–68). Newbury Park, CA: Sage Publications.

McLeod, M. (1986). Victim participation at sentencing. *Criminal Law Bulletin, 22,* 501–517.

McLeod, M. (1988). *The authorization and implementation of victim impact statements.* Washington, DC: National Institute of Justice.

Meredith, C., & Paquette, C. (2001). *Report on victim impact statement focus groups.* Ottawa: Department of Justice Canada.

Myers, B., & Arbuthnot, J. (1999). The effects of victim impact evidence on the verdicts and sentencing judgments of mock jurors. *Journal of Offender Rehabilitation, 29,* 95–112.

Orth, U. (2002). Secondary victimization of crime victims by criminal proceedings. *Social Justice Research, 15,* 313–326.

Orth, U. (2003). Punishment goals of crime victims. *Law and Human Behavior, 27,* 173–186.

Paciocco, D. (1999). *Getting away with murder: The Canadian criminal justice system.* Toronto: Irwin Law.

Parsonage, W., Bernat, F., & Helfgott, J. (1992). Victim impact testimony and Pennsylvania's parole decision-making process: A pilot study. *Criminal Justice Policing Review, 6,* 187–206.

Petrucci, C. (2002). Apology in criminal justice setting: Evidence for including apology as an additional component in the legal system. *Behavioral Science and the Law, 20,* 337–362.

Pizzi, W. (1999). Victims' rights: Rethinking our "adversarial system." *Utah Law Review, 2,* 349–367.

Prairie Research Associates. (2004). *Multi-site survey of victims of crime and criminal justice professionals across Canada.* Ottawa: Department of Justice Canada.

President's Task Force on Victims of Crime. (1982). *Final report.* Washington, DC: Government Printing Office.

Ranish, D., & Shichor, D. (1985). The victim's role in the penal process: Recent developments in California. *Federal Probation, 49,* 50–57.

Reeves, H., & Mulley, K. (2000). The new status of victims in the UK: Opportunities and threats. In A. Crawford & J. Goodey (Eds.), *Integrating a victim perspective in criminal justice: International debates* (pp. 125–145). Aldershot: Dartmouth.

Report of the Standing Committee on Justice and Human Rights. (1998). *Victims' right: A voice, not a veto.* Ottawa: Standing Committee on Justice and Human Rights.

Roberts, J. V. (2003). Victim impact statements and the sentencing process: Enhancing communication in the courtroom. *Criminal Law Quarterly, 47,* 365–396.

Roberts, J. V., & Edgar, A. (2006). *Judicial perceptions of victim input at sentencing: Findings from surveys in Canada.* Ottawa: Department of Justice Canada.

Roberts, J. V., & Erez, E. (2004). Communication in sentencing: Exploring the expressive and the impact model of victim impact statements.

International Review of Victimology, 10, 223–244.

Rubel, H. (1986). Victim participation in sentencing proceedings. *Criminal Law Quarterly, 28,* 226–250.

Sanders, A. (2002). Victim participation in criminal justice and social exclusion. In C. Hoyle & R. Young (Eds.), *New visions of crime victims* (pp. 171–122). Oxford: Hart.

Sanders, A., Hoyle, C., Morgan, R., & Cape, E. (2001, May). Victim impact statements: Can't work, won't work. *Criminal Law Review,* 447–458.

Shapland, J., Villemore, J., & Duff, P. (1985). *Victims in the criminal justice system.* Aldershot: Gower.

Sherman, L., & Strang, H. (2003). Repairing the harm: Victims and restorative justice. *Utah Law Review,* 15–42.

Stolle, D., Winick, B. J., & Wexler, D. B. (2003). *Practicing therapeutic jurisprudence: Law as a helping profession.* Durham, NC: Carolina Academic Press.

Sumner, C. J. (1987). Victim participation in the criminal justice system. *Australia and New Zealand Journal of Criminology, 20,* 195–217.

Talbert, P. (1988). The relevance of victim impact statements to the criminal sentencing decision. *UCLA Law Review,* 36, 199–232.

Tontodonato, P., & Erez, E. (1994). Crime, punishment and victim distress. *International Review of Victimology, 3,* 33–55.

U.S. Department of Justice. (1998). *New directions from the field: Victims' rights and services for the 21st century.* Washington, DC: U.S. Department of Justice.

U.S. Department of Justice. (2002). *Victim input into plea agreements.* Washington, DC: Office of Victims of Crime.

Verdun-Jones, S., & Tijerino, A. (2004). Four models of victim involvement during plea negotiations: Bridging the gap between legal reforms and current legal practice. *Canadian Journal of Criminology and Criminal Justice, 46,* 471–500.

Victorian Sentencing Committee. (1988). *Sentencing: Report of the committee.* Melbourne: Attorney General's Department.

Villmoare, E., & Neto, V. (1987). *Victim appearances at sentencing hearings under the California Victims' Bill of Rights: Executive summary.* Washington, DC: U.S. Department of Justice.

Walsh, A. (1986). Placebo justice: Victim recommendations and offender sentences in sexual assault cases. *Journal of Criminal Law and Criminology, 77,* 1126–1171.

Wemmers, J. (1996). *Victims in the criminal justice system.* Amsterdam: Kugler.

Wiebe, R. (1996). The mental health implications of crime victims' rights. In D. Wexler & B. Winick (Eds.), *Law in a therapeutic key: Developments in therapeutic jurisprudence.* Durham, NC: Carolina Academic Press.

Zedner, L. (2002). Victims. In M. Maguire, R. Morgan, & R. Reiner (Eds.), *The Oxford handbook of criminology* (3rd ed., pp. 419–456). Oxford: Oxford University Press.

Zeigenhagen, E. (1977). *Victims, crime, and social control.* New York: Praeger.

NOTES

1. It is important to note that in some cases—particularly rape—it may be to the advantage of the victim to be spared the need to testify, which carries the likelihood of cross-examination. Indeed, this is one of the justifications for imposing a less severe sentence on offenders who plead guilty.

2. The difference between VIS and VPS is spurious. In this chapter we use the term VIS as a generic term to denote the impact materials victims submit at or for sentencing.

3. Practical concerns include the adverse impact that victim input or allocution may have on court resources and scheduling in an already overburdened judicial system. These and other themes reappear in the recent criticisms of the reform, suggesting that the phrase "victim input into sentencing" is a euphemism for increasing sentence severity, constituting exclusionary criminal justice politics that act to blur the overlap between offenders and victims (see Sanders, 2002).

4. Of course, although sentencing guidelines reduce this effect, it has always been true that defendants may receive varying sentences depending on how sympathetic, articulate, or persuasive they may be.

5. See Ashworth (2002), Sanders, Hoyle, Morgan, and Cape (2001), and Edwards (2001) for discussion.

6. See, for example, Ashworth (2000) and Edwards (2001). The argument about the violation of defendant rights may have some face value; one instinctively assumes that victims' and offenders' interests are in opposition to each other. However, there is little evidence showing that violations of defendants' rights have occurred in the VIS context, violations that the court could not prevent or, if having occurred, could not correct, as it often does with other violations of rights.

7. For further discussion, see Erez (1994) and Roberts (2003).

8. Edwards (2001) describes in detail the multiple rationales used by politicians and members of legislative bodies in the United States, England and Wales, as well as South Australia to convince relevant constituents to pass VIS legislation. Edwards argues that these multiple rationales result in incoherence and at times contradictory justifications that may create problems in implementing the ensuing reforms.

9. It may be harder for laypersons to lay aside an emotional appeal for a particular sentence. One study using simulated jurors found that subjects who heard victim impact evidence "imposed" harsher sentences (Myers & Arbuthnot, 1999). This may be an argument in favor of sentencing by judges rather than juries, but that is a story for another day.

10. Prosecutors in these studies, however, expressed skepticism about judges' interest in the impact of the crime on the victims, and whether they actually considered the VIS when sentencing (Davis & Smith, 1994; Erez & Rogers, 1999).

11. We use the term *effect*, but most of these studies are correlational in nature. Victims who submit a statement at sentencing may differ from those who decide not to participate. Differences in satisfaction levels may reflect previctimization differences in attitudes as much as the effects of submitting an impact statement.

12. Victim satisfaction also tends to increase when victims are informed about the factors that judges consider in determining sentences and know that their views are one of these considerations. Simply put, studies show that the more victims understand the sentencing process, the more satisfied they are with it (Department of Justice Canada, 1990; Erez et al., 1994; Gardner, 1990; Hagan, 1982).

13. Some victims' rights reflect a punitive, nonrestorative perspective. There is nothing restorative, for example, about the desire expressed by relatives of murder victims to witness the execution of the offender. Similarly, some restorative justice initiatives that result in a relatively mild outcome for the offender are vigorously opposed by victim rights' advocates.

14. See Herman and Wasserman (2001). Some critics have referred to the idea that victims play a role in offenders' reentry as "victims in the service of offenders" (see Ashworth, 2000).

15. Continental legal systems, such as the one used in Germany, which allow victims a role in the prosecution as adhesive prosecutor, restrict the application of this law to victims of serious crime.

16. See Stolle, Winick, and Wexler (2003). The commonality between restorative justice and therapeutic jurisprudence is explored in Braithwaite (2002).

17. See, for instance, Cole (2003) and Roberts and Edgar (2006).

18. See Cassell (1999).

19. Cassell (1999) concludes that the curriculum of law schools in the United States propagates this legal culture by the absence of any study materials related to victims' rights and interests.

The Need for Victim Impact Programming

In 1991, my sister-in-law was sexually assaulted and murdered. The impact from that horrendous crime devastated our family, turning my world upside down, and setting me on a personal mission to prevent that kind of pain from touching other innocent families.

Around that time, Tennessee's First Lady, Andrea Conte, was forming a grassroots movement to prevent crime and assist victims. I welcomed the opportunity to join her efforts to "do something" about violent crime. The group evolved into a nonprofit victim advocacy organization called You Have the Power (YHTP) and in 1998, I became its executive director. If you had told me in 1991 that I would someday be working with incarcerated men and women, I would never have believed you. I didn't like offenders. I didn't believe or care that any of them could ever change and thought them to be heartless victimizers only concerned with satisfying their own selfish impulses.

VERNA WYATT AND VALERIE CRAIG

Recidivism rates and my personal experience supported my thinking. The man who murdered my sister-in-law was a repeat offender, and most of the victims I came in contact on a daily basis were victims of repeat offenders. I knew the consequences of their actions first hand. I saw that same devastation with every victim of crime that I encountered. In my opinion, these offenders did not deserve any special attention or consideration. I wanted the offenders locked away in harsh living conditions forever so they would never have the opportunity to hurt others again. "It's what they deserve," I thought.

However I had an epiphany that drastically changed the way I thought about the incarcerated and how we should be treating them. About six years ago I met an ex-offender who, upon leaving prison, completed college, earned his master's degree, and started a nonprofit organization that ministered to at-risk youth. He was living a life that blessed the community in a powerful way. After getting to know him, I realized how our community would have suffered if he had not received a second chance and chose to make a difference.

Not long after this, the Tennessee Department of Correction Victim Liaison asked me if I would speak to a class of inmates and share my personal story of victimization. This new program incorporated victim impact education for the inmates. My first encounter of sharing my story with inmates was very powerful—not only for the inmates, but also for me. The men in that class clung to my every word. Concern showed on their faces as I spoke. Afterward, many of them apologized to me; some offered to pray for me; others asked about forgiveness. Some of them may have been conning me, but I am certain on that day my story touched the lives of those offenders in that room. I left the prison thinking if only one inmate begins to think of victims as human beings, if only one inmate consid-

What Victim Impact Class Participants Say

"I broke into houses and I always thought that I just made my victims angry. But I understand now that it was a lot worse than that. I made them angry, I made them feel violated. They don't feel safe in their own home. I will never make another person feel like that again. Whenever I heard about victims, they were faceless. But you've made it more real to me. Your class has made a bigger impact on me than anything else in this program."

"This is a very important class because you get to see crime through the eyes of the victim. The hurt and disruption that they constantly deal with because of someone else. I see how my decision making affects other people's lives. This class makes the pain feel real. I wasn't raised to hurt people like this and I'm not gonna continue to do so. This class has played a major role in my desire to change!"

"I have really learned a lot from this class. I had never even thought about the victims' point of view or the way they thought or felt because of what I had done to them. I won't live the same life style again when I leave. I will be more accepting to change and being more aware of the people around me and their feelings."

ers the pain victims endure when victimized and changes his behavior because of it, then it was worth sharing my story with them.

My next jolt of reality came when an Assistant Commissioner of Corrections told me, "Verna, 97 percent of the inmates who are incarcerated are returned to the community. How do you want them coming back?" My head had been stuck in the sand for so long, hanging on to the idea of "locking them away and throwing away the key." Now I was faced with a black and white fact—97 percent of the incarcerated population will leave prison. It was sobering. It was time to step back and re-evaluate my mission outlook. If I was truly dedicated to preventing victimization, and if this statistic was correct, then how could I, as a victim advocate, ignore this population that is clearly capable of victimization? It was a no-brainer! Inmates need attention, not because they deserve it, but because we do.

The Importance of Victim Impact

At first glance, it may appear counter-intuitive for victim advocates to work with inmates.

However, the truth is victim advocates and corrections professionals are not adversaries. They share a common goal of "no more victims." Conducting victim impact classes for the incarcerated is a team approach to preventing victimization. Several studies have looked at the effectiveness of victim impact programs across the country. A 2007 Iowa Department of Correction's Victim Impact Report, using two evidence-based studies, concluded victim impact is a contributing factor in reducing recidivism.

YHTP developed its own victim impact curriculum based on our experience as victim advocates. Our program walks the facilitator through the steps of leading a victim impact class and incorporates documentary videos that feature victims of crime who share their stories. For the last four years, YHTP has personally conducted four weekly victim impact classes for incarcerated men and women using this curriculum. As victim advocates, who better to talk about the impact of crime on victims? Our pre- and posttests with class participants show an improvement in the offender's understanding of the impact violent crime has on victims, and anecdotal observations from prison and jail staff indicate an improvement in the general attitude of our class participants.

We've learned from our class participants that the majority of offenders never think of their victim as a human being. Many never even think about their victim at all. One of our offender participants told us, "I've been incarcerated for over 20 years, and I never once thought about my victim until this class." Others let themselves believe the impact of crime on a victim is fleeting. Most offenders do not understand that victimization has a trickle down effect that goes far beyond the primary victim.

Components of a Good Victim Impact Program

The YHTP victim impact curriculum covers 10 topics:

- Accountability.
- Domestic violence.
- Child abuse.
- Drug addiction/drug dealing.
- Driving under the influence.
- Property crime/burglary/robbery.
- Sexual assault.
- Hate crime/gang crime.
- Crimes against the elderly.
- Homicide.

Some programming professionals may believe it is not necessary to cover all these topics because not every offender has committed every crime. However, YHTP believes it is important for the inmate to see that every crime does have an impact, regardless of its nature. Each class begins by telling the offender that we are covering these crimes, not as if we think they have perpetrated them, but because we want them to see the similarities of the victims' ordeals. As we discuss the crime's impact on a victim, the inmate is asked to think about his/her victim and his/her traumatic experience.

We also talk about the difference between guilt and remorse. This

You Have the Power

You Have the Power (YHTP) is a nonprofit, crime victim advocacy group founded by Andrea Conte, former First Lady of Tennessee, who herself is a survivor of violent crime.

YHTP conducts educational programs and trainings, creates training videos, and produces resource guidebooks on topics such as domestic violence, elder abuse, methamphetamine abuse, acquaintance rape, and child sexual abuse.

YHTP DVDs are distributed nationwide to educate professionals and the general public. They also facilitate victim impact classes for inmates at Charles Bass Correctional Complex, Corrections Corporation of America, Tennessee Prison for Women, and Metro-Davidson County Sheriff's Department. YHTP has created victim impact curriculum that is used in Tennessee prisons and other States, and trains facilitators on how to conduct victim impact classes.

For more information about YHTP victim impact classes or curriculum, please contact Sara Kemp, Director of Marketing, at 615–292–7027 or *sara.kemp@yhtp.org*. The group's website is at *www.yhtp.org*.

class is not about guilt or making the offender "feel bad." Everyone in the world has done something for which they are ashamed. The past cannot be changed. However, guilt is very self-focused. It's all about "how bad I am" and "how no one can ever trust or forgive me, including myself." Remorse on the other hand is victim motivated. "I can't believe what that victim is experiencing because of my actions." It is understanding the pain, the frustration, the financial expense, and the long-term impact for the victim.

Guilt holds back any kind of progress, but genuine remorse is a catalyst for changing behavior and making amends. We want remorse from our class participants. Also, all these crimes are discussed because knowledge is power. Everyone knows or will know a victim of crime. When released, offenders will have information about these crimes that will allow them to respond appropriately to those in their sphere of influence who suffer victimization.

Core issues are discussed in every class because they are the root of self-destructive and criminal behaviors. Addiction, violence, anger, depression, and promiscuity are

often mistaken for core issues, when they are actually symptoms of core issues. Although symptoms must be treated, they are not the root cause of negative or criminal behavior. Offenders must identify the source for their symptoms, which is often early exposure to family violence, childhood trauma, or sexual abuse. This is not an excuse for committing crime—offenders must take responsibility and accept the consequences of their actions.

There is absolutely no excuse for victimizing behavior. However, there are "explanations," and it is very important to understand what motivates negative behaviors in order to address them. Knowledge of core issues help offenders have a "light bulb moment," realizing they are not crazy or a bad seed. By connecting those dots, they can now work on their symptoms more successfully by tackling the issues that drive the symptoms. Because many core issues are tied to child sexual abuse and growing up in homes with domestic violence, more time is spent in our victim impact classes talking about the dynamics of these crimes and the long-term impact for the victim.

YHTP uses four different teaching methods: discussion, outlines, videos, and speakers. Outlines are used for each of the 10 topics. Following the outline, we discuss the crime with the inmate, bringing to light what offenders are thinking. This also provides an opportunity for the facilitator to address any denials, minimizations, or justifications. Videos featuring real life victims of crime and real life offenders allow inmate participants to see and hear the information in another format, promoting an interesting discussion. One of the most effective teaching tools is the use of survivors and successful ex-offenders as speakers.

Many survivors, even of the most intimate crimes like sexual assault and child sexual abuse, are willing to come to correctional facilities to speak to incarcerated inmates. Victims share their experience with the hope that their story will keep one inmate from victimizing behavior after they are released. The impact for the offenders hearing the victim's story is very powerful and often dramatic. In the four years we have been conducting victim impact classes, every victim who has come inside the correctional facilities has said that it was a very good experience for them. If facility guidelines allow, we also include successful ex-offenders as speakers. They provide a model of appropriate accountability and are an example that anyone can change, regardless of their past.

Who Are the Facilitators?

Facilitators must both understand victim impact issues and believe offenders can change. If either of these concepts is missing, the class will be less effective. The facilitator needs to understand most offenders have experienced some kind of victimization in their past which set them on a negative path in life. However, at the same time, they must be clear that past history is never an excuse to victimize others. Although the inmate was a victim of some kind of trauma in the past, they are in prison because they became victimizers.

Two facilitators are better than one when it comes to managing the group dynamic, especially for groups of 10 or more participants. While one facilitator leads the discussion, the other can monitor the group's response and provide additional insights. A good back-and-forth of facilitator presentation keeps the class more interesting. There is also less chance of burnout as sole responsibility of the class does not fall to one person. The facilitators should also be able to manage discussion and present opposing viewpoints without being defensive or argumentative. They must be open and inviting yet able to establish firm boundaries and respectfully confront denials, minimizations, and justifications.

Best Way To Measure Offender Progress

Pretests and posttests measure an offenders' knowledge about victim impact before and after the class. YHTP statistics indicate that 85 percent of offenders improve their scores from pre- to posttests. These tests include several true/false questions such as:

- If I left my car unlocked, I'd be asking for someone to steal it.
- Women who wear sexy clothes are asking to be raped.
- If you are jealous, it shows your partner how much you love them.
- Drug dealers do not really have victims.

In addition, personal surveys are administered to gain understanding of offenders' past history of victimization, substance abuse, and criminal behavior. They provide a view of how offenders interpret their personal experiences. The surveys are given at both the beginning and end of class time to see if the offenders view their personal experiences differently after taking the class. While the focus of the class is to help them understand victim impact, it is critical that they also begin looking at

Inmates need attention, not because they deserve it, but because we do.

their past to understand the reasons behind their criminal behavior. Of course, the ultimate goal is no more victims and reduced recidivism.

Challenges Encountered During Victim Impact Class

Some offenders may struggle with illiteracy, learning disabilities, or medical issues. The facilitator must be sensitive to these needs while balancing them with accountability. For example, an individual who cannot read or write can still listen and participate in class discussions. If offenders have medical needs that take them away from class, the facilitator needs to arrange for them to make up work such as writing an essay on the missed topic.

Some offenders will always present a bad attitude or act rudely. Certain behaviors such as sleeping, not paying attention, disrespectful talk, refusing to complete class work, or consistently arriving late are not tolerated. The facilitator must first try to talk directly with the offender about the behavior. If the problem does not improve, the facilitator may talk to the offender again or assign additional work. For example, if an offender falls asleep while a guest speaker is talking, have them write an apology letter to the speaker and assign an appropriate essay topic.

In group settings, people often feed off each others' negative attitudes. In this situation, confront the entire group first without naming individuals. The offenders can monitor each other's behavior, holding everyone accountable. If not, speak

one-on-one to the individuals causing trouble. If problems persist, it may be necessary to have them retake the class or remove them from the program.

Some sessions with difficult topics, such as family violence and sexual abuse, may be difficult for offenders as they may trigger feelings about childhood victimization. This is a healthy response, and the facilitator needs to be prepared to offer options on how to handle such feelings. These options may include individual counseling, talking with a trusted friend, or journaling.

Victim advocates and corrections professionals must work together to prevent victimization. Prisons and jails are constantly plagued by staffing and budget problems—for most, implementing a victim impact program will be a challenge. However, if we are serious about changing the revolving door nature of the correctional system, victim impact is as necessary as substance abuse, life-skills, and chaplaincy programs. ∎

Verna Wyatt began as YHTP Executive Director in 1998. She became a vocal advocate for victims after her sister-in-law and best friend was sexually assaulted and murdered in 1991. Ms. Wyatt serves on the Tennessee Peace Officer Standards and Training Commission, Tennessee Judicial Selection Commission, and Tennessee Sex Offender Treatment Board. In 2005 she was given the President's Award from the Tennessee Association of Chiefs of Police. She may be reached at 615–292–7027 or verna.wyatt@yhtp.org.

Contributing to this article was **Valerie Craig,** Director of Education for YHTP since 2002. Ms. Craig gives numerous presentations every year on such topics as domestic violence, elder abuse, child sexual abuse, acquaintance rape, and internet dangers. She was formerly associated with Senior Citizens, Inc., as the Victory Over Crime Coordinator, providing case management to senior victims of crime. She is a graduate of Middle Tennessee State University with a bachelor of science degree in child development and family studies with an emphasis in gerontology. She may be reached at 615–292–7027 or valerie.craig@yhtp.org.

REMEDYING THE FINANCIAL IMPACT OF VICTIMIZATION

by William G. Doerner and Steven P. Lab

INTRODUCTION

Victims lose out not only as a result of the criminal act but also from participating in the criminal justice process. The criminal justice system alienates the victim, making him or her feel like an outsider to both the offense and the system processes. The victim is little more than a witness for the state. The emphasis is not on making the victim whole. Rather, it is on processing the offender. Judging from citizen disillusionment with the criminal justice system, there is a clear need to take some bold steps to ameliorate the victim's suffering.

If a victim's decision to avoid formal contact with the criminal justice system stems from a rational cost–benefit assessment, then the system needs to entice victims back into the system with economic incentives.

There are a variety of ways whereby victims may recoup some of their monetary losses stemming from the victimization episode. Some alternatives include restitution, civil litigation, insurance payments, and victim compensation. While each method has the potential to restore the victim to his or her pre-crime state, the victim faces new obstacles when using these methods. Likewise, each option holds a different potential for drawing victims back into the criminal justice system. This chapter looks at restitution, civil litigation, insurance payments, and victim compensation as means of both restoring the victim's losses and bringing the victim back into the criminal justice system.

OFFENDER RESTITUTION

Offender restitution involves the transfer of services or money from the offender to the victim for damages inflicted by the offender. The idea of restitution predates the formal criminal justice system. Prior to the advent of a formal system of social control, victims were responsible for apprehending the offender and exacting payment for any loss or harm. Restitution was clearly outlined in various early laws, such as the Code of Hammurabi and the Justinian Code. The idea of offenders making restitution to their victims largely disappeared once the state assumed responsibility for apprehending and prosecuting offenders. While this new system of justice did not prohibit restitution, the practice gradually fell into disuse and was largely ignored.

The 1960s saw a renewed interest in offender restitution. A variety of factors contributed to this movement. They included the recognition of the victim in the 1967 President's Commission reports, the growing concern for identifying alternative methods for dealing with offenders, and the societal movement toward concern for crime victims. The awakening acceptance of restitution at that time was not accompanied by myriad new legislation. Rather, it was pointed out that restitution was an already existing sentencing option that the courts very rarely invoked.

The 1982 President's Task Force on Victims of Crime recommended that restitution become the norm in criminal cases. Later that same year, the "Victim/Witness Protection Act" went so far as to require federal judges to give a written explanation for why they did not require full restitution in a case. By 1990, 48 states had specific legislation dealing with restitution as a separate sentence or as an additional requirement to another sentence (Shapiro, 1990). Today, more than one-third of the states have a constitutional amendment that gives victims a right to restitution (Office for Victims of Crime, 2002a).

Some states have followed the federal lead and now require judges to make offender restitution a mandatory part of sentencing unless there are extraordinary circumstances to suggest otherwise (Office for Victims of Crime, 2002a). At least one state now imposes a civil restitution lien order upon convicted criminal offenders. A *civil restitution lien* means that the sentencing court, at the request of the victim, levies a claim against any real or personal property the convicted offender currently possesses or may come to own (see, e.g., Florida Statutes, 2016, § 960.29–960.297). What this means is that victims can recover any damages or losses from any assets the offender accrues.

⊕ **WEB ACTIVITY**

Many jurisdictions have established materials for both offenders and victims to explain restitution and how to comply with restitution. An example may be found at **http://www.victimsofcrime.org/docs/restitution-toolkit/f1_ca-restitution-guide.pdf?svrsn=2.**

The Rationale for Restitution

The rationale for restitution involves the needs of victims. Victim losses are a key driving force behind the growth of restitution legislation and the use of court-ordered restitution. A survey of Pennsylvania judges revealed that compensating victims was the most important reason for restitution (Ruback & Shaffer, 2005). Other factors, however, are also apparent in the adoption of restitution as a sentencing alternative (see Box 4.1).

Many restitution programs are couched in terms of benefits for the offender. Rehabilitation is hailed as the most potent outcome (Barnett, 1981; Galaway, 1981; Hofrichter, 1980; Hudson & Galaway, 1980). Forcing the offender to pay or perform service to the victim allows the offender to see the pain and suffering his or her actions caused. Rather than simply punishing the individual, restitution is supposed to provide a therapeutic or rehabilitative response to

---

BOX 4.1 COMPETING RATIONALES FOR RESTITUTION

- Restoring the victim to the pre-victimization condition.
- Rehabilitating the offender.
- Providing a less restrictive alternative to incarceration.

- Deterring the offender from future criminal activity.

Source: Compiled by the authors.

deviant actions. The rehabilitative argument is particularly appealing whenever restitution is tied to maintaining gainful employment or entering a job training program (Hillenbrand, 1990). In these instances, offenders help their victims while positioning themselves for legitimate opportunities in the future.

Proponents tend to regard restitution as a less restrictive alternative than normal processing, which would normally take the form of incarceration. Labeling arguments, which fault system intervention as the cause of further deviance, support restitution as a means of mitigating future offending. Rather than leading to deviance, restitution assists the offender in refraining from subsequent criminal activity.

Restitution also carries a deterrence effect (Tittle, 1978). Deterrence assumes that people will continue to commit deviant acts only as long as there is a positive payoff. By mandating repayment to the victim, restitution returns the offender—at least financially—to the exact same position held prior to the unlawful act. Coupling restitution with a fine or imprisonment can produce a negative balance between the outcome of the offense (assumed pleasure) and the system's response (pain). Following the basic hedonistic arguments underlying deterrence, the offender would be better off not committing the offense in the first place. Restitution, therefore, can produce a specific deterrent effect on the punished offender and may even provide general deterrence (i.e., influencing others through example).

Types of Restitution

Galaway (1981) outlines four variations on the general theme of restitution (see Box 4.2). The first, *monetary-victim restitution*, most closely fits the general public's impression of restitution. Under this arrangement, the offender makes direct monetary repayment to the victim for the actual amount of harm or losses incurred. While this is considered direct payment, in practice payments are actually routed through the court or probation office, which then turns the funds over to the victim. This process is particularly useful in cases where the victim does not wish to have any further contact with the offender.

The second form is referred to as *monetary-community restitution*. This type of restitution entails payment by the offender to the community rather than to

---

BOX 4.2 TYPES OF RESTITUTION

- Monetary payments to the victim.
- Monetary payments to the community.
- Service performed for the victim.
- Service performed for the community.

Source: Compiled by the authors.

the actual victim. This option may be used for several reasons. For example, it may not be possible to identify a tangible victim in cases involving vandalism of public property. A victim may be unwilling to participate in a restitution program, or the court may be reluctant to use restitution to the victim in the sentencing of an offender. In some instances, this monetary-community restitution may actually be a method whereby the community simply recoups funds it previously made available to the victim. In essence, the community provided "up-front" restitution to the victim that would now be replaced by the offender.

The remaining restitution categories are closely aligned with the first two, except that they substitute service in place of financial payments. Both *service-victim restitution* and *service-community restitution* require the perpetrator to perform a specified number of hours or type of service (or both) in lieu of making cash payments. These forms of restitution are most common in situations in which the offender does not have the ability to make monetary compensation (such as in the case of unemployed individuals and juveniles). Service to the community may act as repayment for restitution that the community made on behalf of the offender or may be a way to pay for court costs and/or harm to the general populace. In any event, the important feature is that the offender must satisfy the debt established through his or her victimizing behavior.

Evaluating the Impact of Restitution

As with many programs, evaluations of restitution have evolved from simple examinations of attitudes and processes to studies of such outcomes as recidivism, cost savings, and diversion. In general, restitution has enjoyed a warm reception from victims, offenders, the general public, and system personnel (Gandy, 1978; Gandy & Galaway, 1980; Hudson & Galaway, 1980; Keldgord, 1978; Kigin & Novack, 1980; Novack et al., 1980).

However, despite the general acceptance of restitution, relatively few offenders are required by the courts to pay restitution. Table 4.1 presents data showing that in only 18 percent of state felony cases and 12 percent of Federal District Court cases is the felon ordered to pay restitution as a part of the sentence. In the case of property offenses, where it is generally easier to document the amount of the loss, fewer than three out of ten felons in state courts are ordered to pay restitution. Restitution orders clearly vary by the type of offense. The median level of restitution imposed in Federal District Courts is relatively low, ranging from a high of $8,157 in larceny cases to a low of $1,500 in firearms/weapons offenses.

The initial wave of restitution evaluations was mostly *process evaluations*; that is, the emphasis was on the number of offenders handled, the amount of time

TABLE 4.1 Percent of Felons with a Penalty of Restitution and the Median Restitution Ordered

Conviction Offense	State Courts	Federal District Courts	Median $
All Offenses Violent Offenses	18%	12%	
Murder	13	31	6,423
Sexual assault	18	7	2,412
Robbery	18	51	6,020
Aggravated assault	18	20	2,000
Property Offenses			
Burglary	27	64	2,100
Larceny	26	63	8,157
Drug Offenses	14	1	1,500
Weapons Offenses	8	9	1,500
Other Offenses	13		

Source: Rosenmerkel et al, (2009); and Maguire (2010).

participants took to make restitution, the completion rate for restitution orders, and other similar program achievements. Those eligible to receive restitution include not only the crime victim but also his or her family, insurance companies, victim support agencies, and government agencies that assist victims (Office for Victims of Crime, 2002a). The losses covered are likewise broad. Beyond costs for property loss or damage, restitution can cover medical expenses, lost wages, funeral expenses, mental health counseling, and other costs associated with the crime and its aftermath (Office for Victims of Crime, 2002a).

Most programs report a high offender compliance rate with restitution orders (Kigin & Novack, 1980; Lawrence, 1990; Schneider & Schneider, 1984). However, success varies according to the type and level of supervision provided to probationers (Ruback & Shaffer, 2005; Schneider & Schneider, 1984). For example, the use of specialized collection units, particularly those located outside of the courthouse, has been found to be less effective at collecting funds compared with those programs located within the courthouse (Ruback et al., 2004; Ruback & Shaffer, 2005). The simultaneous imposition of other sanctions, such as fines and imprisonment, may also hinder or delay offender payments. The Office for Victims of Crime (2002b) suggests that all court-ordered payments be collected under a single system to address this problem. Finally, restitution programs have been found to be quite economical. They can handle a large number of individuals at a relatively low cost (Hudson & Galaway, 1980).

Studies that look at the impact of restitution upon victims and offenders are known as *outcome evaluations*. The amount of money collected and funneled to victims is one key result that is assessed. Unfortunately, systematic information on the amount of restitution ordered is not available. Data from 2004 to 2010 show that the total amount of restitution collected, nationally, rose from $20 billion per year to over $55 billion in 2010 (Offices of the United States Attorneys, 2016). See Figure 4.1.

Another major outcome to assess is offender recidivism. Challeen and Heinlen (1978) report 2.7 percent recidivism for restitution clients, compared with 27 percent for similar offenders sentenced to jail. Recidivism declined in three out of four programs by ten fewer offenses per 100 youths (Schneider, 1986). A six-year follow-up of offenders who were diverted into a restitution program also showed significantly lower recidivism (Rowley, 1990). More recently, Ruback and associates (2004), examining the impact of restitution before and after it was made mandatory in Pennsylvania, found that offenders who paid a greater proportion of the ordered restitution had lower recidivism than those who did not make as many payments.

While these results appear encouraging, Schneider and Schneider (1984) caution that the value of restitution depends on how well the program is administered. When restitution becomes an agency priority, the results are promising. However, outcome measures lag when restitution is handled as an added-on condition and is not a top agency concern. Programs that aggressively target restitution generate more successful performances and lower

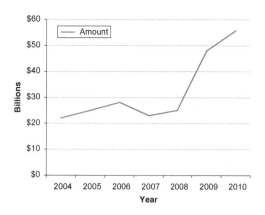

FIGURE 4.1
Restitution Collected

Source: Offices of the United States Attorneys (2016).

recidivism rates (Ervin & Schneider, 1990; Ruback et al., 2005; Ruback & Shaffer, 2005).

Problems and Concerns with Restitution

Despite both the theoretical attractiveness and positive outcomes of restitution, there are a variety of problems and concerns facing the practice. At the very outset is the need to apprehend and adjudicate the offender (Galaway, 1981; Hillenbrand, 1990). The Uniform Crime Reports shows that less than 20 percent of all property crimes (which are most amenable to restitution) are cleared by an arrest. Restitution, therefore, is possible a maximum of one-fifth of the time. Beyond arrest statistics, many offenders are not convicted, thereby mitigating any possibility of restitution.

The Office for Victims of Crime (2002a) notes that a major impediment to restitution is the victim's failure to request such compensation. While many states require prosecutors or the court to notify victims of their right to request restitution, there is no guarantee that such notification actually takes place. Notification also does not mean that the victims will make the request. One solution to these problems is to make restitution a mandatory part of sentencing in all criminal cases (Office for Victims of Crime, 2002a; Ruback et al., 2005).

A third stumbling block is the inability of offenders to pay restitution (Office for Victims of Crime, 2002a). Most offenders come from lower class segments of society. It is naive to assume that these individuals will have the necessary means to make restitution. In some cases, statutes outline provisions in which restitution is ordered but commences at some future date when the offender will have the ability to pay (Office for Victims of Crime, 2002a). Another potential solution is assisting offenders in finding employment. The provision of jobs to offenders requires either public funds or substantial cooperation from the private sector, both of which may face problems. First, jobs may not be available. Second, opponents argue that more worthy law-abiding citizens are denied jobs in favor of offenders.

A fourth major issue is demonstrating and calculating the loss and the appropriate level of restitution (Office for Victims of Crime, 2002b). While a dollar figure for stolen or damaged property should be easy to identify, questions arise concerning depreciation for older, used property and the value of sentimental items for which monetary compensation is hard to determine. Some offenses may leave victims with psychological damage, for which setting a dollar figure may be more demanding. Difficulty also arises when attempting to set a level of service for restitution (Harland & Rosen, 1990). How much work or time offsets monetary loss, physical pain, or psychological suffering? In almost every attempt to order restitution, the court is asked to go beyond its legal expertise and become involved in the decisions that would be better made by a doctor, psychiatrist, economist, or accountant.

Another major area of concern deals with the question of the proper philosophy of the criminal court. Thorvaldson (1990) argues that restitution moves the emphasis of the criminal justice system from society to the victim. Under restitution, the victim is seeking personal redress rather than acting on behalf of society. Consequently, restitution diminishes the importance of criminal processing and sentencing (Thorvaldson, 1990). Many individuals also see restitution as inappropriate for cases in which offenders receive a prison or jail term (Office for Victims of Crime, 2002a). Basically, critics claim that restitution shifts the court from a criminal orientation to a civil orientation. Instead of focusing on the offender, the victim becomes the focus of the process.

 **WEB ACTIVITY**

Issues with restitution have been identified by many organizations. One such organization is the National Committee for the Prevention of Elder Abuse. They have offered their insight and comments at **http://www.preventelderabuse.org/ elderabuse/issues/restitution.html.**

Several other issues carry potential problems for restitution. The current criminal justice system is not set up to administer such programs (Shapiro, 1990). Indeed, there is little coordination among agencies on monitoring restitution orders or sharing information on compliance with such orders (Office for Victims of Crime, 1998b). Further, there is little evidence that restitution will have a deterrent effect (Barnett, 1981). Clearly, there are still many reasons to question the efficacy of restitution.

While there are several stumbling blocks to restitution, there are many who believe that improving restitution requires taking steps to institutionalize the practice throughout the criminal justice process. Box 4.3 lists several recommendations made by the *New Directions* project (Office for Victims of Crime, 1998b). Among these recommendations are making restitution mandatory across the nation and making victims aware of their right to restitution. Of equal importance is the building of methods, techniques, and procedures for monitoring and enforcing restitution orders. Finally, the recommendations also include calls for ways in which victims can try to enforce restitution payments, notably through petitioning the court and resorting to civil actions.

CIVIL LITIGATION

Another method of redress for crime victims is the civil litigation arena. Civil lawsuits are the modern version of retribution/restitution practices from the past. The victim or the victim's family has the right to take civil action against offenders to recoup losses and to exact punitive damages. People sometimes call a civil lawsuit a tort action. A *tort* refers to a wrongful act that the *defendant* (the criminal) has committed against the *plaintiff* (the victim). This act has produced some type of loss, usually an injury or damage. The purpose of a tort action or civil litigation is for the plaintiff to recover monetary compensation from the defendant for any physical or psychological harm inflicted by the offender (Berliner, 1989). Thus, any civil lawsuit must be concerned with issues surrounding the liability of the defendant and the collectability or recovery of damages (Office for Victims of Crime, 1997).

There are some important benefits from filing civil suits (Dawson, 1989). Perhaps the most important aspect is the sense of control the victim regains through the court action. As long as the state is prosecuting the case in a criminal court, the prosecutor makes all the key decisions. The prosecutor, not the victim, decides whether to take the case to trial. The prosecutor, not the victim, can negotiate a plea settlement. The prosecutor, not the victim, decides what evidence to bring into court. Once the venue switches from the criminal court to a civil proceeding, the victim is no longer an outsider in the case. Instead, the victim and his or her ensuing problems are the central concern of the court case. The victim has the right to remain in the courtroom throughout the proceedings and has the final say in any settlement decision (National Center for Victims of Crime, 2001).

There are other advantages to pursuing a tort action. In civil suits, the level of proof required is "a preponderance of evidence," whereas in criminal cases, it is "proof beyond a reasonable doubt" (National Center for Victims of Crime, 2001). Even if the defendant is not found guilty in a criminal trial or if the prosecutor elects not to file charges, civil action may remain a viable alternative. In addition, a unanimous jury decision is not necessary in a civil proceeding. A majority or two-thirds decision is enough to gain a favorable verdict. Berliner (1989) notes that juries tend to be sympathetic to victims in civil cases. Furthermore, the defendant (offender) can no longer refuse to testify by invoking the self-incrimination protection (Brien, 1992; Dawson, 1989; Office for Victims of Crime, 1997). The constitutional privilege against self-incrimination pertains to criminal proceedings, not to civil action.

Following one of the most notorious civil suits in history, family members of Nicole Brown Simpson leave the courthouse in 1997 after the jury found former football star O.J. Simpson liable in the wrongful death civil suits brought against him following his acquittal in the criminal trial for the murder of Nicole and her friend Ronald Goldman.

CREDIT: AP Photo/Susan Sterner

Despite these advantages, there are a number of drawbacks to civil remedies. First, many victims are unaware of the option of pursuing a civil suit or how to find an appropriate attorney. These problems are exacerbated by the fact that many attorneys are unaware of this avenue of redress for crime victims. These problems are slowly being addressed by the establishment of referral agencies or groups around the country and through state legislation that emphasizes victims' rights to civil recourse (Office for Victims of Crime, 1998b). Second, as with restitution, the offender must be identified and located. There may be no possibility for civil action if the offender is unknown. Third, civil cases require the victim to hire an attorney and pay some filing fees before the proceedings begin (Barbieri, 1989). In effect, lower income victims are barred from the civil system. Unless the victim is awarded a sizable sum of money, he or she may actually lose money after paying a guaranteed minimum fee to the attorney. Even with large awards, attorneys typically secure at least one-third of the award as a fee.

Fourth, some victims suffer further damage as a result of the lawsuit. Information about the victim's past behavior, character, and personal situation are all open to detailed scrutiny. This type of examination may cause further psychological and emotional harm to the victim (Barbieri, 1989). Fifth, civil suits are time consuming and may take a period of years to resolve. During this interval, the victim must have continued contact with the offender, which could bring further discomfort.

Finally, because most offenders have little or no income, there is little reason to expect any recovery, even if the victim wins his or her suit. One innovation many

states have attempted, to advance a victim's ability to attach an offender's assets, is the passage of so-called "*Son of Sam" provisions.* After New York serial murderer David Berkowitz (nicknamed "Son of Sam") was apprehended, he stood to gain millions of dollars by selling book and media rights to his story while his victims and their families received nothing. The idea that a criminal could gain a small fortune from his heinous acts prompted the passage of a new law that allowed the state to confiscate any royalties and place the monies into a compensation fund.

Despite a flurry of similar legislation, these regulations were declared unconstitutional by the U.S. Supreme Court *(Simon & Schuster v. Members of the New York State Crime Victims Board et al.,* 1991). The Court ruled that this statute violated the First Amendment protections against censorship because it "singles out income derived from expressive activity for a burden the State places on no other income, and it is directed only at works with a specified content" (p. 487). As a result, these monies are no longer earmarked for confiscation and payment to crime victims. However, more recent incarnations of "Son of Sam" laws make it easier for victims to bring civil suits to collect any profits made by offenders as a result of their criminal activity (see Table 4.2).

TABLE 4.2 Possible Defendant Resources to Consider When Recovering a Civil Judgment

Source of Income

Wages
Benefits (pension payments and annuities)
Unearned income
Trust fund income
Tax refunds
Government entitlements

Property and Holdings

Personal property (cars, jewelry, etc.)
Real property (home, land, etc.)
Bank accounts
All debts owed to the defendant
Financial holdings (stocks, bonds, etc.)
Partnership interests
Future interests in real and personal property through wills, trusts, etc.

Source: Office for Victims of Crime (1997).

Another possible avenue for victims is to file a *third-party civil suit* (Carrington, 1981; Castillo et al., 1979). In these instances, a victim sues a government entity, business, or corporation, such as a landlord, the managing corporation of a shopping center, or any other responsible body.

The argument developed during litigation of a *third-party suit* concerns the issue of whether the defendant's negligence failed to establish or maintain a safe and protected environment. Here, the victim must demonstrate two things.

First, the criminal episode must be a foreseeable event. One can satisfy this requirement by documenting other offenses that have occurred on the premises or by showing that the area has a reputation for being a high-risk location. Second, either the third party must have failed to take appropriate steps to curtail further criminal events or its efforts must have fallen woefully short.

Suppose, for example, that an unknown offender assaults and robs a tenant who is returning to his apartment in a housing complex. Neighbors have complained to the landlord on several occasions that the lighting in the halls is broken, non-residents have been seen roaming the area, and there have been other similar criminal incidents in the past. Despite this information, the property manager has taken no remedial action. Under these circumstances, a victim may be able to hold the landlord responsible for ignoring a known hazard.

Whether through civil litigation against an individual offender or against a third party, victims need to be made more aware of this avenue for recourse. The Office for Victims of Crime (1998b) has offered several recommendations to enforce the use of civil litigation (see Box 4.4). These recommendations range from simply informing victims of this response, to developing consulting networks that can assist in litigation, to changing the laws in order to allow victims more time in which to bring claims in civil court.

BOX 4.4 SELECTED RECOMMENDATIONS FROM THE FIELD FOR CIVIL LITIGATION

- Crime victims should be fully informed of their legal rights to pursue civil remedies.

- State and local networks of civil attorneys who have experience representing crime victims should be expanded.

- Increased efforts should be made to identify consultants with the expertise to testify on issues relevant to victimization in civil and criminal cases.

- Civil attorneys should provide training to victim service providers on civil remedies for crime victims.

- Statutes of limitations for civil actions involving child abuse cases should be extended.

- States should examine statutes of limitations for civil actions relating to other criminal acts to determine whether they should be extended to provide a meaningful opportunity for crime victims to obtain needed relief.

Source: Compiled by the authors, from Office for Victims of Crime data.

PRIVATE INSURANCE

Another method for alleviating the losses due to crime entails private insurance. Most homeowner insurance policies have provisions for the recovery of lost and damaged property. Likewise, health insurance policies typically allow payments for injuries sustained as a result of criminal incidents.

The use of insurance to offset the effects of crime does have several shortcomings. Foremost among these is that citizens must purchase the insurance. The fact that many people cannot afford insurance premiums effectively places such protection beyond their reach. Of course, this observation assumes that insurance is available to purchase in the first place. Many inner-city locations are in such crime-infested areas that private insurance companies refuse to do business there. This problem carries enormous ramifications. Lack of insurance leads to further gentrification and more urban decline in these blighted areas. This situation became so grave that the federal government now underwrites crime insurance for commercial enterprises and residents in high-crime areas.

Some people also argue that viewing insurance as a means of offsetting crime losses actually penalizes the victim further by assuming that it is the victim's responsibility to take action and avoid crime. Another problem is that most insurance policies have a deductible amount that reduces the cash outlay to victims. Deductibles of, say, $200 or $500 effectively eliminate any insurance payments for many crimes. In general, while insurance is a possible method for recouping losses, it is not an appealing means in many instances.

VICTIM COMPENSATION

Victim compensation takes place when the state, rather than the perpetrator, reimburses the victim for losses sustained at the hands of the criminal. While it is true that some victim compensation operations derive money from offender restitution, the state is the entity that has direct contact with the victim.

Victim compensation is not a new concept. These remedies once existed in such historical places as ancient Greece and Rome, biblical Israel, Teutonic Germany, and Saxony England (Jacob, 1976; Schafer, 1970). For a variety of reasons, this practice fell into disuse during the Middle Ages. Modern interest in victim compensation came about as a result of the advocacy efforts of Margery Fry. Fry, an English magistrate, played a prominent role in the passage of victim compensation laws in New Zealand in 1963 and in Great Britain in 1964 (Edelhertz & Geis, 1974) (see Table 4.3). In the U.S.A., California launched its victim compensation program in 1966, followed by New York and Hawaii. As one might imagine, there are a number of parallels between the Great Britain legislation and the American programs (Greer, 1994).

TABLE 4.3	Landmarks in Crime Victim Compensation
1963	First victim compensation legislation passed in New Zealand.
1964	Victim compensation legislation passed in Great Britain.
1966	California begins first victim compensation program in the U.S.A.
1977	National Association of Crime Victim Compensation Boards created.
1984	Federal Victims of Crime Act passed.
1986	States receive funding from Victims of Crime Act (VOCA) for first time.
1988	VOCA amended to require states to pay benefits to domestic violence and drunk-driving victims.
2002	All 50 states, the District of Columbia, U.S. Virgin Islands, Puerto Rico, and Guam have established compensation programs.

Federal efforts in the U.S.A. for victim compensation began in 1964 but did not win approval until the passage of the "Victims of Crime Act" (VOCA) in 1984. The VOCA initiated a process whereby the federal government would provide victim compensation for federal offenses and federal funds for state compensation programs. The source of these funds came from fines, bond forfeitures, and special assessments levied on convicted individuals and businesses.

As Figure 4.2 shows, VOCA has been responsible for the flow of significant amounts of money into state compensation programs. The Crime Victims Fund has received more than $20 billion in deposits since it began in 1984. In 2012, the Crime Victims Fund generated approximately $2.8 billion for distribution and, in 2014, it generated another $3.6 billion (Office for Victims of Crime, 2015).

The fluctuations in deposits since the late 1990s are attributable to several large fines paid by corporations (Derene, 2005). Fund disbursements fall into several prioritized categories (Office for Victims of Crime, 2011). In FY 2016, $20 million was set aside for investigating and prosecuting child abuse cases. Almost $38 million was set aside to improve services to victims in federal cases. More than $4.5 million went to the Federal Victim Notification System. Office for Victims of Crime (OVC) discretionary grants received $29.4 million of the remaining funds. The remaining funds were divided between state victim compensation programs ($179 million) and state victim assistance programs ($379 million) (Office for Victims of Crime, 2016b). All 50 states, the District of Columbia, and the U.S. Virgin Islands benefit from these funds. In FY 2012, more than $394 million was paid in state compensation to 186,773 claimants, an average of approximately $2,110 per claim (Office for Victims of Crime, 2016b).

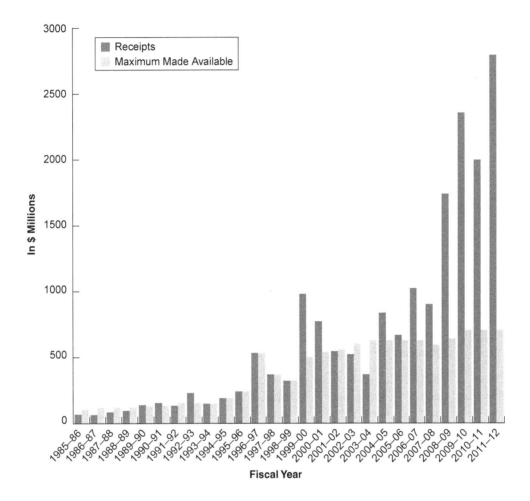

FIGURE 4.2
Crime Victim Fund Deposits

Source: Office for Victims of Crime (2016b).

 **WEB ACTIVITY**

More information on the operations of the federal victim compensation program and funds may be found at **http://www.ovc.gov/pubs/reporttonation2015/crime-victims-fund.html.**

In addition to providing money, the VOCA helped standardize state crime compensation laws. The initial flurry to pass compensation provisions produced a variety of rules and regulations that differed from one state to the next. To be eligible to receive the federal VOCA funds, states had to follow a series of program guidelines. For instance, some states were granting compensation only to victims who were state residents. VOCA regulations called for the removal of state residency requirements, among other things. In order to reach a better understanding of just what victim compensation entails, the following sections describe some of the more salient characteristics of these statutes.

Philosophical Bases

Proponents feel that government has the obligation to provide victim compensation for two distinct reasons. The first view is the *social contract* argument. This perspective maintains that government, through its system of taxation and provision of services, engages in an unwritten contract to care for the safety and well-being of its citizens. Citizens, according to this perspective, have relinquished the power of law enforcement to government in exchange for protection. The experience of being a crime victim, through no fault of one's own, represents an affront to this agreement because the government has failed to keep its promise. As a result, it is incumbent upon government to restore victimized citizens to their former status.

The second philosophical position is the notion of *social welfare*. Government attempts to provide a minimum standard of living for its disabled, deprived, and unfortunate citizens. This position holds that innocent crime victims fall into this category because they suffer deprivations that are not self-induced. As a result, government should extend its welfare practices and come to the rescue of crime victims because they are, in effect, deprived.

The argument one chooses to embrace carries important ramifications for other features of victim compensation. For example, if one adheres to the social welfare view, one might endorse a "financial means test." Under this scheme, only poor people should be eligible for compensation benefits. However, if one adopts the social contract notion, then compensation should be available to everybody, regardless of their financial status.

A third reason offered for victim compensation deals with the use of compensation as an enticement to lure victims back to the criminal justice system. Earlier we noted that many victims refrain from contacting the authorities because of the additional costs inherent in doing so. They are responding to a simple cost–benefit analysis. Compensation, however, can alleviate much of the monetary loss associated with the offense. Therefore, it is possible that compensation can tip the balance of the cost–benefit equation and bring victims back into the system. Not only does compensation carry the potential to promote goodwill between the criminal justice system and citizens/victims, it may also result in more crime clearances and (eventually) lower crime through the apprehension of more offenders.

Compensable Acts

Most programs restrict victim compensation to three categories of victims. The first group includes victims of personal injury crimes and the family members of victims who were killed. All expenses related to physical injuries, including mental health services/counseling and lost wages, are covered (National Association of Crime Victim Compensation Boards, 2007). Payments typically cover medical expenses, losses related to missed work, and mental health treatment of the victim (and family, in the case of the victim's death). Conversely, victims are rarely compensated for losses due to property crimes. Only a handful of states have provisions allowing payment for property loss or damage (Parent et al., 1992).

The second group is "Good Samaritans." Under *"Good Samaritan" provisions*, a person who is hurt or killed during an attempt to prevent a crime from taking place or while attempting to capture a suspected criminal is entitled to compensation. The thinking here is that society owes a special duty to anybody who acts above and beyond the normal duties of citizenship—that altruism should be encouraged, not discouraged.

The final category specifically includes anyone who is injured while coming to the aid of a law enforcement officer. Some states stipulate that people who do not help a police officer when he or she asks for assistance are guilty of a misdemeanor. Thus, it makes sense to compensate citizens when they act on behalf of a police officer.

There are also some people who are specifically not eligible for compensation. For example, most states prohibit compensation for law enforcement officers and firefighters. The thinking here is that their actions are part of the job and that other programs, such as workers' compensation, are more appropriate vendors (Parent et al., 1992). Other excluded persons include prison or jail inmates and individuals involved in organized crime.

Eligibility Restrictions

One restriction on compensation is to ensure that an offender is not *unjustly enriched*. This is primarily a concern in domestic violence cases in which the victim still resides with the offender. Rather than simply exclude domestic violence victims from receiving compensation, the VOCA and its 1988 amendments require states to establish guidelines for determining whether compensation would be "appropriated by [the offender] or used to support him in a *substantial way*" (National Association of Crime Victim Compensation Boards, 2007). States are required to have written guidelines that apply to *all* crimes, not just domestic violence offenses. One way to alleviate such concerns is the use of provisions, such as those in Minnesota, that allow compensation if a domestic violence victim will prosecute the offending party or is in the process of seeking a legal separation or a divorce.

A number of states have a financial means test on the books. In other words, the victim must suffer serious financial hardship before an award will be forthcoming. As we mentioned earlier, one philosophical basis for establishing a victim compensation program is the social welfare argument. While a financial hardship test stems from this orientation, it is also a mechanism to cap program expenditures. Interestingly, if a state compensation program operates under a financial hardship restriction, it is not eligible for federal victim compensation funds.

Another condition that affects eligibility is victim involvement or *contributory misconduct*. The victim must not share any criminal responsibility for the event. In other words, victim precipitation reduces one's standing for a compensation award. For example, suppose that John challenges Peter to a fight. Peter accepts and during this pugilistic event he breaks John's nose. Depending on how the state's provisions read, the compensation board may deny John's claim completely or it may reduce the size of the award in proportion to the amount of victim contribution to the criminal incident.

One additional eligibility criteria concerns the availability of other forms of assistance. Victim compensation is universally viewed as a *source of last resort*. That is, all other avenues for compensation must be exhausted before compensation benefits are forthcoming (National Association of Crime Victim Compensation Boards, 2007). Payments go to victims only after all alternative sources of funds are exhausted. Other sources include workers' compensation, disability benefits, insurance policies, offender restitution, private donations, Medicaid, Social Security, and, possibly, civil lawsuit awards. Any payments from a compensation program are reduced by an appropriate amount corresponding to funds received from such alternative sources. In order to avoid undue hardship on victims, programs typically make awards and subsequently recover any funds available from other sources.

Awards

States vary in the cap or limit they will pay per claim. Typically, caps range from $10,000 to $25,000, although the state of Washington has a $150,000 maximum, while New York has no cap on payments for medical losses. Some states require a minimum loss in order to prevent the program from being inundated by frivolous claims that are costly to investigate. Many states also make emergency awards when victims or survivors face immediate financial hardship (Office for Victims of Crime, 1998b).

Crime compensation covers such items as lost wages, medical bills, prosthetics, funeral expenses, and, in some instances, mental health counseling. Most programs do not set aside any monies for pain and suffering or for property damage. Indeed, only five programs allow for pain and suffering, and eight make awards for property damage (Parent et al., 1992).

A recent addition to the items that victim compensation can pay is costs that arise from forensic medical examinations. A standard police investigatory practice is to transport sexual assault victims to a medical facility for physical examination. As Chapter 9 will explain, this examination consists of two parts: gathering physical evidence from the victim and providing medical treatment to the victim. Some compensation boards reimburse applicants for the medical portion of the examination but reject payment for the evidentiary aspects. This practice led a U.S. Department of Justice report (1986: 17) to comment that "[f]orcing sexual assault victims to bear this cost is tantamount to charging burglary victims for collecting fingerprints." The "Victims of Crime Act" of 1984 makes funds available for qualifying victim compensation programs to pay for forensic examinations.

The award itself can take several forms. The payout may be in a lump sum, in periodic installments, or in partial amounts. Some states permit victims in dire need to receive a small emergency award, pending the outcome of a full investigation. Some compensation agencies pay vendors (such as doctors and hospitals) directly to prevent victims from skipping out on their bills.

Funding

An important political issue for many people concerns funding sources. While some states extract monies from the general tax structure to underwrite victim compensation, a more popular funding mechanism is the offender. According to the National Association of Crime Victim Compensation Boards (2007), most state compensation programs receive funds primarily from fines and fees levied on offenders, with approximately one-third coming to the states from the Crime Victims Fund. Funding also comes from monies recouped through offender restitution payments to the state. Most programs receive *no* general revenue funds from the state.

Reporting Crime and Applying for Compensation

One prominent feature of victim compensation is its close alliance with the criminal justice system. Virtually every state requires that the crime be reported to the police within a relatively short period of time (typically 72 hours). Victims must also cooperate fully with the police investigation and cooperate completely with the prosecution of the case should the state attorney or district attorney pursue that option. There are also deadlines for when victims must apply for compensation. Failure to abide by any of these requirements results in an automatic claim denial and the repayment of any compensation benefits that the victim may have received already. The Office for Victims of Crime's *New Directions* project (1998b) calls for a relaxation of the reporting and claims time frames and for allowing the initial report to

 WEB ACTIVITY

A great deal of other information on victim compensation is available from the National Association of Crime Victim Compensation Boards at **http://www.nacvcb.org/** and the National Association of VOCA Assistance Administrators at **http://navaa.org/**.

be made to non-law enforcement agencies, such as counselors or medical personnel. The current requirements represent a very calculated attempt to bring victims back into the criminal justice system.

DOES VICTIM COMPENSATION WORK?

As noted earlier, a substantial number of victims elect not to report their victimizations to the police. Those victims who do contact the police may choose not to prosecute. One reason for this lack of involvement in the criminal justice process appears to be that victims realize they can minimize their losses by avoiding the legal system. If the decision to not cooperate with the system stems from an economic appraisal, then the system needs to lure victims back with financial incentives.

Some observers contend that victim compensation fits this bill. Failure to report the crime to the police, assist in the police investigation, and cooperate completely with the prosecution of the offender can automatically produce a compensation claim denial. Victim compensation, therefore, amounts to an economic incentive that serves to entice the victim back into the legal process. Compensation administrators routinely tout their programs as promoting greater victim cooperation with the legal machinery.

Macro-Level Effects

Victim compensation administrators generally assume that their programs increase victim participation in the criminal justice system. If this is correct, certain macro-level effects should appear. A *macro-level effect* refers to a change in some group or organizational characteristic. Because victim compensation laws mandate crime reporting, cooperation with the authorities, and participation in court cases, certain systematic effects should surface. Victim compensation programs should produce an increased rate of violent crimes known to the police, a higher proportion of known crime that is violent, and an increased proportion of violent crimes cleared by the police.

An examination of four states operating a victim compensation program found no support for any of these expectations (Doerner et al., 1976). A replication using victim compensation programs from several Canadian provinces did not uncover any evidence for the proposed effects (Doerner, 1978a). Because both studies utilized official data, it is possible that shortcomings within the data influenced the findings. As a result, another analysis examined self-reported victimization data (Doerner, 1978b). Utilizing the National Crime Panel Surveys from 26 cities made it possible to test two hypotheses. First, it was anticipated that compensating jurisdictions would record higher rates of violent crime reporting than would non-compensating areas. Second, it was expected that reporting rates for property crime in compensating and non-compensating jurisdictions would be similar in both types of jurisdictions because these offenses were not compensable. The findings revealed that areas with compensation programs had similar rates of reported violent and property crimes. Thus, these studies suggest that victim compensation did not stimulate an increase in crime reporting.

Although these studies failed to uncover any discernible effects, the possibility still exists that victim compensation programs do influence conviction rates. However, an analysis of Canadian provinces revealed similar conviction rates for violent and property offenses in both compensating and non-compensating jurisdictions (Silverman & Doerner, 1979). As a result, the researchers concluded that victim compensation did not alter conviction rates.

In sum, these studies do not provide any consistent empirical evidence in support of the contention that victim compensation positively affects other components of the criminal justice system. This conclusion takes on much greater importance in view of the fact that the evidence is derived from studies conducted in two different countries and with data from official, as well as non-official, sources. Despite the conclusion of no macro-level or organizational effects, it still remains to be seen whether victim compensation programs generate any micro-level or individual effects.

Micro-Level Effects

Several researchers have pointed out that certain micro-level effects should materialize. A *micro-level effect* refers to any changes in a person, such as being more satisfied with the criminal justice system if a person received compensation. To test this assumption, Doerner and Lab (1980) mailed a questionnaire to victims who had applied for crime compensation in Florida. Following the advice of program officials, they divided the study participants into a group who received compensation and a group who was denied compensation. The expectation was that compensated victims would express more favorable attitudes toward criminal justice personnel and would be more likely to cooperate with these personnel in the future than would non-compensated applicants.

The results showed that compensated victims were more satisfied with the crime compensation officials than were non-compensated victims. However, a similar sense of satisfaction did not accrue to the police, to the state attorney, or to the judge. While compensated victims were more likely to say that they would register a claim with the crime compensation program in the event of a future victimization, they were not inclined to cooperate with other system personnel. Thus, it would seem from this study that victim compensation programs do not generate a "spillover" or a halo effect to the remainder of the criminal justice system.

The foregoing results suggest that victim compensation programs have had little impact on the attitudes and views of the public toward the criminal justice system. This suggests that the future of compensation must not rely on arguments that it benefits the criminal justice system or society. Rather, an appeal to the social welfare and social contract arguments holds much more promise.

Problems and Concerns with Compensation

Besides the potential impact of compensation on the criminal justice system, it is possible to evaluate these operations in terms of the number of victims served and the extent of services provided. Early program evaluations found a number of readily identifiable deficiencies (Brooks, 1975; Doerner, 1977; Meiners, 1978). Just about every program was deluged by the number of claims it had received. Given the small number of staff, some claims required more than a year for processing. Rejection rates exceeded the 50 percent mark, and the availability of victim compensation remained a well-kept secret. These observations led one researcher to forecast that unless these problems were corrected, "victim compensation programs will not significantly reduce the plight of the crime victim in our society and will remain a prime example of a misguided social program" (Doerner, 1977: 109). More recently, Newmark and associates (2003) reported that 87 percent of claims were approved for payment.

These concerns appear to have diminished as the programs have matured. A phone survey of victims in six states revealed that the average processing time for claims is only ten weeks (Newmark et al., 2003). At the same time, almost a quarter of the victims believe this processing time is too long. The Office for Victims of Crime (1998b) offers several recommendations that could further increase the number of awards as well as speed up the making of awards. These suggestions include the use of new technologies for filing and processing claims, greater cooperation among agencies in processing claims, and integrating victim compensation more closely with other victim assistance functions and programs.

While recent figures on awards appear impressive, they fail to tell us the extent to which all eligible victims are being reached and served by compensation programs. Considering the total number of compensable offenses reported to the police, whether the victim was culpable, and the availability of insurance to cover losses, there were approximately 168,000 victims eligible for compensation in 1987 (Parent et al., 1992). Less than half of these crimes, however, resulted in a compensation claim. Many victims are not applying for or receiving compensation. One reason for this gap may be the relative anonymity within which many compensation programs operate (Newmark et al., 2003). That is, most victims do not know about the programs (McCormack, 1991). Greater outreach is needed to make victims aware of compensation programs (Office for Victims of Crime, 1998b).

Toward Restorative and Community Justice

by Michael Braswell, John Fuller, and Bo Lozoff

Peacemaking criminology has the potential to be effective at many levels. We have already discussed how personal transformation and institutional change can be envisioned by peacemaking criminology. While each of these levels of change are important, there is another opportunity to implement peacemaking that is rapidly gaining momentum around the world as an effective and humane way to deal with offenders. Community justice is emerging as an alternative to the traditional criminal justice system. While there are many variations of the community justice theme, we will concentrate on a process termed *restorative justice* as a way to demonstrate how positive change can occur outside the criminal justice system.

Community justice as practiced by the restorative justice movement cannot be called a new phenomenon, but rather a return to the days when conflicts were resolved at the level of the family, clan, group, and community. The emphasis of community justice is not on the punishment of the offender, but on the restoring of the relationship between the offender and victim, as well as on maintaining order and social and moral balance in the community. Community justice therefore has a broader mandate than the traditional criminal justice system. It must satisfy the concerns of several constituents and produce a result that is viewed both as just and satisfying. In other words, the limited institutional goals of clearing a court docket or ensuring that an offender is punished are not enough for community justice. A more inclusive and healing result is the goal.

Before we discuss the underlying principles of restorative or community justice, we need to examine why the criminal justice system is so unsatisfying in giving people a sense that crime is being dealt with in an effective manner. At the heart of the dissatisfaction with the criminal justice system are two issues. The first issue of concern is the general feeling that the criminal justice system does not work very well, particularly in reflecting the interests of the victims of crime. When an offender commits a crime against an individual, the state takes the case away from the victim and prosecutes it as its own. In point of fact, the state replaces the victim as an aggrieved party and uses its own values and constraints to decide on a disposition. The Norwegian criminologist Nils Christie argues that the conflict between the offender and victim are property that the state takes away.[1] The offender and victim no longer have the opportunity to resolve the case in a mutually satisfying way, and hope of repairing the relationship is diminished.

A second issue of concern with the traditional criminal justice system is its failure to change the criminal behavior of the offender. The over-reliance on punishment that is the hallmark of the criminal justice system ignores some of society's other important goals.[2] The determination of guilt or innocence and the imposition of a punishment are inherently short-sighted activities. If offenders are consistently embittered by their interaction with the criminal justice system, and the issues that contributed to their deciding to violate the law are not addressed, then we should not be surprised that when they are released from prison that they recidivate. A mean-spirited or apathetic criminal justice system will produce a mean-spirited, former inmate who feels he's got nothing to lose. While it is true that an emphasis on punishment does try to achieve the goals of retribution, deterrence, and incapacitation, viewing of the offender as an enemy rather than a family member or neighbor facilitates a punishment mentality that inevitably becomes a self-fulfilling prophecy. The restorative justice movement seeks to reclaim the offender and repair the relationship with the victim and community. Ultimately, this form of justice can be healthier for all concerned.

Underlying Principles of Restorative Justice

Before we examine the process of restorative justice it is useful to look at the underlying principles. Ron Claassen, from the Center for Peacemaking and Conflict Studies at Fresno Pacific College, lists these principles that will guide our later discussion.[3]

1. Crime is primarily an offense against human relationships, and secondarily a violation of the law (since laws are written to protect public safety and fairness in human relationships).

2. Restorative Justice recognizes that crime (violations of persons and relationships) is wrong and should not occur, and also recognizes that after it does there are dangers and opportunities. The danger is that the community, victim(s), and/or offender emerge from the response further alienated, more damaged, disrespected, disempowered, feeling less safe and less cooperative with society. The opportunity is that injustice is recognized, the equity is restored

(restitution and grace), and the future is clarified so that partici-pants are safer, more respectful, and more empowered and coop-erative with each other and society.

3. Restorative Justice is a process to "make things as right as possi-ble" which includes: attending to needs created by the offense such as safety and repair of injuries to relationships and physical dam-age resulting from the offense; and attending to needs related to the cause of the offense (addictions, lack of social or employment skills or resources, lack of moral or ethical base, etc.).

4. The primary victim(s) of a crime is/are the one(s) most impacted by the offense. The secondary victims are others impacted by the crime and might include family members, friends, witnesses, criminal justice officials, community, etc.

5. As soon as immediate victim, community, and offender safety con-cerns are satisfied, Restorative Justice views the situation as a teachable moment for the offender; an opportunity to encourage the offender to learn new ways of acting and being in the com-munity.

6. Restorative Justice prefers responding to the crime at the earliest point possible and with the maximum amount of voluntary coop-eration and minimum coercion, since healing in relationships and new learning are voluntary and cooperative processes.

7. Restorative Justice prefers that most crimes are handled using a cooperative structure including those impacted by the offense as a community to provide support and accountability. This might include primary and secondary victims and family (or substitutes if they choose not to participate), the offender and family, com-munity representatives, government representatives, faith com-munity representatives, and school representatives, etc.

8. Restorative Justice recognizes that not all offenders will choose to be cooperative. Therefore there is a need for outside authority to make decisions for the offender who is not cooperative. The actions of the authorities and the consequences imposed should be tested by whether they are reasonable, restorative, and respective (for victim(s), offender, and community).

9. Restorative Justice prefers that offenders who pose significant safe-ty risks and are not yet cooperative be placed in settings where the emphasis is on safety, values, ethics, responsibility, accountabil-ity, and civility. They should be exposed to the impact of their crime(s) on victims, invited to learn empathy, and offered learn-ing opportunities to become better equipped with skills to be a pro-ductive member of society. They should continually be invited (not coerced) to become cooperative with the community and be given the opportunity to demonstrate this in appropriate settings as soon as possible.

10. Restorative Justice requires follow-up and accountability structures utilizing the natural community as much as possible, since keeping agreements is the key to building a trusting community.

11. Restorative Justice recognizes and encourages the role of community institutions, including the religious/faith community, in teaching and establishing the moral and ethical standards which build up the community.

It is easy to see how restorative justice principles encompass the concerns of peacemaking criminology. Additionally, the idea of community justice is emphasized. While some of the issues that are embedded in restorative justice can be addressed by the traditional criminal justice system, it is clear that an alternative philosophy is needed. In other words, the restorative justice, community justice, and peacemaking criminology concepts all require the traditional criminal justice system to focus much more broadly on the welfare of the victim, community, and offender. The limited focus on guilt or innocence and punishment are insufficient to achieve the type of healing result that is part of the community justice model.

Given the underlying principles of restorative justice, it becomes useful to ask some questions about the traditional criminal justice system. How did the criminal justice system get to the point where conflicts are taken away from individuals and made crimes where the state is considered the aggrieved party? Is justice concerned only with the punishment of offenders? Is it dysfunctional for society to keep insisting on more and more punishment when it seems not to be effective? Is there a point where the criminal justice industry begins to advocate policies that are more concerned with narrow vocational and economic interests rather than broader concerns of justice?

The Promise of Community

We all live in communities. By this we mean something beyond living in a physical neighborhood. To live in a community means that the individual is connected by social and economic ties to a group of other individuals. The concept of community can become confusing in postmodern times when one knows someone thousands of miles away through the Internet much better than his/her next-door neighbor. Nevertheless, the person next door has the potential to be a friend or a real pain in the neck, depending on just how well you both fulfill the expectations of being neighbors. Those with whom we share this sense of community are partners in developing a physical and shared world. Whether we personally like our neighbors or not, we alternately cooperate and oppose them in our daily lives. They have a tremendous potential to contribute to our quality of life depending on whether they help in times of need or break into our homes and steal our belongings.

This sense of community is what makes stable society possible. In traditional societies, the community did the work that the criminal justice system does in more complex societies. For example, anthropologist William Ury, a leading scholar on conflict resolution, explains how the Bushmen in Africa use the community to resolve conflicts:

> When a serious problem comes up, everyone sits down, all the men and women, and they talk and talk—and talk. Each person has a chance to have his or her say. This open and inclusive process can take days—until the dispute is literally talked out. The community members work hard to discover what social rules have been broken to produce such discord and what needs to be done to restore social harmony. A *kgotla*, which is what they call their discussion, serves as a kind of people's court except that there is no vote by the jury or verdict by the judge; decisions are made by consensus. Unlike a typical court proceeding where one side wins and one side loses, the goal is a stable solution that both disputants and the community can support. As the group conversation proceeds, a consensus about the appropriate solution gradually crystallizes. After making sure that no opposition or ill will remains, the elders voice this emergent consensus.[4]

It can be argued that the differences between the traditional Bushmen society and modern industrial society are vast and that making any kind of comparison between social institutions is fraught with problems. However, the intent of describing the process the Bushmen use for resolving conflicts is to suggest the adversarial way that is used in our court system is not necessarily something that is part of the natural evolution of social institutions. The intent of demonstrating how the Bushmen settle differences is to argue that for the vast majority of the time we have had human social institutions, cooperation and consensus have been important ingredients of stable societies. The contemporary criminal justice system is a relatively recent method for deciding how conflicts get resolved and, as we have previously stated, the results are not particularly satisfying.

Can the community be effective in resolving conflicts in contemporary society? Ury argues that it can. The same processes that are effective in traditional societies can work today. In looking at the declining juvenile crime rate in Boston, Ury credits the community.

> The key, according to Boston Police Commissioner Paul Evans, was "collaboration." The entire community was mobilized. The police worked closely with teachers and parents to search out kids who had missed school or whose grades had dropped. Local government agencies and businesses provided troubled youth with counseling, educational programs, and after-school jobs. Social workers visited their homes. Ministers and pastors mentored them and offered a substitute family for kids who almost never had two and some-

times not even one parent at home. Community counselors, often ex-gang members, hung out with gang members and taught them to handle conflict with talk, not guns.[5]

What is unique about the contemporary attempts to use the community in resolving conflicts is the partnering of the community with the government. It is easy to forget that in the larger context, government officials and community members live in the same neighborhoods. In traditional societies, the community performed the functions of government. Today, the social institutions of government have encroached into many of the arenas of the family and community to the point where the influence of the community has lost much of its relevance. The goal of restorative justice programs is bringing the community back into the conflict-resolution process. This involves looking at criminal acts in a more comprehensive and inclusive way. It expands the scope of focus beyond the conflict between the offender and the government by including the victim, other interested parties such as the families of the victim and the offender, and the community itself.

Restorative justice also measures success in a way that is different from the traditional criminal justice system. Rather than worrying about clearing the court docket with plea bargains that leave all parties unsatisfied or even bitter, or keeping score by the number of years of incarceration meted out to an offender, restorative justice is concerned with the healing of relationships and of reclaiming stability in the community. These are, admittedly, more difficult goals to measure but real social justice is a more complex value than the more limited concerns of the contemporary criminal justice system. Real social justice represents a more long-term, rather than short-term, view, and promises to be longer lasting and less likely to see repeated problems.

Finally, restorative justice in the community is superior to the traditional criminal justice system because of the responsibility it places on the offender. Rather than having something done to him or her, the offender must actively participate in the healing process of the community, the victim, and ultimately him or herself. This healing process might be as simple as an apology to the victim, or it might mean paying restitution to recompense the victim's loss. The offender might be required to perform some type of community service to repay the damage done to public property or the social order. But, most importantly, from a restorative justice perspective, the offender must willingly and actively participate in his or her own healing. This might include traditional treatment methods such as drug and alcohol programs, or it could include having offenders publicly take responsibility for their actions and engage in community education programs designed to prevent others from making the same mistakes.

Forms of Restorative Justice

The idea of restoring the damage done by crime is appealing in theory but requires well-thought-out programs to become effective. Simply putting the offender and the victim in the same room together without some guidance or structure is a recipe for disaster. The unresolved conflict could quickly escalate into harsh words and/or violence. There is a process designed to aid the victim and offender in resolving the conflict to their mutual satisfaction. This process is called Victim-Offender Reconciliation Programs.[6]

Victim-Offender Reconciliation Programs (VORP)

Victim-Offender Reconciliation Programs are designed to bring the victim and offender together to forge a resolution to their problem. With the help of a trained mediator, they take proactive roles in inventing creative options to the traditional criminal justice system sanctions. By empowering the victim and offender to suggest and agree upon solutions to their conflict, the VORP process helps resolve disputes in such a way that the outcomes are long-lasting. Victim-Offender Reconciliation Programs may not be appropriate for many cases, so the voluntary participation of the parties is essential. While the term reconciliation implies that both the victim and offender need to reconcile, many times the victim has no motivation to work toward a middle ground because he/she has done nothing wrong for which to recant. Therefore, the term mediation might be a better description of what happens in these programs.

There are three basic objectives to these programs:

1. To identify the injustice

2. To make things right

3. To consider future actions

In the traditional criminal justice system, it is often the case where the victim and offender never get to hear and understand the other's side. The conversation in the traditional criminal justice system is filtered through the police, prosecutor, defense attorney, and the judge. In this adversarial process, the victim and offender are often driven farther apart by positional bargaining. The VORP process gives them the opportunity to meet face-to-face and explain their injuries, motivations, and concerns. In the process of this mediation they often come to understand, sometimes for the very first time, exactly what the other side was thinking. They ask questions of each other. The victim can put a human face on the loss, and the offender has a chance to show remorse. This step of identifying what the injustice has resulted in is, therefore, useful to the victim who gets to tell his/her story and to the offender who gets to explain his/her actions.

Once the facts of the case are agreed upon, or at the least each side has had an opportunity to gain an understanding of the other side's behavior, the stage is set to develop an outcome that makes things right. For the offender this might include such things as an apology, restitution, return of valuables, or any number of other ways to repair the harm done to the victim. For the victim, the setting right of things may include receiving these reparations from the offender in exchange for forgiveness. In many conflicts, the disputants have ongoing relationships whereby the repair of that relationship is important to repair the harm caused by the crime. Simply becoming financially whole often is not enough to satisfy both parties, especially when they may be related. Forgiveness, if sincere, can be a powerful healer and a profound way to correct an injustice.

Once an agreement has been reached, it is written up and signed by both parties. This then becomes part of the court record and has the impact of a legal document. Depending on the jurisdiction, this agreement can be ratified by the criminal court and any violation can result in the offender having to appear before the judge. Alternatively, this agreement can become the basis for a civil suit by the victim against the offender for failure to comply with the conditions.

The agreement may specify the conditions of future actions that could include a payment schedule for restitution, agreement to enter into a treatment program for drug or alcohol abuse, or a pledge to stay away from the victim. In order to prevent the conflict from recurring, this dimension of agreements for future actions can specify how any ongoing relationship might be monitored by the Victim-Offender Reconciliation Program.

Family Group Conferencing

Family Group Conferencing is an extension of the Victim-Offender Reconciliation Program. It involves not only the victim and the offender, but also other parties including family members, the arresting police officer, representatives from the community and/or the government. A mediator coordinates the conference and allows each to have their chance for input. An outcome is agreed upon that accomplishes several goals. First, it resolves the conflict outside the traditional criminal justice system. Secondly, the victim and offender have a chance to confront each other and have their side of the story heard. Thirdly, there is an opportunity for other affected parties to provide input and express their concerns. And finally, the agreements that are forged strengthen the ties of the parties and ultimately of the community. Family Group Conferencing is a process that began in New Zealand and was adopted in Australia and eventually in the United States. The Family Group Conferencing model is used most extensively in the juvenile court where the concern for the offender's welfare is considered as important as the victim's.[7]

Victim-Offender Panels (VOP)

It is not always feasible or appropriate for the victim and offender to meet and try to work out their conflicts. For example, in the case of rape, the victim may be so traumatized that any contact with the offender would be harmful. Also, there are many instances in which the offender is not known and therefore not available for conferencing or reconciliation. This does not mean, however, that some of the benefits of conflict resolution cannot be employed. In these instances Victim-Offender Panels are useful.[8]

Victim-Offenders Panels allow victims to address offenders who have committed the same types of crimes as the victims have experienced. The victims do not confront the individual who harmed them directly, but rather, they confront an offender who has harmed someone else. The idea behind these panels is to allow the victim to express the nature and depth of harm they have experienced to offenders. The victim, thus, plays an educative role in showing offenders the human damage that their crimes can cause. Offenders get to see that their actions have consequences for others and can reflect on the harm they may have caused to their own victims. The result, hopefully, is that offenders will change their anti-social attitudes and behaviors.

Victim-Offender Panels have been shown to be effective with carefully chosen victims of drunk drivers and with victims of burglary. The exact process that these panels provide may vary, but the idea is to give victims a chance to tell their story and to give offenders an opportunity to see how their crimes impact on other people. Again, there is no chance for reconciliation in Victim-Offender Panels because the victims never meet the actual offender, just someone who has committed the same type of crime.

These three types of restorative justice practices demonstrate a very different philosophy from the traditional criminal justice system. They all aim at helping both the victim and the offender and, to a broader extent, the community. Critics of these practices would point to the consequences for the offender, claiming any reconciliation that the offender agrees to cannot include enough punishment to satisfy the concerns of justice. This myopic view of justice, one concerned with the amount of punishment, is inconsistent with restorative justice principles. For the long-lasting resolution of the conflict, and the ultimate well-being of the community, punishment has proven to be ineffective.

Reintegrative Shaming

How can restorative and community justice programs effect real change in the offender? For many individuals, looking at restorative justice for the first time, the idea that punishment is not paramount is disturbing. It appears to these observers that the offender is "getting away" with the crime when there is not substantial punishment. For those who embrace the restorative justice concept, however, there is a more powerful process at work than punishment. John Braithwaite contrasts shaming and punishment by calling attention to the symbolic nature of each:[9]

> Shaming is more pregnant with symbolic content than punishment. Punishment is a denial of confidence in the morality of the offender by reducing norm compliance to a crude cost-benefit calculation; shaming can be a reaffirmation of the morality of the offender by expressing personal disappointment that the offender should do something so out of character, and, if the shaming is reintegrative, by expressing personal satisfaction in seeing the character of the offender restored. Punishment erects barriers between the offender and punisher through transforming the relationship into one of power assertion and injury; shaming produces a greater interconnectedness between the parties, albeit a painful one, an interconnectedness which can produce the repulsion of stigmatization or the establishment of a potentially more positive relationship following reintegration. Punishment is often shameful and shaming usually punishes. But whereas punishment gets its symbolic content only from its denunciatory association with shaming, shaming is pure symbolic content.

Reintegrative shaming casts a stark and powerful light on the offender in a way that is both positive and transforming. This type of shaming (as contrasted with disintegrative shaming or stigmatization) is designed to bring the offender back into the social net of the community. Currently our traditional criminal justice system does little in the way of reintegrative shaming. The way the process now works, it is more likely that the victim feels more shame than the offender. The trial and sentencing that is supposed to be what Goffman calls a "successful status degradation ceremony" has become a spectacle about which many offenders feel little shame. This lack of shame on the part of the offenders occurs because many offenders identify with the deviant label. Their offender identity becomes a Master Status whereby they feel pride and accomplishment from the rejection and stigmatization of society.

Critics of reintegrative shaming point out that it works best in tight-knit, homogeneous societies like Japan. Given the individualistic nature of Western nations like the United States, there is concern that the shaming would not be reintegrative. Many people in the United States are poorly integrated into society to begin with, so the idea that they can be reintegrated becomes problematic. There are vast differences between cultures, according to the critics of shaming, and to expect cultural bound bonds that work in one society to be equally effective in another requires a leap of faith that many are not willing to make.

Some Recent Developments

Gordon Bazemore and Mara Schiff have edited a volume based upon a recent conference focusing on restorative justice's evolution into a broader context of community justice. Kenneth Polk advocates that restorative justice be expanded into the larger arena of social justice, including shifting our emphasis on delinquent and deviant youth to proactively increasing developmental opportunities for youth in general. He suggests the restorative justice movement is at a crossroads; either expand the idea of restorative justice or allow the movement to become one more innovative social control option for the criminal justice system. Mary Achilles and Howard Zehr propose greater, more active inclusion of victims in the restorative justice process, while David Karp and Lynne Walther describe how community reparative boards in Vermont attempt to implement restorative and reintegrative processes within a community justice context. Barry Stuart describes some guiding principles for designing peacemaking circles in communities including accessibility, flexibility, being holistic as part of the empowerment process, incorporating a spiritual dimension, building consensus and being accountable.[10]

In defense of restorative justice, it is just this lack of tightly knit community that restorative justice is trying to inject into the western style of justice. In our postmodern world, we have lost the sense of togetherness that makes meaningful communities possible. No matter how large our efforts or how many "keep out" signs we have posted in our yards, the reality is that we are connected—we are in this thing called life together. What a person does, good or bad, affects others. Rather than seeing this fragmentation as a reason to dismiss restorative justice, we should see as a challenge. Restorative and community justice principles can facilitate not only the healing of victims and offenders, but also many of the ways institutions interact with individuals in society.

Faith-Based Corrections

One interesting trend in community justice is the reemergence of religion as a legitimate and recognized correctional institution. Pepinsky and Quinney identified religious and humanistic intellectual traditions being influential in the development of peacemaking criminology and in an earlier chapter (Chapter 2) we discussed how a variety of religious and wisdom traditions are important precursors. Faith-based programs can provide a spiritual dimension to the rehabilitation of the offender that is not available from other types of programs. For instance, because of the constitutional separation of church and state, government programs must be careful about imposing a religious component into the treatment plan for offenders.

Government programs are limited in their ability to help victims and offenders with faith issues, but faith-based programs are free to explore such issues if the person desires it. By providing practical assistance and opportunities to discuss spiritual and emotional issues in a supportive context, programs can assist victims and offenders in moving beyond their alienation to greater emotional, physical, and spiritual health. Of course, offenders and victims come from diverse ethnic, religious, and cultural backgrounds. They may have varying cultural assumptions about managing anger, grief, and stress. They may be deeply involved in other religions or may be hostile to religion. Programs offering a spiritual component must be sensitive to this and be able to help the victim or offender gain the most from their own tradition and support network.[11]

Faith-based programs can encourage positive changes in offenders in both community-based and institutional environments. Even in prison—even on death row—faith-based experiences can transform lives. While on death row for almost 13 years, Willie Reddix described an inner peace he had found by referring to it as a "quiet light." Walter Correll, an inmate on death row in Virgina, wrote, "Right now I may be on death row, but with Jesus in my life it's life row." (see Chapters 4, 6, and 7 for other examples).

Community Justice and Peacemaking

The purpose of this chapter is to establish the connection between peacemaking criminology and community and restorative justice. Having a correctional system that accomplishes the goals of changing the offender's antisocial behavior and protecting the community requires something that the traditional criminal justice cannot provide. In fact, as we have previously pointed out, the reliance on punishment does little to change the offender's behavior and, in fact, often results in a community that is further threatened with new victims who are harmed. Something else is required to bridge the need for change in an offender's life and the need for the protection of the community. A bridge of compassion recognizes the harms and fear shared by offenders and victims, but also offers a way back into the community for each as well. Community justice is a context where much restoration can take place.

Questions

1. Describe the two issues concerning the traditional criminal justice system that people find unsatisfactory and thus propose a form of community justice. Are these problems ones that can be fixed within the context of the traditional criminal justice system?

2. Ron Claassen presents some underlying principles of restorative justice. Give a brief summary of these principles. Which of them are at odds with the traditional criminal justice system? Which of these principles do you think is most important for healing individuals and the criminal justice system?

3. Explain how the community is intregal to the idea of restorative justice. Is the way the term community is used in restorative justice the say as our everyday understanding? What would a restorative justice program that is integrated into the community look like?

4. What is reintegrative shaming? Speculate on how this principle might be misused in the criminal justice system. Is reintegrative shaming something that can be adapted to the materialistic culture of the United States?

5. Are faith-based correctional programs likely to be effective within the peacemaking criminology context? How might the issues of separation of church and state be addressed within faith-based correctional programs?

Notes

[1] Christie, Nils (1977). "Conflicts as Property." *The British Journal of Criminology,* 17(1):1-15.

[2] Irwin, John and James Austin (1994). *It's About Time: America's Imprisonment Binge.* Belmont, CA: Wadsworth.

[3] These principles are taken from Ron Claassen's web site (www.fresnp.edu/pacs/rjprinc.html). The content has not been edited and they are printed with permission.

[4] Ury, William (1999). *Getting to Peace: Transforming Conflicts at Home, at Work, and in the World.* New York, NY: Viking. 5.

[5] Ury, ibid. p. 10-11.

[6] Van Ness, Daniel and Karen Heetderks Strong (1997). *Restoring Justice.* Cincinnati, OH: Anderson, p. 69-72.

[7] Van Ness and Strong. ibid. p. 73-74.

[8] Van Ness and Strong. ibid. p. 74-76.

[9] Van Ness and Strong. ibid. p. 117.

[10] Van Ness and Strong. ibid. p. 128.

[11] Bazemore, Gordon and Schiff, Mara (eds.) (2001). *Restorative Community Justice; Repairing Harm and Transforming Communities.* Cincinnati, OH: Anderson Publishing Co.

[12] Arriens, Jan (ed.) (1997). *Welcome to Hell.* Boston, MA: Northeastern University Press, p. 25.

Credits

CPSIA information can be obtained
at www.ICGtesting.com
Printed in the USA
LVHW101913100419
613688LV00020B/51/P